Advance Praise for ISIS Defectors

"Some stories deserve to be told. And some truth is more terrifying than any fiction. This book is both." —**Abigail Rodriguez**, Documentary filmmaker and VP of Development, Outrun the Sun Productions

"In a world searching for answers to explain the ISIS phenomena, Anne Speckhard is a treasure trove of information. The insights she has gleaned from interviewing hundreds of terrorists and now this new body of work—thirty-two ISIS defectors/returnees reported upon here, collected with her research partner, Ahmet Yayla,—challenges some hard held assumptions about violent extremism and Islam. And puts us on the path to understanding the real motivations behind so many people joining the Islamic State."
—**Jeff Swicord**, Journalist, Voice of America Television

Anne Speckhard, the American psychologist and Ahmet Yayla, the Turkish police officer, are a unique research team; by collecting authentic defector voices they have exposed, like nobody before them, the moral depravity of the Daesh 'Caliphate'. The damning evidence against the so-called 'Islamic State' is here for all to see—I cannot think of a stronger counter-narrative."
—**Prof. Em. Alex P. Schmid**, Editor-in Chief, *Perspectives on Terrorism*

"Anne Speckhard and Ahmet S. Yayla have given us one of the best—if not THE best—look into the twisted world of ISIS/Daesh, detailing the process of these interviewees' recruitment, fighting, torture and brutality, eventual disillusionment and attempts at defection. It should be critical material for everyone responsible for addressing the threats posed by this group and its advocates; and important educational material for use in fighting against their efforts to recruit more vulnerable individuals to their cause. The authors are to be commended for their work." —**Dr. Alistair D. Edgar**, Executive Director, Academic Council on the UN System, Associate Professor of Political Science, Wilfrid Laurier University

"A key component of defeating ISIS is telling the world what ISIS is really like—from the inside. By having ISIS defectors tell their stories, Anne Speckhard and Ahmet Yayla are doing a great service with their new book."—**Peter Bergen**, author of *United States of Jihad*, Vice President at New America, and CNN's national security analyst.

"Great insights from courageous CVE work by Anne Speckhard, Ph.D. and Ahmet Yayla, Ph.D. on their *ISIS Defectors Interviews Project*. Their groundbreaking effort will open new doors to discredit the ISIS narrative through firsthand testimonials of those who were brave enough to expose the terrorist group for what it really is. I eagerly look forward to further application of their work." —**Michael A. Brown**, Research Fellow at RAND Corporation

"If anyone is qualified to write on this subject it is Anne Speckhard. When you have read this book, as well as her others, you will almost be able to call yourself an expert on the subject. When Anne writes about a topic you will know that she has done her homework so thoroughly, right down to interviewing the most unlikely people, and placing herself in potentially dangerous situations. When you have read *ISIS Defectors* you will not only have a thorough understanding of what makes the ISIS fighters tick, but you will also have no illusions about their goals to conquer as much of the world as they can by their singularly brutal methods. This book is another masterpiece by Anne Speckard and her research partner, Ahmet Yayla."
—**Joe Charlaff**, Middle East Correspondent for *Homeland Security Today*

"The so-called Islamic State presents an unprecedented global threat. Since my encounter with Anne Speckhard in Iraq interviewing terrorist suspects, she has produced many notable works. Her latest, with Ahmet S. Yayla, is essential reading for both scholars and practitioners!" —**Professor Rohan Gunaratna**, Author, *Inside al Qaeda: Global Network of Terror* Columbia University Press

"In their book, *ISIS Defectors: Inside Stories of the Terrorist Caliphate*, Anne Speckhard and Ahmet Yayla ask the key question: why do people join the group? As importantly, they ask it of the right people: men and women who fought for, or otherwise supported, the so-called Islamic State. These personal accounts of defectors provide invaluable insights for those working to counter the ISIS appeal, and add significantly to our understanding of how the organisation works and where it is most vulnerable. The book shows us that although ISIS is known for its cold-blooded ruthlessness, there are many of its members who are disgusted by its brutality and repelled by its hypocrisy." —**Richard Barrett**, Senior VP at the Soufan Group

"In her latest book, Dr. Anne Speckhard, with her research partner, Dr. Ahmet Yayla, explores the intersection of psychology and terrorism via their in-depth interviews with ISIS defectors. This is fascinating stuff, in large part, because of Dr. Speckhard's expertise in psychology and her ability to elicit candor from her interview subjects. This book belongs on the shelf of anyone with an interest in the phenomena of ISIS and its legions of young recruits."—**Carol Rollie Flynn**, Former Senior CIA Executive

"Anne Speckhard and Ahmet Yayla's report of their daring and courageous interviews of ISIS defectors exposes important insights into the group's recruitment process that are crucial to countering violent extremism (CVE) work. More importantly, their book illuminates the reasons why these individuals left ISIS. This information not only has implications for interventions designed to prevent individuals from joining ISIS, but also has practical applications for discrediting ISIS by exposing their hypocrisies and failures. This book is a must-read for anyone interested in knowing more about why individuals join and leave terrorist groups, particularly those in the CVE field." —**Sara Zeiger**, Senior Research Analyst, Hedayah, The International Center of Excellence for Countering Violent Extremism, Abu Dhabi

"Unveiling the seditious nature of IS, which is the epitome of terror in the true and wide sense of the word, is almost a sacred task. Dr. Speckhard's and Dr. Yayla's book is a pioneering and illuminating work that brings first hand, authentic stories of defectors from IS's ranks; which is a significant contribution to the in-depth understanding of the processes and dynamics that run in the veins of this fascist, contemporary phenomenon. As proven in her former works, Dr. Anne Speckhard is again standing at the forefront of updated, relevant research contributing to the promotion of the deeper understanding in the field of counterterrorism. Their book will probably be a cornerstone work for more researchers on the subject matter and encourage more truthful stories that eventually will follow and be publicized when this so-called 'Islamic State' is eventually shattered, even if Salafi jihadism will probably plague us for a much longer time."—**Yoram Schweitzer**, former Israeli intelligence officer, and Director of a Research Program on Terrorism and Low Intensity Conflict, Institute for National Security Studies, Tel Aviv University

"The self-proclaimed Islamic State has dramatically changed the political, economic, and security landscape of the Middle East. Of the many ways to better understand and then combat the group, learning directly from defectors has high value and can provide information and insights unavailable from any other source."—**Howard J. Shatz**, Senior Economist, RAND Corporation, co-author of Foundations of the Islamic State: Management, Money, and Terror in Iraq, 2005-2010

"Dr. Anne Speckhard provides psychological insights like we have never seen before. The detailed accounts of real life case studies of violent extremists collected with her research partner, Dr. Ahmet Yayla, transform our understanding from the 'theoretical' to the 'empirical'. This brilliant work is definitely another milestone in the right direction towards an evidenced-base approach to preventing and countering violent extremism." —**Maqsoud Kruse**, Executive Director of Hedayah, The International

Center of Excellence for Countering Violent Extremism, Abu Dhabi

"Two intrepid researchers set out to hunt down disenchanted ISIS cadres who dared to speak out and denounce the so-called Islamic State. An extremely timely read put together by action-based researchers in the thick of the battle in this enormous fight against evil!" —**Rita Cosby**, Emmy-Winning TV/Radio Host and Best Selling Author of *Quiet Hero: Secrets From My Father's Past*

"Nothing beats the inside view and now you have one—of ISIS. Brace yourselves."—**Mubin Shaikh**, Islamic Radicalization and Counter-terrorism Expert, coauthor of *Undercover Jihadi: Inside the Toronto 18*

"Anne and I have known each other for many years and frequently exchanged views on a wide variety of terrorism-related topics. Too date, there are some reports, articles and interviews with ISIS defectors, but none to the extent of Dr. Speckhard and Dr. Yayla's research detailed in *ISIS Defectors: Inside Stories of the Terrorist Caliphate*. In the last year, Anne has travelled the world to identify, locate, gain access, understand and interview returned or defected terrorists, amongst others in Belgian cities such as Brussels and Antwerp. This book, ISIS Defectors, describes a large number of valuable cases, which provide unique insights—amongst others the ISIS defectors' call not to join them—to policy makers, prevention workers and operational members of the police, intelligence and security services, working in the domains of radicalisation, extremism and terrorism. This book is a must read!" —**Stephan Van Hauwe**, Head of Security and Operations, Antwerp World Diamond Centre

"In ISIS Defectors: Inside Stories of Confronting the Terrorist Caliphate Dr. Anne Speckhard and Dr. Ahmet S. Yayla reveal the Holy Grail of CVE: striking interviews with fellow human beings who survived the horror of the so-called "Islamic State" from the inside, revealing the duality of perpetrator and victim within the same person. As terrifying and infuriating as these true stories are, ISIS Defectors conveys the crucial truth that all concerned are indeed as human as anyone else, cultivating an understanding that is the antidote for violent extremism of all sorts. Recalling my days as a leader of white supremacist hate groups 20 years ago, then adding all I've learned as a CVE consultant and peace educator for the past 8 years, it's become clear that people get involved in violent extremism when basic human needs aren't met. This brave work by Drs. Speckhard and Yayla corroborates my conclusion, citing needs from identity, purpose, and belonging, to simple food and water as levers pulled by Daesh to cultivate fear and hatred around the world. ISIS Defectors is an utter deconstruction of false Caliphate narrative, and is far deadlier to Islamist extremism than any bullet or bomb could ever be."—**Arno Arr Michaelis IV**, Author, Speaker, CVE Consultant and Peace Activist, Former White Power Skinhead

ISIS Defectors

Inside Stories
of the Terrorist Caliphate

Anne Speckhard, Ph.D. & Ahmet S. Yayla, Ph.D.

First published 2016
By Advances Press, LLC
McLean, VA

Editor - Susan K Barnett, www.impact-communications.com
Cover Design - Jessica Speckhard, www.SpeckhardSavc.com
Book Publicist – Susan K Barnett, www.impact-communications.com
Cover photo - A snapshot of one of our defectors speaking on video
Interior photos courtesy of ISIS Defectors and Islamic State

Library of Congress Control Number: 2016944462

ISBN 978-1-935866-71-8– ISIS Defectors – Hardcover
ISBN 978-1-935866-72-5– ISIS Defectors – e-pub

Dedication

To our families and the brave people we worked with in this project—who risked their own lives making it possible for us to dare to interview ISIS. From Ahmet: to my lovely wife and my children. From Anne: to my husband, children and grandchild who make our home a place filled with love—an antidote to life's evils.

Table of Contents

"When I am sitting alone, it comes to me, this picture of the person who was executed and I get frightened, I think inside me, there is terror."

- **Bint Aisha, ISIS Defector**

Prologue - They Risked Their Lives to Speak

They've been radicalized and battle hardened. They know what it feels like to decapitate a fellow human. They've seen women and children strap on vests and blow themselves up for the cause. And they've risked their lives to escape.

ISIS Defectors: Inside Stories of the Terrorist Caliphate breaks new ground, detailing the stories and reflections of dozens of men, women and even children who joined the ISIS jihad, but became so disgusted and disillusioned, they defected.

With unprecedented access, from September 2015 to May 2016, the *ISIS Defectors Interview Project* conducted in-depth interviews that include thirty Syrian ISIS defectors who successfully escaped ISIS and are currently hiding out in Turkey (fighters, wives of ISIS fighters, and even children who joined ISIS); two European returnees whose defections are unclear; six parents of Europeans who went to Syria to fight—some are still alive and inside ISIS and some are dead.

Each in-depth interview (some that took up to five hours) is a window into ISIS reality in full-living horror. From motivations to joining; the manipulation of children and their use as suicide bombers; the treatment of women; ISIS' sex trade; finances through seizures, taxation, oil sales and sex slaves; unexpected allegiances among political enemies; the killing of Sunni Muslims; mental health consequences and more, we have gathered stories, photos, and videos that are remarkably consistent and have never been seen before now.

ISIS is the most powerful, ruthless and well-funded terrorist group in recent history. Since its 2014 claim of establishing a "Caliphate", ISIS has unleashed an unprecedented and prolific social media recruiting drive that has attracted up to 30,000 foreign fighters from more than one hundred countries—at times drawing a flow of 1500 foreign fighters per month.[1]

Both the CIA Director, John Brennan, and former Defense Intelligence Agency (DIA) Director, LTG Mike Flynn, warned after the deadly 2015 Paris attacks that these brutal killings were a sign of things to come.[2] FBI director, James Comey, has confirmed that there are over one thousand active ISIS investigations in the U.S., across all fifty states.[3] Though it appears that ISIS did not directly command the San Bernardino, California terrorist killers, one of them had pledged her *bayat* (allegiance) to ISIS before carrying out their attack.[4] We know that ISIS orchestrated the Paris and Brussels bombings, and inspired the Orlando dance club massacre, attacks that occurred during the time we were conducting our interviews.

While a political solution in the war-torn area of Syria and Iraq is a necessary precondition to the total defeat of ISIS, given the nature of the proxy war that ISIS represents, and the complex web of regional actors that profit from the actions of ISIS, that's not a likely outcome in the near future. Military actions can degrade the group and its ability to recruit and finance itself, but ISIS is so embedded in civilian areas that the collateral damage of military strikes will likely fuel more terrorism rather than curb it. And it will send terrorist cells underground.

Thus, discrediting the group's ideology is essential to stopping its online recruitment.

We believe that disillusioned ISIS defectors who tell their authentic stories about life inside the Islamic State are *the* most influential tool to counter ISIS' robust propaganda and prevent others from joining. ISIS produces thousands of slick recruiting videos, memes and tweets. For this reason, most of our interviews have been recorded on broadcast quality video with the interviewee's permission. We are packaging these into short video clips, memes, written and audio stories to feed onto the Internet and social media, to counter and compete head-on with ISIS's successful and (as of yet) unchallenged online campaign. Some of the photos and links to our video clips are included in this book. More can be found at the *International Center for the Study of Violent Extremism's* website, www. ICSVE.org. (We warn you, some are very graphic.)

The defectors undertook a gravely dangerous journey to defect from ISIS and most have risked their lives to speak to us. All have willingly given us cautionary statements for Westerners and others who might be considering joining ISIS. We will use these statements, alongside their first-person accounts of life inside ISIS, to discredit the terrorist group from the inside.

For our part, this work did not come without its own dangers to us—from personal threats from ISIS inside southern Turkey where the bulk of these interviews took place to narrowly missing ISIS attacks in Belgium.

We are not journalists. We are academics and security experts, with additional expertise in psychology and law enforcement. We have published scientific papers and written books on terrorism primarily for scholarly consumption (many of which can be found on our website). This project and resulting book and videos, partly self-funded and partly funded by a donor who wishes to remain anonymous, are meant to be both useful to scholars as well as accessible to general readers.

ISIS Defectors: Inside Stories of the Terrorist Caliphate is a true-life narrative of our journey, and the face-to-face meetings with those who have been inside the most brutal terrorist group in recent history. We have changed the names of all those who need to hide their identities, and withheld or changed identifying information to prevent ISIS from hunting them down for revenge. Though edited to avoid redundancy, we were struck by the remarkably consistent interview answers and information provided throughout the thirty-two defector interviews. As a trauma psychologist, I also saw clear posttraumatic reactions to recalling events they lived under ISIS.

To all those who are concerned about terrorism and finding strategic ways to counter ISIS' successful online tools of recruitment, if you would like to support our work, please visit our website at www. ICSVE.org and donate.

Anne Speckhard, Ph.D.

Ahmet S. Yayla, Ph.D.

International Center for the Study of Violent Extremism (ICSVE)

Chapter One - Venturing into ISIS Territory

Ahmet's voice was serious. Although I knew he was relatively fearless, I heard fear in it.

"Anne, we were followed today," my Turkish research colleague, Ahmet S. Yayla, announced over Skype when I logged on to take part in the interview. It was six-thirty in the morning Washington, D.C. time, November 7, 2015—but already afternoon in Şanlıurfa, Turkey, where Ahmet and his family live.

"I'm asking for an armored car. I'm going to find out what's happening," he grimly explained, adding, "I'm leaving now."

I glanced at my interpreter sitting next to me, locking eyes with her. Mona and I knew this was dangerous work, but now a real life situation was unfolding that felt like it was out of a novel. It was occurring right in the room with us, while we sat staring powerlessly into the computer monitor, trying to grasp the situation that was happening an ocean's width away.

"They are already here so they will give you the interview," Ahmet added, in his ever-responsible tone of voice. And with that he left.

"They" were a cameraman, English-to-Turkish interpreter, and a recent defector from ISIS who had agreed to not only tell his story to us, but to do so on camera. This will be our eleventh interview with an ISIS defector. We are speaking to men, women and children, all of whom had been inside ISIS and escaped. The work is unprecedented.

Venturing into terrorist territory has been a way of life for me over the past fifteen years. Traveling throughout the Middle East, Europe, and the former Soviet Union, I've personally interviewed nearly five hundred terrorists and extremists, from leaders to foot soldiers, meeting with them in most cases out in the field—that is—in their homes, cafes, streets, alleyways. I've even sat inside their prison cells, talking to thwarted suicide terrorists who willingly unstrapped their bombs, or were stopped before detonating themselves and their targets. In the cases of suicide bombers who have 'martyred' themselves, I've interviewed their widows, parents and other family members and close associates—sometimes staying overnight in the homes of these terrorists.[5]

I've interviewed the hostages of suicide terrorists—individuals who sat beside, and talked face-to-face, with terrorists in an activated state with bomb belts strapped to their bodies and bombs strewn throughout the theater or school (i.e. Dubrovoka Theater in Moscow and Beslan School in North Ossetia) while they threatened to kill themselves, as well as the hundreds of hostages they held, if their demands were not met.[6]

When I talked with terrorists, my questions were always focused on trying to understand what put them on the terrorist trajectory. And since I'm a research psychologist, I also wanted to know if there was anything that could have prevented them from entering, or anything that could have taken them back off the terrorist path—especially before they enacted violence.

I found myself on that fall day, listening helplessly as my colleagues in Southern Turkey sat in a small, sterile, white-walled studio-like room with our video camera locked onto the brown checkered *keffiyeh* wrapped around the head of a former terrorist we'll call Abu Musab (father of Musab); wondering what Ahmet's sudden departure meant for his life and that of his three kids and wife living in a town where two ISIS retribution murders had occurred only the week before. Incredibly, we still carried on with our eleventh interview. Ahmet's colleague stepped in to fill his role as my co-interviewer, translating my English into Turkish and our fixer then translating that into Arabic.

Over the years, as I helped unlock the ways in which ordinary people transformed themselves into terrorist killers, I was invited to consult with governments and international bodies on national security concerns. For instance, in 2006 and 2007, I was asked by the U.S. Department of Defense to go to Iraq to help design and write a de-radicalization program for the 20,000 detainees and 800 juveniles held by the U.S. Coalition forces; what ultimately became known as the Detainee Rehabilitation Program.

In the spring of 2014, I'd attracted the support of a donor who wishes to remain anonymous and the opportunity to pitch its leadership, "I'd like to replicate my earlier work interviewing terrorists, this time capturing stories of disillusioned and disengaged terrorists on video," I'd told the two women and four men in power suits seated around a polished wood conference table. "I think human stories, the stories of terrorists who have become disillusioned and walked away from the movement might be a powerful tool to prevent and dissuade others who could fall prey to groups like ISIS and al-Qaeda. It's a powerful counter narrative. Would you be willing to fund such a project?" I'd asked.[7]

Indeed, the social media campaign of ISIS was cranking out literally thousands of Internet-based marketing materials to seduce in record numbers, susceptible individuals into its group, and Americans along with many other Westerners, were getting caught in its webs of seduction. Attacks in the West were imminent. By fall of 2015, nearly 30,000 foreign fighters had gone to join the Islamic State, over 5000 from Europe alone, and ISIS was going strong—still managing to attract 1000 foreign fighters per month.[8] More than any other terrorist group in history, ISIS has been extremely successful in using the Internet to seduce individuals from all over the globe to travel to Syria and Iraq to join them on the battlefield for a fanaticized "Caliphate". And perhaps even more threatening, they have also been adept at motivating those who don't go abroad but are willing to enact lethal acts of terrorism at home.

"You think you can get former ISIS cadres to talk to you on video?" Stevie Pilatkis, one of the experts from the donor group, asked me. "You got them to talk before, but will they speak on video this time around?"

"I can get former terrorists to talk to me," I answered, looking around at the grave faces of the men and women interested in making my project happen. "But I don't know if I can capture any former ISIS cadres on video. I'm good at winning trust, but I've never videotaped my interviews and I imagine an ISIS defector leaving the battlefield would likely fear for his own life. As well, many would be reluctant to talk on film and basically record confessions that could subject them to prosecution for any crimes committed while an active ISIS member. I think we'll be more likely to find former al-Qaeda, but they may still be instructive and useful for prevention and dissuasion if you want me to try that," I answered. They nodded in agreement and asked me to get to work. The initial funds to launch the project were limited, but at least enough to get the project off the ground—with the hopes of finding more funds down the road if I succeeded.

So in the early fall of 2015, I headed off on a new project, first tracking down the usual suspects—former extremists who had written books or who had turned away from terrorism and were now fighting terrorist groups who were recruiting vulnerable young men and women as they had once been recruited. They were easy to find—Morten Storm, a Danish kid who grew up to become a thug and then aligned with al-Qaeda inspired extremism and had won the trust of Anwar al-Awlaki, the al-Qaeda leader and ideologue, but later turned against him and helped the CIA hunt him down.[9] Yousef Bartho Assidique, a white Norwegian kid who converted to Islam after his mother became deathly ill, but lacking knowledge of Islam as a young convert, fell headlong into a group of extremists discussing the idea of beheading a Norwegian journalist who had insulted the Prophet—only to later be rescued by his mother's love; Mubin Shaikh, a Canadian former extremist who had been an al-Qaeda enthusiast until he traveled to Syria and met a Syrian *sheikh* who turned him back around. When he returned to Canada, he ended up volunteering himself to the Canadian security forces as an undercover agent where he ultimately helped round up the Toronto 18—a group aiming its terror attacks on both Canadian and American government targets.[10]

Once I tracked them down, they all agreed to give video interviews explaining how they had gotten caught up in terrorism and extremism and how they'd also gotten disillusioned along the way, and finally backed away. The project was succeeding, but as I worked my way through these fascinating, dynamic characters, capturing stories that explained how they had gotten ensnared into violent extremism and how it hadn't worked out well for them, the thought of also capturing former ISIS cadres on video ate at the edges of my consciousness. Who better to speak out against ISIS than those who had been on the inside, who had pledged their allegiance to its fantasized "Caliphate" but then, disillusioned or worse, had walked away? What stronger voice could be used to dissuade a young person from getting sucked into the virulent ideology of the Islamic State and hypnotized by its pervasive social media presence than a former ISIS cadre? While the voices speaking out against ISIS and al-Qaeda that I was collecting were powerful, I knew it would be so much stronger to speak to actual ISIS defectors.

But how to find them? And once located, would any ever agree to speak to me, and to speak on video no less? It seemed impossible. But that was before I met Dr. Yayla.

Ahmet, a Turkish former police chief and university professor working in the southern city of Şanlıurfa, Turkey, and I met the way millions of professionals with shared interests meet—on LinkedIn. After he connected with me, I fired off a friendly note of greeting, but in his case, I couldn't resist tacking on an impetuous question—just in case.

"P.S. I am working on a project interviewing former jihadis, if you have any from ISIS that I can interview let me know!!" I quipped, never imagining he would reply in the affirmative.

"Maybe we look for an opportunity to work jointly on a project involving ISIS?" he wrote back. "[I'm] at the Syrian border living with PKK and ISIS." Halfway around the world, Ahmet had been thinking the same thoughts about pursuing interviews with defected ISIS cadres. It was September 2015. He, too, realized the importance of capturing the voices of disillusioned ISIS cadres that could tell what was happening inside territory under ISIS rule. Ahmet had in his illustrious career as a counter-terrorism police chief already interviewed thousands of terrorists from groups including the PKK, ISIS, DHKP/C, Hezbollah, al-Qaeda, TIKKO, and many other terrorist organizations active in Turkey that had ceased their existence over the years.

Ahmet had recently retired from his police work to become a university professor at Harran University in Şanlıurfa and was serving as chair in the Sociology Department. Realizing the importance of where he sat—on the southern edge of Turkey, not far from an extremely porous border that allowed ISIS cadres and their materials to pass back and forth from Syria—his town already housed nearly a half million Syrian refugees. Ahmet was sure that among them were ISIS defectors. Indeed, his town, its name often shortened to "Urfa," was referred to as a rest and relaxation point in Turkey—by ISIS cadres. It was also a common destination for extremist Europeans traveling through Turkey to meet up with their ISIS handlers to take them across the border into Syria and Iraq, to join the terrorist jihad.

Ahmet also wondered how to find and contact those who had disengaged and if he could persuade them to talk. He'd been trying to work his way into their trust for almost a year at that point. From his point of view, he was interested in details of how they recruit, train, indoctrinate, and operate but he was more than willing to include a research psychologist on his team. He had already put out feelers to the people smugglers in the area—raunchy characters he knew from his former work as a police chief—people that would likely be able to steer him to the right Syrians to approach for interviews. It turns out, I had popped my impetuous question at the opportune moment for our collaboration to begin.

Our partnership started the journey into ISIS territory that you will read about in this book, talking to actual ISIS insiders who "drank the Kool-Aid" of the so-called "Islamic State", which offered them of a fantasy of building a "Caliphate" in Syria and Iraq, and from there expanding around the world.

Through his former policing contacts, Ahmet was slowly but surely finding a way to locate these disillusioned former ISIS cadres hiding out in Turkey, and win their trust. Most were recent defectors. As Ahmet convinced them to talk, at first they only allowed us to record their voices. Later as their trust grew, they agreed to appear on video but only anonymously and with their identities hidden from view. They wrapped their faces up in a *keffiyeh* and many also wore sunglasses to hide their eyes. But once hidden from view, they were willing to tell on camera their inside stories of the terrorist group that had overtaken their lands and briefly overtaken their hearts and minds. These were battle-hardened men who had fought for ISIS (alongside two boys and three women—the wives of ISIS fighters, two having served in the *hisbah* [ISIS's police force]). Now they had crossed over—into Turkey and out of ISIS—and were willing to speak out to discredit and to denounce one of the most virulent terrorist groups to date. ISIS was now their enemy and they were willing to tell what life was really like under ISIS. But to do so we had to be present with them, to record their words and capture their stories on video, and Ahmet—who was there in person—had just received a threat on his life.

Chapter Two - Warnings

Henry Barrett's words came back to haunt me. Just two months before, I had found myself facing off with Henry, the legal officer overseeing this project. "Listen Anne, there's no interview, no matter how good, that is worth you ending up in the trunk of a car. That's just not worth it," he'd said, as I looked anxiously and determinedly around the room. It was just four days before Ahmet and I were scheduled to start the first of our ISIS interviews. But here I was, back in the donor's boardroom, seated around that gleaming conference table under fluorescent lights. Their side of the table was animatedly discussing my project and upcoming trip to Şanlıurfa, Turkey, to do these ISIS defector interviews face-to-face. The project was only just beginning, but now it was looking like it could get grounded before taking off.

I nodded and swallowed, trying to push out of my mind the image of me in a trunk. "If Ahmet is who he says he is, I'll be fine on this first trip," I argued. "He's the former Chief of Police for the area so I am quite sure he's armed and can judge the security situation pretty well. I'm planning to stay at his home and I won't be apart from him at any point in time," I reasoned—determined to salvage the trip. This was an amazing chance to talk to actual ISIS defectors in person and I was determined not to scrap it.

But I'd made a crucial mistake. I'd brought up my security and my reliance on Ahmet for safety, by asking Jeff Levy, the project officer, if they had any way to check out Ahmet. That's when the room erupted into a vigorous discussion of how the project could blow up if anything went off course.

"If you check on the State Department's travel advisory, it warns against travel there and even U.S. government officials aren't currently allowed to travel to the south of Turkey because of the security situation," Stevie said. "You'd be traveling on our funds. Imagine the article in the *New York Times* if something happened..." he said, looking around the table with his eyebrows raised and shaking his head in the negative. I sensed growing opposition to my upcoming trip, as they lined up in a defensive posture; though I wasn't sure if their concern was as much for my safety as for their careers and reputation if something went awry.

While they discussed the bureaucratic aspects of things going wrong, I also wondered about my personal safety, remembering how Ahmet had assured me that I could stay with him and his family in the security of his home. But another part of my mind was suspicious. *How can I know he is who he says he is? What if he needs money—I'd make a high value hostage being married to a now retired U.S. Ambassador. He doesn't have any real loyalty to me—it might be really tempting to sell me...*

I knew of cases in Turkey where fixers had intentionally sold western journalists to ISIS who later turned up as hostages—and beheaded. My heart raced as I quietly calmed my fears and rationally argue my case.

"*If* he's corrupt and wants to sell me, then I could end up in that trunk. I'm not keen on becoming another bride of ISIS," I joked, trying to make light with a reference to a book I'd recently published.[11]

"I know from past experience interviewing terrorists that if I keep going back into the same places, then there will probably be talk about me and that could be dangerous," I explained, relying on my years of experience doing interviews in terrorists' territory. "Right now, though, I think he hasn't told anyone who I am, only that he's got an American psychologist that will be sitting in the room with him." I didn't mention that Ahmet had also asked me to lecture at his university and offered to take me around town to see the historic sites.

Did they advertise the university event? My mind raced. *We could be walking around the old city and I could be nabbed with, or without, his involvement…I need them to check this guy out!*

The whole hubbub had its origins in an e-mail I received ten days earlier when Jeff, the project lead in the donor's office, had written to ask me about my travel plans for the project. He was making sure all the funds were in place and to double check on where I was planning to travel.

"You mentioned plans to conduct interviews in Şanlıurfa in Turkey," Jeff wrote, after receiving my plans, and proceeded to rattle off the State Department's travel advisory and ban. "We are concerned about this." He went on to suggest getting others to collect the interviews rather than going myself, adding, "Anywhere close to the borders with Iraq and Syria would be of concern to us (100 percent about safety)."

When I called to discuss it with him, however, he seemed less forbidding and told me that I *could* go—that I would just have to go as a university researcher, not representing their donor organization. After I agreed to those terms, I thought I had evaded Jeff's concerns and could continue on unimpeded.

But then Jeff had called this meeting, just days before I was scheduled to leave for Turkey. I thought it was just a routine meeting but I made that crucial mistake when we got together. "Jeff, did you ever ask your security contacts if they were able to vet Ahmet Yayla?" I had asked. "Because my security in going to Urfa pretty much depends on he being who he says he is." And that question had kicked off this stormy debate. The board members continued knocking it around the table, while I tried to placate them back into accepting that good counter-terrorism research always has some elements of risk.

But I knew they were talking sense—even I shared their concerns about ending up an ISIS hostage, or dead, as I tried to not let my fears get the best of me. But I also didn't want to give up this remarkable opportunity to be on this inaugural trip into ISIS defector territory. Everything was set up. Ahmet had identified and contacted six former ISIS defectors; we planned to have them come in, one-by-one, and we would complete all six interviews while I was in Urfa. I was pretty sure I could fly under the radar this first time. I wanted to get the lay of the land—make sure we got a good start.

"Why don't you have your security guys check him out and then we can decide from there?" I asked, hoping that if Ahmet checked out we could move ahead. Maybe after that we could find a safer way to keep going; or maybe the research wouldn't turn out to be worth it. But if we never got started we'd never know.

The group nodded as I talked, but I could see they were worried. The meeting ended with a "We'll get back to you," but that I shouldn't fly in four days as planned, until I heard from them.

As I left the meeting Jeff reached out to stop me. "I know we already discussed the travel advisory and government travel ban to the south of Turkey by e-mail," he said apologetically.

"Yeah, I thought we had resolved it," I answered, sighing.

"The discussion went all the way up the ladder," Jeff confided. "They're not against you going, but concerned. And I guess it's complicated—whether or not you are going as a university professor or representing our organization and if you are using our funds for your travel…"

We walked out of the boardroom together.

Crap! I thought to myself once I was out on the street and walking away from the gleaming glass and steel office building. *Why did I share my concerns about Ahmet with them?* I berated myself. The interviews were already set up. I had my plane tickets. This was bad.

I was fuming with frustration—this wasn't the first time I had been blocked by obstacles thrown in my path by bureaucracies. While I was trying to pursue my own research career, independent of my husband's high profile roles as a U.S. Ambassador, I'd learned my first hard lesson when we served in Minsk, Belarus.

I had just begun a Chernobyl liquidator project in which I agreed to interview the liquidators—the cleanup workers—who had evacuated the local populations and covered over the exploded nuclear facility that had spewed radioactive particles all over Belarus and the surrounding area when it exploded in 1986. I had my funding in place and the project was ready to move when a diplomatic row ensued. Out of fears that the U.S. was spying on him, the President of Belarus took over the neighboring U.S. Ambassador's residence along with other diplomatic residences in the same compound. As the U.S. Ambassador to Belarus, my husband, Daniel, was recalled to Washington for over a year until the situation was politically resolved. When we naively asked about my going back to work on the Chernobyl project during this interim, Daniel was told by his State Department bosses that if he valued his career he would stop me from returning to Minsk. Blocked. I was furious. I even made him ask if this "advice" applied to a private U.S. citizen or specifically to his wife who took no salary from the State Department. That's when they made it clear about valuing his career and the need to "control" his wife.

The same happened when I started interviewing terrorists. U.S. State Department officials came to our door early one morning when I was in Israel, having just come out of Gaza. They sheepishly asked my husband if he knew where I was, and if I was perhaps "pulling a Patty Hearst" (referring to the granddaughter of the publishing magnate who was famously kidnapped and co-opted into joining the leftist terrorist group, the Symbionese Liberation Army) since I'd been—according to them—"hanging out with" Hamas. Daniel set them straight, informing them that I'm a university professor who routinely interviewed terrorists, and that no, while I might have been meeting to talk with them, I wasn't joining Hamas any time soon.

Then when he was serving as the U.S. Ambassador to Greece I had research funding to interview Hezbollah cadres in Lebanon, but when I shared my plans with the U.S. Embassy's regional security officer, he blocked my travel to Beirut.

Thus I had gotten used to bureaucratic roadblocks and had learned, for the most part, to avoid discussing my plans with the U.S. State Department while Daniel was an active ambassador. Now as I started my ISIS defector project, with Daniel retired from State and no longer the spouse of a high-level diplomat, I once again saw that bureaucracy might still become my enemy. Even a private donor was referencing the State Department's travel advisory and blocking me! Ugh! It hadn't taken long to run into them—yet again.

As I grumbled my way back to my car I reflected on what I was about to embark on—*if* the donor could get over their concerns and allow me. It was early November of 2015 and the trees were ablaze in color. The sky was brilliant blue and the sun shone brightly. Some of the red and yellow leaves had already fallen onto the sidewalks and they made pretty abstract patterns that filled my mind as my thoughts wandered far away— across the ocean.

With our shared security expertise, Ahmet and I had gotten to know each other over e-mail and started discussing how we might be able to collaborate. He told me that he had twenty years of experience "interrogating terrorists from all kinds of backgrounds," and started keeping me informed about his outreaches into ISIS defector territory— going to the nearby Akçakale Refugee Camp to meet with a woman whose family had been executed by ISIS. "She has a strong and bitter story I will listen to. I've also scheduled a visit to Adiyaman prison to visit an ISIS member who was imprisoned for other crimes." He tacked on a sidebar about the appalling political situation in Turkey: "There has yet to be any one person detained or imprisoned as a result of ISIS related investigations in my country!!!" he noted with obvious disgust.

Indeed, up to that time the Turkish government had turned a blind eye to thousands of Westerners moving across Turkey as they streamed into ISIS territory inside Syria. Ahmet was well aware that counter-terrorism police were stopping Europeans who arrived to Şanlıurfa in southern Turkey, only to receive instructions to let them go, everyone knowing full well they were on their way into Syria to join ISIS. Likewise, Turkish security forces did little to nothing to stop the free flow of ISIS cadres and equipment moving in and out of Turkey across the border shared with Syria. Aside from being the buffer zone between ISIS-held territory and Europe, Turkey also serves as the outer border of NATO, yet they were not stopping the flow of foreign fighters into or out of ISIS.

Turkish Prime Minister Erdogan had his own interests to consider, interests that he consistently put before his commitments to the EU and NATO. By offering ISIS passive, if not active support, he got a two-for-one deal. He supported toppling Bashar Assad, Syria's ruthless dictator, and supported ISIS fighting the PKK—keeping a group that had created problems for Turkey for decades—well occupied. And as the Russians would soon claim in December of 2015, it appeared that Prime Minister Erdogan's son was also benefiting from a brisk trade in embargoed oil originating from ISIS.[12] Likewise, some donors in Qatar and Saudi Arabia were apparently using Turkey to funnel cash for weapons purchased and shipped through Turkey to ISIS cadres which made it likely that Turkish authorities could also take their cut from these supply chains as well.[13]

The politics with ISIS and Turkey were about to heat up a few notches further, but Ahmet and I were not yet aware of what was to come, although Ahmet did forewarn me that we might want to start our joint project soonest as our window of opportunity to get our interviews might be limited. "Turkey is going through a turbulent time which is becoming more powerful as we approach the election time," he wrote. "So, I assume even widespread, violent demonstrations could be initiated if things go really viral as people have begun to talk about it openly…"

Ahmet was enthusiastic about having an American partner join his research. He had completed his masters and doctoral study in Texas and worked extensively with U.S. Embassy officials and U.S. military in his counter-terrorism work. He loved working with Americans and was in fact hoping someday to move back to the U.S. and be hired as a university professor. For that he needed to write and publish books and articles in English on exactly these topics, and I could help him. But we still needed to overcome the obstacles to our potential collaboration.

As we laid plans to collaborate, I asked Ahmet if he thought the former ISIS members would agree to give us interviews on video.

"Those ISIS people, they don't like the camera," Ahmet wrote back. "I am not sure if I can persuade them to talk to the camera even if their faces are blurred and voices are changed. *They are afraid. One simple mistake can cost their lives.* So, this might be an issue. For this reason, I only audio record," he explained. "I could push the limits, but really, I don't know."

I explained to Ahmet why I was hoping to get actual former ISIS cadres speaking on video about the group's ideology, what life had been like under ISIS, and especially why they had become disillusioned and quit. "I want to put edited video clips of them speaking out about ISIS on the Internet to fight with ISIS in the social media space—to discredit and delegitimize ISIS and their ideology," I explained. "My project is for the purposes of prevention and dissuasion."

We began making plans for me to travel to Şanlıurfa, Turkey. As I got ready to buy my plane tickets I downplayed fears for my personal safety. How could I do otherwise? How could I continue to go out and interview terrorists if I focused on the danger? But I could not resist writing one last time, to question Ahmet, "One thing that is a concern is how do we know the people we are talking to are authentic and that they have actually defected? And of course safety is a concern," I added, trying to sound nonchalant.

"Safety is also my ultimate concern," Ahmet wrote back, understanding what I was thinking. Maybe he even read my mind. *Could I trust him? Did he have any monetary motive to sell me to ISIS?* I found myself asking myself this question once again. By then, more than one Turkish fixer had admitted selling Westerners to ISIS. My mind raced back to another kind of video. *I'd make a great hostage and beheading, married to a former U.S. Ambassador…*

"Please do not forget," Ahmet wrote, doing his best to reassure me, "I was the Chief of Police here for four years before I passed to the University. So, never, ever would I put you in a dangerous position. I will be with you all the time while you are here. Plus, Urfa is considerably safer compared with the rest of the south and east of Turkey. Anyways, you should be comfortable with your security here. My wife also speaks English and she will join us as her time allows. You are also welcome to stay at my home."

"That's great, I'll stay with you," I answered, jumping at the possibility of staying in the safety of his home, as I had already conjured up the vision of ISIS terrorists learning I was in Urfa and breaking into my hotel room in the middle of the night to drag me off.

Ahmet replied by reassuring me that he was a "family man" and that I would be safe staying with him. That made me laugh—as that was the least of my fears. He also sent lovely photos of his family—his wife smiled from behind wide sunglasses as she held her arm lovingly draped around the shoulder of her eldest boy. They had three boys, ranging in age from six to eighteen; the family looked happy and united. He also sent a picture of Osman, the six-year-old smiling as he posed at his school desk on his first day of school. He had dark black hair, was wearing a turquoise shirt as he smiled into the camera lens. Ahmet's wife wore a headscarf wrapped softly around her head and shoulders and the way she held her lithe frame, covered from head to toe in a fashionable made her look chic and relaxed, albeit conservative enough to "cover" herself. Staring at their photos I felt eager to meet them all in person.

There remained the other looming question, how did we know the ISIS cadres we were interviewing had really defected? *Maybe they would murder us both for having tried to interview them!* Again, Ahmet reassured me, "I have experience of interviewing over five thousand terrorists." He was quite sure they were not fakes and had truly defected.

With the offer to stay at his home, I was in. Discussing dates, Ahmet asked that we wait until after *Eid al-Adha*, the Islamic Feast of the Sacrifice commemorating Abraham's willingness to sacrifice his son to God as it was an important feast for gathering his extended family at home. As I bought my plan tickets to Urfa for early November, our project started to take on momentum. "I spent Friday talking to three ISIS guys and taking notes..." Ahmet wrote. He'd already been talking to Syrians refugees who had fled from ISIS rule and had gradually worked his way into talking to actual ISIS cadres who had also fled the group and were now in hiding in Turkey.

Four days from leaving—I was now on pins and needles waiting for the donor's permission to go, and silently wondering if I should just go on my own personal funding if their answer was negative.

Their e-mail arrived two days later: "XXX [the donor group] is impressed by your determination and commitment to Countering Violent Extremism. As to the discussion concerning your proposed travel to Southern Turkey next week: <u>XXX Does NOT approve of your travel to Southern Turkey and we are adamant that you NOT conduct any work on behalf of XXX in Southern Turkey.</u>"

It was a Friday and Henry Barrett, the fund's legal advisor to the project, had asked to meet me for lunch before this latest eruption. At lunch we discussed the e-mail.

"Are you still going to go?" he asked.

"I can't use the funder's money and go," I answered, incredulous that he was even asking the question.

Shaking his head, he laughed and added, "I told them, knowing you, that you'd be unlikely to stop..."

Were they telling me to go anyway? Pushing the responsibility solely onto my shoulders? Was I supposed to disregard their e-mailed demand?

If so, I probably shouldn't ask. So I didn't.

We finished our lunch, parted and I phoned Ahmet, asking what he thought of the donor's worry over the State Department's travel ban, telling him I could travel to Istanbul, but was blocked by my funder due from going all the way to Şanlıurfa where our interview subjects were to be located.

"You'll be safe here!" he protested, disappointment filling his voice. "We just moved the beds around in the boys' room to make a place for you," he added.

"Would it be possible to move the location of our interviews? To bring our subjects out of the banned travel zone?" I asked, grasping at possibilities to save the project. I didn't want to let it slip out of our hands.

"I've worked so hard to win their trust," Ahmet answered after a brief pause, concern filling his voice. "I don't want to do anything to make them suspicious. I already had one angry at me because we met in public. They are very frightened about getting caught and killed by ISIS. I think they trust me now and the place I've set up," he explained.

I nodded listening; what he said was absolutely legitimate. My mind raced for an answer. *Should I ignore the funder's instructions? Pay my own way? Would they discontinue the project if I went on my own?*

"Why don't you Skype in?" Ahmet suggested.

"Skype in?" I'd never done an interview remotely before. I'd traveled everywhere—to terrible places to meet terrible people. *Skype in?*

"Come to Istanbul and join the interviews by Skype. You can even ask questions if you want," Ahmet offered. I considered his idea. "Then after we finish the first six interviews, I'll fly to Istanbul and meet you in person."

I knew it was the only way to do the project without taking crazy risks and getting the donor furious at me. I just didn't realize what the costs would be to Ahmet and his family.

Chapter Three - *Cubs of the Caliphate*

"They trained us some days on [suicide] bombing and other times on weapons training," Ibn Omar is telling us. He is now fifteen-years-old but his voice is still boyish.

"The one who becomes a 'button', how do they prepare him, what do they tell him?" Ahmet gently probes.

"Button" is the word Ibn Omar and others use to describe the children—some as young as ten-years-old—who are encouraged to become vehicular suicide bombers. Ibn Omar calls them a "button" because they are taught to push a button (or brake) inside a rigged car to detonate its payload as they drive at high speeds into checkpoints and enemy lines.

Ibn Omar (his name means Son of Omar) has been explaining to us how young children, the so-called *Cubs of the Caliphate*, are indoctrinated and trained to be 'martyrs'. "They teach him about the car, how it's rigged up, and you go near it to see that you push the button and it will explode," Ibn Omar explains. "They tell them to blow themselves up among the unbelievers—the infidels. The guy who taught us religion taught this. He taught us, 'When you get to that car and push the button you will go to Paradise.'"

Ibn Omar is leaning forward in his chair, his entire head wrapped in a black and grey checkered *keffiyeh*. He's placed dark sunglasses atop that. Even though his face is hidden, it's obvious from his boyish frame and his small plastic-sandaled feet relentlessly tapping against the chair leg, that he's still a child. He clearly doesn't want to be recognized. He's very likely terrified that ISIS can hunt him down and kill him for having defected from their ranks. At fifteen, he's already a hunted man.

This boy is the ninth of our thirty interviews we will wind up doing with ISIS defectors from Syria, during this first phase of our project. The first six interviews were completed with me joining in via Skype from Istanbul. As a counter-terrorism expert, I've read a lot about ISIS, but hearing from actual insiders and in great detail, is mind-blowing.

By now we are a tight team, two weeks into our well-established pattern of having me Skype in for the interviews, which is working far better than I had imagined. After the sixth interview we have gained enough trust that defectors now agree to let us move from audio only to also video recording, including Ibn Omar.

I'm now back in my office in Washington, D.C. sitting with Mona, my Arabic translator by my side. Ahmet is in another makeshift video studio in southern Turkey with Murat, a graduate student helping him interview the boy. For security reasons, we are shifting interview locations but they all look the same—a non-descript white studio. I am utterly glued to my computer monitor, listening intently, but unable to see because the Internet connection in Ahmet's area is so weak that we don't risk turning on the video. Listening, I feel barely able to exhale. When Ibn Omar was a member of ISIS, he was only thirteen-years-old.

He began his seven months inside ISIS at a training camp for children where he was taught military tactics and *shariah* law as defined by ISIS. He continues to tell us about the "buttons". "The younger ones— who were naive—would be told to take a car and park it in a certain place. When they pressed the brake to stop, it would explode. The older ones who were convinced and willing, once they got to the location, they would press the button and blow themselves up." Ibn Omar's voice suddenly breaks with emotion. He is unable to finish his thought. Ahmet watches his knee bouncing up and down as his foot taps on the edge of his chair.

How evil and cynical an adult must be to tell a young child to forfeit his life in this way, I think to myself.

"Would you rig the cars, or would they come to you from elsewhere, ready?" Ahmet asks, reflecting his police focus on operational details of terrorist actions.

"The cars are prepared in Tell Abyad [a Syrian border city divided with Akçakale in Turkey] in hangers that [normally] store grain," Ibn Omar explains, his voice quiet; he sounds depressed.

"When they take the young kids to the explosion … how do they teach them to do it?" Ahmet queries.

I hear a deep sigh. "They don't teach them. They tell them to drive until they reach their destination, then pull the handbrake and wait. When they pull the handbrake, the car explodes." He is starting to open up— maybe Ahmet's fatherly style is beginning to help him speak about things that are clearly painful for him. I can't believe we are talking to a kid who almost became a suicide bomber and who has this depth of knowledge about how children are manipulated into going to their deaths.

Ahmet, I've found, is a skilled interviewer. It's hard to get a trauma survivor to open up. To do so you need to be the type of person who is able to ask the right questions in the right way, and then not only hear difficult material and hang in there with it, but also be able to hold the other person's painful emotions so they won't shut down. Ahmet has his own police interrogation style, but he is also gentle, and his heart is good. I'm pleased to see that he does very well in these face-to face interviews, which, as a research psychologist, makes me feel better about not being there in person.

On my side, I listen carefully with my psychologist ears and interject questions by typing them into Skype chat so as not to disturb their rapport. Ahmet asks my questions when the timing feels right. We've found it's better this way. It's jarring for the subjects if I suddenly chime as a disembodied voice. Although I do say hello at the beginning of each interview when Ahmet introduces me as an American research psychologist who is assisting him with the interviews, Ahmet makes very little of my involvement and our subjects usually forget I'm there. I had assumed at least some would wrongly accuse me of being from the CIA, but surprisingly none of them has ever questioned my presence. Here sexism works in my favor. As a woman I'm quickly discounted, left to actively type questions and comments as we go along.

And joining by Skype does have some advantages. We can converse silently about where the interview is going, how to respond to painful and often shocking material, and decide what we should ask next—all without interrupting the flow of the interview. While we have a consistent list of prepared questions that we want to cover, we let our subjects tell their stories naturally and insert our questions in ways that help them open up rather than shut down. All of our subjects have endured trauma and prefer to avoid many subjects, so it takes patience and skill to circle around and return to painful issues in ways that help them to begin to slowly talk. Likewise, they often surprise us with new information. So we take a semi-structured approach to the interviews, which are lasting several hours each, and follow as the defectors lead us into the inner workings of one of the most brutal terrorist groups in history.

"Those who would go [as suicide bombers]. Do they give them pills or anything?" Ahmet asks.

"Some of them take pills," Ibn Omar explains, a fact that is confirmed by a former ISIS commander we later interview.

"What type?"

"No one knew," the boy responds. "They were small pills that they would open and give to you." Later we learn from the commander that it's a sedative.

Ahmet asks about what the kids ate before going on their suicide missions.

"Everybody eats together at the camp. Some people eat before they go. Others don't."

"How many people that you knew went to blow themselves up?"

"From what I know it was about fifteen that went to blow themselves up," Ibn Omar's responds, not acknowledging if he knew any of them.

"When one of you were taken to carry out an explosion what would the other kids say?" Ahmet is now unable to keep the horror from invading his own voice.

"They would all say he's going to Paradise."

"Tell us about when your friend went to blow himself up. When you guys would spend time together, what did you talk about?"

"Some people said he went to Paradise, some said he didn't. Some said he was a martyr, blew himself up amongst infidels and killed many. We'd keep discussing that."

"After the bombing would you celebrate at the camp, or not?"

"They would just fire shots [in the air] and shout, '*Allahu Akbar!*' [God is greater!]"

"Where were the targets for suicide bombings?"

"Kobanî [also known as Ayn al-Arab, a city in northern Syria, located immediately south of the border with Turkey], the Syrian regime, the Free Syrian Army and the Kurds," Ibn Omar lists the usual enemies of ISIS and the fighting that took place in Kobanî between the Kurds and ISIS when ISIS took over Kobanî.

"Would these cars target checkpoints, military outposts, or homes?"

"No, the targets were checkpoints or military outposts. They'd come toward it speeding up and then blow himself up."

We have heard from those who served in the Free Syrian Army, prior to becoming ISIS fighters, that ISIS routinely sent Syrian child suicide bombers to checkpoints placing the opposing soldiers in the horrific position of having to judge whether or not to shoot an approaching child or flee from their post to avoid a potential explosion.

"Was there ever a suicide bomber who didn't carry out the attack and ran away?" Ahmet asks, as I hope the answer is yes, many!

"No. They don't run because they don't know what will happen.

It's not up to them." I feel sickened imagining that young children tricked into getting behind the wheel of a car do not understand that they are driving to their deaths.

"How old were the older ones?"

"School is divided in two groups, younger and older. The older were twenty-years-old and above. The older ones are convinced— sometimes they compete for who goes first." Ibn Omar sounds deeply depressed describing it.

"Why do they want to blow themselves up?" Ahmet asks.

"They blow themselves up because whoever blows themselves up around infidels will go to Paradise," he answers sullenly. Clearly he doesn't buy it.

"Who told you this?"

"The *sheikh*."

"Are the suicide bombers afraid?"

"No," his voice now devoid of emotion. Like many trauma survivors he's likely learned to dissociate his emotions from conscious awareness when they are overwhelmingly painful.

"Why weren't they afraid?"

"I don't know. They were convinced," Ibn Omar again answers flatly, offering no explanation. He clearly wishes to avoid remembering. "I started to see them taking the younger kids. They'd tell them they'll go to Paradise. There were some who didn't want to go, they'd tell them to drive the car somewhere and they would detonate it. I started to see a lot of people going but I wasn't convinced. I tried to take leave—when they approved my leave, I left them."

Ahmet, guides him back to the Cubs' training camp. "What about the older kids that would compete to go? Tell us about that."

"The older ones—once one of them drove a big truck with the bed filled with bombs. He was going to blow himself up. He and his friend argued about why he was picked to go before."

"Where did he blow himself up?"

"*Al-Farqa,*" Ibn Omar answers, naming a small village we don't know.

"So, tell us how you joined ISIS," Ahmet asks, going back to the beginning.

"I'd see them [ISIS] when I would go back and forth to the city," Ibn Omar explains, referring to going to and from his work in the countryside as a cotton harvester. He like many poor kids in his region was no longer in school at age thirteen. "I'd meet them and talk to them. Once I got to know them, I'd go to their local base. They asked me to join them in *ad-Dawlah* so we could carry out jihad for Allah." Ibn Omar is using the formal name, *ad-Dawlah*, meaning 'the State' ISIS insists its members use this designation. "They said they'd give me a car and a weapon and I could take whatever I want, and do whatever I want, and then I joined them." Ibn Omar's family was very poor and a young kid getting a car in Syria is unthinkable—a boy's dream.

"At this point, they [ISIS] had taken over your village?" Ahmet asks.

"Yes."

"When they took your village, how did they treat you?"

"In the beginning when they first took control, they treated us well and later they treated us badly."

"How? What did they do?" Ahmet gently asks.

"I saw them flog people for smoking. People were executed. Sometimes they took small kids who stole groceries and cut their hands off." *This done by an organization that claims to base itself upon Islam, a religion that is to be charitable to the poor,* I think to myself with disgust. The ISIS version of Islam—we will learn from many others—starved the locals to force them join. Ibn Omar is now sitting silently—likely shut down by what he's quietly remembering.

"When ISIS took over, what did your parents do? Where did they work? How were the family finances? How did you live? Was food readily available?" Ahmet peppers the boy with questions to open him back up.

"Some days it was and some days it wasn't," he answers dully.

"Why wasn't there food?" Ahmet again asks gently.

"There was no work," he answers, mirroring many of the other defectors who told us that when ISIS takes over, they control all the resources and jobs and only those who sign on with them can work and feed their families.

"Why did you want to join them?" Ahmet probes.

"They say jihad and that you'll go to Paradise," naiveté still echoing in his voice.

"How much time passed between you meeting and joining them?" Ahmet asks.

"Fifteen days."

I gasp hearing it. These days, those who join ISIS, both in Syria and in the West, radicalize so fast. It's a security nightmare for the international community trying to figure out who's going to be the next to board a plane for Syria, or mount an attack at home.

"What happened after you asked to join them?"

"They loaded us on a bus and took us to their training camp. There were a lot of us."

"How many of you were there?"

"About thirty."

"Were they all from your village?"

"No, some were from other villages and were also brought to the camp."

"When you went, did you tell your parents?"

"No."

"You ran away with them?"

"Yes."

"Tell us what happened," Ahmet asks, trying to coax the boy

into telling his story rather than giving short clipped answers to avoid remembering his time in ISIS.

"When they put us on the bus, they had the Qur'an playing. After we reached the camp we started training."

"Where was the training camp?"

"In *Tabqa.* " This city is near the Tabqa Dam, located on the Euphrates River, forty kilometers [twenty-five miles] upstream from Raqqa, the ISIS stronghold.

"How was the camp? Was it big? Were there more students?"

"Yes, there were more, the training camp was a big school," Ibn Omar responds. "There were about five hundred—just kids." *So many children!*

"So how was life in the camp? How did you wake up at this camp?" Ahmet asks, continuing his fatherly, gentle tone.

"At the *adhan* [call to morning prayers], they fired two shots in the air and woke all the young fighters and took us to pray. After we prayed they took us to shower—in cold water—until sunrise." Ibn Omar's head now hangs low. But Ahmet asks him what type of training he had at the camp and Ibn Omar seems to open up to that question.

"Military training with wooden rifles, not real ones. They placed ropes above and below us and we'd crawl in between them. Then they made us crawl through muddy trenches with barbed wire above us. They had a tire run that was about fifteen meters long. Then we had to jump through a big ring of fire. First we'd train on the rifle, we lie on the floor, and pull the wooden trigger." In some ways I can imagine these activities as adventures for a young boy, but of course that wasn't the case.

"After that, we'd train on the Russian [Kalashnikov rifle]. Then *Sheikh* Abu Musab—he'd come and train us in [physical] exercises. After that, Saifallah Al-Serbi taught us religious studies. And after that, they take us to offensive [classes]. We'd run and shout, '*Allahu Akbar!* ' and carry the flag and they would throw flash-bang grenades around us. After about a month they took us to *ribat* [border patrol of ISIS territory]."[14]

"So what did you do in *ribat*?" Ahmet asks.

"Sometimes they let us fire blank shots. They taught us to drive pick-up trucks. They taught us to fire the DShK (Dushka) 32, BKC," he lists heavy weaponry. "Then we started going to places near Kobanî. Before I quit, they wanted to teach me, and some of my friends, how to 'button'," Ibn Omar now admits, his voice again getting heavy and dull. He then pauses, hangs his head and sighs deeply. Even though I can't see his face it is clear to me that he has shut down.

In March of 2015, ISIS had already recruited at least four hundred children over a three-month time span for military training and hard-line indoctrination, according to the British-based human rights monitoring group, Syrian Observatory for Human Rights. The children were recruited near schools, mosques and in other public areas—some with their parents' consent and others without.[15] ISIS needed these children to fill in its ranks. The Turkish government had finally begun to tighten up its border with Syria, so the flow of foreign fighters slowed, and Coalition air strikes were taking their toll. So ISIS leaders ramped up their recruitment of younger cadres from the local populations. When ISIS captured Mosul, Kurdish officials reported that one hundred twenty-seven children between the ages of eleven to fifteen were kidnapped and forced into militant training to carry out terrorist operations—including suicide missions.[16]

"They use children because it is easy to brainwash them," Rami Abdulrahman, the head of Syrian Observatory for Human Rights reported.[17] "They can build these children into what they want, they stop them from going to school and send them to IS [Islamic State] schools instead." As early as August of 2014, ISIS released a video showing child cadres proudly performing chants, songs and military formations in front of the Chechen ISIS leader Omar al-Shishani, and in the summer of 2015, ISIS released that first infamous video of a child beheading a prisoner.[18] In that horrifying video, a boy who looks to be about ten-years-old, dressed in camouflage and with a black headdress, his face uncovered, takes a small knife in his hand as he approaches a regime soldier who is lying on his stomach, hands tied behind him. The boy ruthlessly pulls his victim's head up, holding him by the hair and proceeds to slit his throat and then behead him. After severing his head, the boy holds it up triumphantly to the camera.[19]

Until then, boys as young as twelve had been shown in videos executing their victims at gunpoint and children had been shown alongside proud displays of severed heads, but no child had yet been filmed carrying out a beheading. A new low, even for ISIS.

"Tell us about your religious studies," Ahmet redirects the conversation, understanding that the boy does not yet want to open up about almost being sent on a suicide mission.

"The lessons were given by Abu Juleybiba al-Libi."

"Which verses did they teach you [from the Qur'an], which books, which *sheikhs* or writers?"

"I don't know. He would just tell us a verse and sometimes he would just preach."

"How many in each class?"

"Each religious class was twenty [students]."

"Can you describe the schedule of your day?" Ahmet asks, again trying to get into the details.

"Training began at 7 a.m."

"The military training?"

"Yes – until *adhan al-maghrib* [call to sunset prayers]." He sounds exhausted.

"And the religious studies?"

"From the *adhan al-maghrib* [call to sunset prayers] until *adhan al-isha* [call to evening prayers]."

"How long did you stay at the camp?" Ahmet coaxes.

"About a month."

"What was the name of the camp?"

"Its name was *The Martyr, the Sheikh Abu Musab al-Zarqawi Camp*, [named after the late leader of al-Qaeda in Iraq who was assassinated in a 2006 U.S. military bombing raid], and our division was the *Cubs of the Caliphate*."

"Who told you to become a 'button'?" Ahmet asks, honing in again on the painful subject.

"*Sheikh* Abu Musab." This is most likely a *nomme de guerre* of one of the fighters who named himself after the now deceased former al-Qaeda in Iraq leader, al-Zarqawi.

"How did you respond?" Ahmet probes.

"He started taking some of my young friends. They took them to pick-up trucks and told them to drive and it turned out there were bombs in there." Recounting what he witnessed—ISIS leaders tricking kids into suicide missions—Ibn Omar is now skirting nearer to the horror which he narrowly escaped.

"Some of us took leave, then quit and came to Turkey," he tells Ahmet with finality.

Ahmet brings him back into the camp once again, "What did they train you to target?" Ahmet asks.

Ibn Omar names two towns we don't recognize, "*Al-Karat* and *Al-Farqa,* and the Free Syrian Army."

"How many of your friends went?" Ahmet pushes.

"A lot. A lot of people I knew."

"From the same training camp?"

"From the same and others."

Ahmet moves to the time after his graduation from the *al-Zarqawi* training camp. "After your training was completed and you were deployed, where did they take you?".

"[After], we finished military training, they took us in pick-up trucks and buses. They took us to Raqqa. Then it was Deir [ez-Zor]. Then on the border with Iraq there are some camps. We went into the camp then we went back to *ribat* [border patrol] and Kobanî. For four or five days they gave us tours in the area," he answers, describing a tour of ISIS-held territory intended to instill in these boys the "glory" of the "Caliphate". "They showed us the fight on the front line. How the *mujahideen*, like us, were fighting."

"They got you excited?"

"Yes. When we saw them we felt everything was going well for them [ISIS]," he explains in his boyish voice.

"Tell us about the beheadings. Who were they, why? Did you agree with it?" we ask, circling in again on the horrific.

"In the beginning, I thought that those who were beheaded were infidels. Adulterers were killed and stoned. Some were thieves. Some practiced magic. Some were traitors. Some others had their hands cut off for stealing. Some wrote letters to women, some were informants to the Syrian regime."

"Was anyone killed in front of you?"

"Yes, and the older recruits would do it. Sometimes they let the seven and eight-year-olds do it, either with a knife or a gun." I can't help but gasp imagining a seven-year-old beheading a grown man.

"Was there any incident when someone was killed in front of you at the camp?"

"Yes." *Back to the monosyllabic answers—he's shutting down, I* think.

"How were they killed?"

"Al-Zarqawiya."

"What's that?"

"A big knife." Named after the former leader of al-Qaeda in Iraq, the precursor organization to ISIS, this is also the name of his youth camp.

"Did any of your classmates execute anyone?"

I recoil as we wait to hear the answer.

"Yes."

We don't ask him directly if he beheaded anyone, as we decided before embarking on this project, for ethical reasons, we would not ask anyone directly what crimes they may have committed. We know they could be prosecuted for self-incriminations and we might feel bound to turn them into the authorities as well—ethical dilemmas we prefer to sidestep.

"How did it make him feel?"

"He felt he was close to God."

"Tell us about your friend."

"They took him, we asked him where he was going, and he told us he was going to perform an execution. He came back happy."

"What did he tell you when he came back?"

"He was proud because despite the fact that he [the prisoner] was much older, [my friend] was able to cut his head off and he couldn't stop him." I am now forcing myself to listen and not turn away.

"How was he able to cut off his head?"

"The person's hands are tied, so he pulled his hair back and sawed across his neck until he was beheaded." Ibn Omar makes a sawing motion with his hand as he describes it, I see later when we watch the video of his interview. I get the strong feeling that Ibn Omar was present for this beheading, but we decide not to ask.

We are speaking to Ibn Omar in November 2015. He'd been in Turkey seven months by then. The events Ibn Omar is recalling occurred before ISIS publicly released that first video showing a boy beheading a Syrian prisoner.

"Didn't you want to behead anyone like your friend did?" Ahmet asks, skating very close to our ethic of not asking our subjects to incriminate themselves.

"No, I didn't want to behead anyone."

"Why? *Ad-Dawlah* does this all the time. Why didn't you want to do what they do?" Ahmet goads just a bit.

"No, I don't want to like cutting anyone's head off."

"Why?"

"I just didn't want to," Ibn Omar answers. We suspect that he likely was involved, especially as other defectors have already told us that to graduate from the *shariah* training camps, there is the required ritual to behead a prisoner as proof of having adopted ISIS ideology and committed to the Islamic State. The trainees are given a prisoner and a knife before they make their *bayat* [pledge] to ISIS. There is every reason to believe that Ibn Omar faced the same fate at age thirteen.

"In the beginning when they used to execute people in front of you, did it make you happy or sad?"

"There were some that were sad, but that was deep down. You had to act happy and shout, '*Allahu Akbar!*' If you weren't happy you'd be punished."

"Personally, were you happy or upset in the beginning?"

"I would get upset."

Later we learn from other defectors that ISIS held prisoners in Tabqa for the sole purpose of using them at the end of *shariah* trainings.

"Tell us about your friend that performed the execution. Tell us the whole story. How he went and then came back to tell you about it."

"They came and picked him up in a truck and told him he was going to execute an infidel…They took him, the *al-Zarqawiya* and the infidel from Tabqa to Tell Abyad, to the traffic circle. They tell everyone in the mosque the day before to come, and the next day people gather. They bring the prisoner. Sometimes they just shoot him in the head." He doesn't want to remember.

"How did your friend kill him?"

"My friend took him to the traffic circle, put him on his knees, and beheaded him. Blood squirted everywhere. Then he put the severed head on the floor next to his body." I feel my stomach flipping over in horror, again wondering if he was actually there witnessing it and even replaying it now in his mind.

"What did your friend tell you when he came back from the camp?"

"They brought the infidel, the apostate, and I cut his head off with *al-Zarqawiya*. I got money as a prize and could take extra leave."

"Did you have any nightmares because of what you saw?"

"Some people dreamt they were being executed by beheading. Others didn't [have any nightmares]," he responds, saying nothing of his own dreams and neither confirming nor denying whether he actually witnessed this beheading by his friend. ISIS practices *Takfir*—declaring other Muslims who don't adhere to their version of Islam as apostates, worthy of death.

"So if you're not with them, you're not Muslim? "Why?" Ahmet asks.

"I don't know." He's just a kid.

"You worked with them at the training camp, they didn't tell you why?"

"No. If you don't join *ad-Dawlah* and pledge your loyalty to Abu Bakr al-Baghdadi you are an infidel. Some of the local [ISIS] fighters said they now knew that their father was an infidel and that as soon as they could, they would take leave and would go kill him."

"These were some of your classmates?"

"Yes."

Beheading your own father. Totalitarian regimes around the world are all the same in this regard—turning children against their own families.

Ibn Omar is the perfect young candidate to be inducted into a group like ISIS. He's a naive, a believing Muslim who doesn't know his religion and can't read the Qur'an, so he can't verify or discredit what he's being taught. He's living in a conflict zone and still probably sees things rather black and white like the pre-teen that he is. His father has been disempowered with the lack of work that came with the conflicts, and powerful men therefore will appeal to him when he feels frightened about the future and is looking for a pathway to manhood.

"How do you feel now about *ad-Dawlah*, are they right or not? Tell us why?" Ahmet asks. In this project we are interested in gathering voluntary statements from ISIS insiders willing to denounce the group, because we believe the voices of those who walked away are the most powerful to discredit ISIS and its ideology.

"Wrong. They kill innocents. They say they are an Islamic State but they aren't Islamic," he responds. "They allow and forbid things as they please. They take cigarettes from traders and sell them to other traders. Most of them take pills. That's why I wasn't convinced."

"Where were they taking pills and taking cigarettes from traders?"

"They take all the cigarettes off the market, after a week the cigarettes reappear on the market." Interestingly, in some of the ISIS propaganda films, cigarettes are burned for a public "show", but apparently at other times they are quickly resold on the market.

"How were you convinced in the beginning that they were an Islamic State and now you aren't?"

"Once I joined them I saw." *Exactly,* I think, *an insider knows the truth.*

"After you ran away from home, did you miss your family?" Ahmet asks. I think about the pictures Ahmet sent when we were first getting to know each other, of himself and his wife with their three sons and how he talked about his boys when we met in person in Istanbul. He's a very concerned father and that comes out as he interviews Ibn Omar.

"No," Ibn Omar answers, surprising me.

"Why didn't you miss them or try to talk to them?" Ahmet asks with kindness.

"It's forbidden. The moment you set foot in the camp they tell you to forget your family," Ibn Omar exhales another long sad sigh.

"Why did they tell you that?"

"So you don't run and keep going back and forth and they [the family] will convince you to quit."

"Personally, didn't you miss your family?"

"No." Ibn Omar learned to separate himself from his feelings about missing his parents—expressing them could have ended in death.

"You believed in them [ISIS] and liked them, or did you just want to run from your family?"

"No, I liked them [ISIS] a lot, but now I don't want them," his voice is flooded with disappointment that fades into another silence.

"Didn't you have a friend that you confided in and said you missed your family?"

"There were friends like that, but we're scared to speak to them because people will inform them [ISIS] and they worried we'd run away or something."

"Why can't you quit?"

"Because they do bad things, and if you want to quit, they won't let you."

"Why?"

"Because it is forbidden." Ibn Omar, like so many of the ISIS defectors we talk to has learned to accept what is *haram* [forbidden] according to ISIS, and that they are *to hear and obey* without question. A refrain we will hear repeated often.

"Tell us about the training and why you didn't miss your family," Ahmet pursues.

"We arrived at the camp and began our training. My friends and I would sit and talk. After we finished our training for the day, we'd go to religious studies. Everything was normal. Towards the end, when they started telling us about 'buttons', then I stopped liking them. After that, they weren't important to me." Ibn Omar's disillusionment came as he realized they were being trained as cannon fodder for a group that had no interest in their welfare.

Ahmet wants to get into the details of the daily routine at the children's camp. Even the seemingly mundane was a means for manipulation.

"What did they give you for breakfast?" Ahmet asks.

"Dates and yogurt. That's it."

"Did it fill you up?"

"No." Ibn Omar wraps his arms around his small body and his foot again taps nervously on the chair leg.

"Why would they give you so little to eat?" Ahmet asks.

"So when we fight, we can withstand hunger."

"Tell us about the meals in that training camp in detail," Ahmet coaxes.

"It was dates and yogurt, and dinner was sometimes chicken, sometimes rice and lamb and bulgur wheat."

"Why wasn't there lunch?"

"Because in battle, sometimes you can't just sit and have lunch."

"When you wanted to sleep, what would you do?" Ahmet asks.

"They would come and tell us to go to sleep. Everybody would go to their bed and sleep. Those who could read Qur'an would and those who didn't know how to read Qur'an went to sleep or he'd pretend to read the Qur'an." I imagine the illiterate among them pretending to be able to read in order to appear pious.

"What time would you go to sleep, approximately?"

"Bedtime was ten p.m. We had to wake up for morning prayers and shower in cold water."

"When they put you in the cold water [in the morning showers], would you play?" Ahmet asks, searching for any shred of normal, playful, boyish behavior in this camp.

"We'd just stay and walk around [in the water] in the winter so we can stand the cold."

"Did you cry then?"

"No, but a lot of people cried. Cried and yelled. They wanted to get out and they [ISIS] wouldn't let them."

"Tell us more details about those who cried."

"There were many who cried. Five or six, every morning. We'd hear them screaming and every time they'd try and leave the water, they would be sent back immediately. I remember when they took us from Tell Abyad to Camp Tabqa, we were in front of the Turkish border. One of us jumped out of the bus and ran to Turkey."

"Tell us about the trainers and *sheikhs*, did they treat you kindly because you were children?"

"No."

"Psychologically—were they caring?"

"No, it was military training. No caring or anything. If you slipped up, they would put your finger in the barrel of a gun and bend it all the way back, almost until it broke." His foot, in its broken rubber sandal, taps relentlessly on the leg of his chair, but his voice is bland and devoid of emotion. He's learned to bury it deep inside, yet his body betrays him.

"They treated you harshly?"

"Yes."

I realize that Ibn Omar has thus far taken no opportunity to exaggerate. Instead, as with most true trauma survivors, he prefers to engage in avoidance and downplay what he's been through.

"Did you have playtime or anything like that?" Ahmet encourages.

"No, just training. It was forbidden to play. Some would try; they would go and play in the trees near the school. They [ISIS] forbade it. They were told to clean the camp and wash the clothes of all the soldiers."

"Not even football [soccer]?" Ahmet asks.

"No, only the older recruits could," his voice sounds tinged with envy. I can almost feel the "sibling" rivalry set up between the elder youth and youngsters at the camp.

"What was the age of the youngest recruit?" Ahmet asks.

"There was one who was seven-years-old. He wanted to join and they accepted. He was one of the security patrol and intelligence."

"How did he get there and request to join?"

"He came to the main checkpoint and asked to join." I try to imagine this small, innocent child appearing at the checkpoint of an ISIS training camp, having no idea what he is getting himself into, yet ISIS is ready to scoop him up. "The soldiers brought him to the *sheikh*. The *sheikh* agreed, and he went through fifteen days of training. After that he became security/intelligence. We didn't speak about leaving or missing our parents in front of him."

"Why?"

"If he were to snitch, the *emir* would punish you."

"The younger recruits, how many of them were there?"

"There were less young recruits than older ones, about fifteen or sixteen of them."

"How old were they?"

"Six-and-a half to seven-years-old. The older kids were between seven and fifteen-years-old." I shake my head in disbelief.

"If your camp housed fifty people. How many of them were under the age of ten?" Ahmet asks, trying to gauge what percentage were really little kids.

"About eighteen of them."

"Were there incidents when families came to ask after their children? Demanding them back?" Ahmet asks.

"Yes."

"Did they get them back?"

"No. Families can't come to the camp, they'll get hit." We assume he is speaking of snipers guarding the camp's entrance or land mines. "They go to the checkpoint that is further away. They say that they are here for their children. So sometimes when the child who is well trained has been at the camp, they are told they aren't there. If the child is not as good of a student, then they allow the family and child to see each other from a distance," the boy explains. I imagine the pain of families and their children, broken hearted and broken down by this ruthless organization that tricked their sons into their cult-like camp.

"Did you miss or crave anything while you were at the camp?"

"If you ask for something, you're told it's forbidden until training is over. After training, you're able to request leave for a day, or a few hours. You'll be given spending money and you can buy."

"Who gives them the money?"

"After you spend time with them, they will give you a salary, and you're allowed to take leave or days off."

"How long do you need to stay with them?"

"Two or three years." Almost a quarter of a young life.

We are always interested in how Europeans engage with ISIS. Ahmet asks if Ibn Omar saw any European fighters.

"American, Chinese and French," he tells us. Whenever I hear about American foreign fighters in ISIS, my ears prick up. *What are they doing there?*

"Did you talk to them?"

"We don't understand them and they don't understand us." Ibn Omar speaks only Arabic.

"What do you think of them?" Ahmet asks.

"They're better than the Syrians."

"Why do you say that?"

"They come for real jihad. Syrians and Egyptians are no good. We always see the Egyptian or Iraqi foreign fighters just here to rule and take money. The Chinese, Americans, and Russians, or any other foreign fighters come for jihad. They go to fight. The Syrians are always behind. The foreign fighters are on the front lines ahead of them," he explains.

Ibn Omar is mirroring a sentiment we have heard repeatedly. Many of the adult defectors have told us that the Western foreign fighters are indoctrinated into militant jihadi thinking before arriving and are "true believers" committed to building the "Caliphate."

"Were there foreign children at the training camp?" Ahmet wonders.

"Sometimes they come with their families, not individually. The whole family comes. A father and son, a man and his brother. Their training camp is separate. The foreigners sometimes come with us, only one or two of them." From others we learn that foreign fighters join training camps grouped by shared language, so likely it was Arabic speaking foreigners in his camp.

"Were there young girls at the training camp?" Ahmet inquires.

"There weren't any. Some women carry weapons in the city. They wear traditional Islamic clothing and their job is to flog."

"Who are these women?" Ahmet asks.

"The women of *ad-Dawlah*; they work for the *hisbah* [morality police]." We will hear a lot about the *hisbah* in this project—the ubiquitous and often sadistic keepers of the ISIS morality code.

We're keenly interested in the treatment of women by ISIS, the roles they play inside ISIS, and the fates of Western girls who travel to become the brides of ISIS.

"How do they treat women in the areas they rule? Do they look for wives?" Ahmet begins this line of questions.

Ibn Omar shares the bit that he knows about. "They look for wives a lot. He marries her for a week and leaves her." One sometimes hears speculation about gang rape of single young women in ISIS controlled territory. This is different. Ibn Omar is saying that ISIS cadres marry and then treat women as disposable. *Is this the so-called, jihad al-nikah? I wonder? Jihad al-nikah* was the likely false rumor that circulated in 2013 about women traveling to Syria to provide sexual comfort for the fighters by marrying them in rapid succession for one night—basically functioning as prostitutes (see Chapter Five and Six).

"Who are the ones that look for wives?" Ahmet asks.

"Foreign fighters, Egyptians. They marry them and leave them after a week," he repeats. We've heard a lot about the Tunisians coming to ISIS because they are unemployed and too poor to be married at home. Sex-starved, they are noted as particularly aggressive toward the local single Syrian women. But now Ibn Omar is telling us about Egyptians who use marriage to prey on women. *It's rape*, I find myself thinking.

Using Skype chat, I ask Ahmet to ask if any of the boys were mistreated or sexually assaulted in the camp.

"No," Ibn Omar answers, then he adds, "There was an incident when an *emir* went to a woman at home and tried to rape her. They [ISIS] suspected him and he ran away to Turkey."

Our assumption is that ISIS must, at least on the surface, be offering something positive, otherwise no one would join or stay in the organization. True, it's hard to leave once in, but we assume there must also be benefits to joining. "When you think back about your experiences with the Islamic State, what good have you learned, what benefits did you attain?" Ahmet asks.

Ibn Omar has no trouble with the question and answers immediately. "They taught us how to pray, and how to perform *zakat*. Some things I liked, some others I didn't. I liked prayer and that they taught prayer, fasting, charity, and all things good. They don't let anyone blaspheme, or drink alcohol, or take drugs, or adultery, or anything like that. They cleaned the country from all [these things]. There was no more theft."

"But there were also things I didn't like. If they don't like someone they would just execute them, cut off their hands, or flog them. If a woman isn't wearing *hijab,* or a hand, or body part is out, then they flog her in the street and no one can intervene. Or the floggers [the *hisbah*] come and hit her. Sometimes they would bring a young child who is innocent and cut off his hand because he didn't want to join ISIS. Because he didn't follow them, they cut off his hand!" I flinch at the barbarous image of a child's hand chopped off for *any* reason.

Suddenly Ibn Omar marches on with a litany of abuses, "Innocent people are punished. They put them in small cages and submerge them in water, cut off hands, flogging…"

"Have you seen cases of torture?" Ahmet asks.

"Yes." The monosyllabic answers appear to return, but this time they don't. Now, about halfway into his two-hour conversation with Ahmet, Ibn Omar appears to feel safe enough to open up more. He has begun to trust that if he does, Ahmet will help him hold his pain in the remembering.

"Where?"

"I don't know, they put us in a van and drove us at night. They'll put five or six in a cage, shut the cage, and submerge it in the water until they almost drown and then they pull them out. They kept torturing them like that." Later, on the Internet, we find pictures and an ISIS video of this practice.

"Who were the people in the cage?"

"No one knew what they did or who they were. Sometimes they put people in a car and they hit it with an RPG [rocket propelled grenade]. Blew them up in the car, or they burn them."

How can he ever be normal after witnessing these things? I ask myself.

"After you pray what do you pray for?" Ahmet is referring to *dua,* personal prayers that follow formal prayer. He poses this surprise question not from our list, but I think it's brilliant—a great way to get at a child's internal mindset.

"When I was with them, I would pray for victory for *ad-Dawlah,* and to destroy the planes and tanks of the Americans, and give Muslims strength. Now I pray *Allah* will give victory to those in the right," he answers, reflecting a common prayer of Islamic tradition.

"Do you pray for your parents?" Ahmet returns to this tender subject. Since fleeing ISIS, Ibn Omar has been separated from his parents who remained in Syria and is living with an aunt and uncle in Turkey.

"Yes, for Allah to bless them and give them a long life and keep them safe for me."

"Do you love your parents?" Ahmet ask.

"Yes." The monosyllabic answers return. As a trauma survivor, his positive and posttraumatic emotions are buried together—to access one he ends up accessing them all. So it's psychologically safer for him to keep them all buried, and avoid feeling anything at all.

"Did you like them more, or the 'Caliphate?'"

"I liked my parents more." Finally, we hear some positive emotions for his family. "Yes, they are dear to me and I missed them but I couldn't leave until I had been with them [ISIS] for five months."

"So, how did you decide to leave them [ISIS]? Tell us in detail what you saw that made you hate them."

"I saw that they were training young children that didn't know anything," once again his young voice wavers with emotion. "If those kids knew that their missions were actually suicide bombings, they wouldn't go. I saw them teaching young kids about explosions. I knew it was only a couple of days before they would teach me about them, too. I decided to quit before they trained me," terror fills his voice.

I think how close he came. *The boy narrowly escaped being put in a bomb-filled car*...

"How did you leave?"

"I requested leave from the *wali* [administrator] to go to Raqqa. I requested a month of time off...People requested either fifteen days or a month off. I requested a month. Some of them went back, but I was one of the ones who didn't go back after my time off." It sounds like he made a case for himself to earn leave before his two to three years of serving ISIS.

"When you went back to your family during your time off, were you convinced to be a suicide bomber? Did your family have to convince you not to?" Ahmet is searching for that turning point, when actionable doubt started to find its way in.

"I saw them training the younger kids; they started training some my age after I left. When I went back to my parents, they asked where I had been and I said with *ad-Dawlah*. I stayed with them for a couple of days and then crossed the border into Turkey."

"How did you feel when you saw your parents after five months of being away from them?"

"It was normal." Here is a traumatized boy—no expression of feelings about the reunion with his family, nothing.

"When you came to Turkey, did your parents send you, or did you come alone?"

"I came alone."

"Why weren't you convinced to become a suicide bomber?"

"I wasn't convinced that if you did it you'd go to Paradise."

"What do you think happened to all those suicide bombers?" Ahmet gently probes, trying to get at what Ibn Omar now believes about so-called 'martyrdom' operations. The boys were all demanded to celebrate and yell '*Allahu Akbar!*' Now, he may be wondering if his classmates are actually rotting in hell, rather than lounging in Paradise.

"I don't know," Ibn Omar dodges the question.

"Tell us about your decision to quit in further detail," Ahmet encourages.

"The older recruits had telephones and they started showing us how innocents were dying and those that should die, nothing was happening to them. We saw people beheaded. Old and young, all were innocent and died, and there were no consequences for the guilty. That's why I quit." By the age of thirteen, this boy has taken on board more than a lifetime's quantity of traumatic bereavement and horror.

"You saw the videos and saw that innocent people were the victims of the bombings, talk to us about that," Ahmet continues to gently coax.

"The *emir* told the camp that some of recruits that had been with them for longer were coming to stay with us for a few days until their base was ready. We would socialize with them and watch video clips on their phones—these videos showed people [being beheaded] proclaiming their innocence. ISIS killed their families. ISIS members denied killing innocents, but we all knew who the killers were at the camp. After I saw the video clips, I decided to leave them. If it weren't for the things I saw, I wouldn't have left them. I would have stayed." Ibn Omar was captivated by the Islamic teachings, and by the dream of building a Utopian "Caliphate" ruled by Islamic ideals where he would be freed of living under Bashar Assad's oppressive regime.

"The other recruits with you that also saw the videos, what was their reaction?"

"They had the same thoughts. Some were scared to leave and others weren't. Those who weren't scared left."

"Are you happy now in Turkey?"

"Yes, I am finally free from *ad-Dawlah*. Everything is forbidden there. In Syria, *ad-Dawlah* imposed a curfew from midnight. Then they moved it to seven p.m. In Turkey, you can go out at anytime. Here is better than there," his voice lightens.

"What do you do in your free time in Turkey?" Ahmet asks.

"I go and look at Syria [across the border]," Ibn Omar answers, his voice is filled with longing.

"You miss Syria?"

"Yes. After I finish picking cotton, I go to the fence and look at Syria," the boy repeats. Ibn Omar is working as a low-paid migrant laborer.

"How do you feel when you look at Syria?"

"I want to go there."

"What's stopping you from going?"

"The Kurds."

"The PYD?" Ahmet clarifies, referring to the Kurdish forces in Syria, the analogue of the PKK in Turkey.[20]

"Yes."

"Why are you scared of them?"

ISIS drastically changed the politics in Tel Abyad, the region in Syria where Ibn Omar is from. It used to be a mixed town with Kurds and Arabs living peacefully side-by-side. But it was overtaken by ISIS, and then retaken by the Kurds, who now often see all Arabs as ISIS who should be hunted down for retribution for all that the Kurds suffered under ISIS rule.

"You don't want to go because you're wanted by them?" Ahmet asks.

"Yes," Ibn Omar lets out another huge sigh.

"When you think about home, what do you miss the most?"

"I miss the whole house. I'd walk around the house, sit at home, walk around the neighborhood and see people. After I finish work, I go look at Syria through the fence. I wish I was home with my parents. I often wish I could go home and sit there and walk in our street. I feel like all I want is just to go back," he answers, dejected.

"How do you see your future in Turkey?"

"I don't have a future in Turkey, only in Syria. I just feel like I want to go back."

"Why do you feel you don't have a future in Turkey?"

"Because this is not my homeland," the boy answers. "I lost everything, my country, our home, and everybody died…" It is then that Ibn Omar, half man and half boy at age fifteen, starts to cry. Ibn Omar, who so narrowly missed having any future at all, sees no future as long as he is held hostage here in Turkey while his town, literally within walking distance, remains inaccessible.

Ahmet stays on the possibility of a future, "If you got married and had children, what would you teach them?"

"I'd teach them to pray and fast, not to do anything wrong."

"Wrong like what?"

"Not to steal, not to drink, not to hit or hurt anyone," he answers, no longer innocent.

"Do you want to get married?"

"No."

"Why?"

"Just because." Ibn Omar is displaying the posttraumatic feature often present in trauma survivors of having a sense of a foreshortened future. After what he's lived through he finds it difficult to believe in any sense of predictability, safety or goodness in the world. He may also feel guilty for surviving when others did not.

"Imagine if you had a lot of money, if you came from a rich family—what would you do?" Ahmet asks, trying to encourage the boy to see possibility.

"I don't know. I'd buy a car. I'd start a business and have apartments on top," he responds.

"Allah created us in this life to live and understand life. Why do I feel like you're so pessimistic?"

"I'd like to always stay this way," the boy answers, his head hanging down.

"You like to be isolated and alone?"

"Yes. I like to always stay alone. I isolate myself. No one to talks to me and I talk to no one. I don't like to get close to people."

"What about your peers, are they isolated like you?"

"They like to mix and mingle; they talk with anyone like normal."

Avoiding interacting with others and social alienation like Ibn Omar is describing is another feature of PTSD. He's going to need a period of security before he'll likely begin believing in any kind of personal future again—but it doesn't look like that can happen anytime soon. He has another, more pressing reason for avoiding mixing with others—if anyone connected to ISIS recognized and reported him— he knows that could result in his murder.

"This situation is because you're coming from war. Everyone who goes through war feels the same way. You should be happy and live life, what you saw is behind you. Be happy, live life," Ahmet, the father, tries to encourage him.

"No, I want to stay like this," Ibn Omar repeats, his voice flat. My guess is that if he opened up his mind to feeling the positive feelings Ahmet is suggesting, all the posttraumatic recall would come rushing in— and he cannot afford that yet, lacking the emotional support he's going to need to help him through it.

"Since you haven't seen your mother in a while, do you think about hugging her? If you saw her what would you do?" Ahmet asks, while I worry that the boy will get upset again.

"I'd greet her and hug her. I'd stay with them and never leave…" he pauses, choked up.

I can feel his sadness as he expels his breath and it makes me want to reach out and wrap my arms around him. I type my feelings to Ahmet, "This boy is killing me—breaking my heart. Is there something he needs? Food or something that I can buy for him?"

Ahmet types back, "He needs shoes and a warm coat. He's wearing broken plastic sandals and he only has a light shirt but the weather has turned cold here. He has no jacket. He works for three dollars a day in a cotton field."

I swallow hard reading this, feeling horrible for what this kid has been through. I point to the text as Mona, the Tunisian translator by my side reads it and also frowns. But she quickly explains to me (we are on mute) that Ahmet should be careful about what he buys the boy. Used clothing is a better choice to avoid calling attention to him or raising any questions about where, and how, he got new clothes. I type that—to be careful what he buys for the boy—though Ahmet has already moved ahead with the interview.

"In Turkey, ISIS is trying to recruit young children your age. Have you heard of this?" Ahmet queries.

"I've heard a little. People talk."

"So are there occasions where they've taken children from here to Syria?"

"Here at our town? No."

"Now you're in Turkey, are you still afraid of *ad-Dawlah*?"

"Once I saw what they were really like, I stopped being scared of them."

"Don't you know they have intelligence in Turkey?" Ahmet asks.

"Yes, I know."

"You're not scared of the intelligence?"

"No."

"Why?"

"They don't scare me."

"On normal days do you have any nightmares that wake you up?" Ahmet asks a question I typed to him. I want to know how this kid is dealing with all of this trauma.

"No."

He's got it buried deep. Most trauma survivors who avoid talking about and remembering what happened, end up facing their traumas at night. Dreams are the brain's way of processing.

He is clearly afraid of ISIS, given he carefully wrapped his face in the *keffiyeh* and sunglasses we offered him to ensure they can't identify and hunt him down for talking to us. He is likely expressing false bravado, or dissociation—burying his fear so deep inside that he can honestly answer that he feels no fear.

Ahmet begins to wrap up our interview. "Imagine you are talking to all the children in the world. What would you say to deter them from joining such a regime? From the heart, what would you say?" Ahmet asks.

"I would tell them not to join this regime, they [ISIS] are not Muslims. They are infidels. They kill innocents. They aren't there for jihad. They are only there for money. Those who join them cannot get out easily. They portray themselves as Muslims, but teach students how to carry out explosions and they say you'll go to Paradise." He starts to softly sob, but continues, "This is all lies. None of it is true. I'd try to convince them not to join *ad-Dawlah*." It's heartbreaking.

Ahmet waits a few minutes and as we do with every defector, we ask if they will volunteer a statement. "Please speak to the camera and tell your sincere feelings to the children of the world," Ahmet says to Ibn Omar.

Ibn Omar nods and sits up tall. He turns to the camera and repeats his hard-learned lessons to his audience, "Don't go with them, they are not an Islamic State. It's all lies. All they do is take ground from the Free Syrian Army and give it to the Kurds, and the Kurds give it to the Syrian regime. You're joining for nothing. They trick people to get them in jihad, but this is not jihad. They just bring them to fight. They just bring people who blow themselves up to get into Paradise. You'll go through this torture for nothing. It's all lies."

"I would tell them not to go," he continues, his boyish voice still speaking directly to the camera, "I tell all the kids in the world don't join *ad-Dawlah* because they are infidels. The children that they recruit they're all gone and they got nothing out of it. They just bring kids so they blow themselves up for their own benefit. The only people that get anything out of it are the high ranking [ISIS members]. Children get nothing. I advise all children in the world not to join them."

Ahmet ends the interview. "We need to go, Anne. It's getting dark here soon." They must travel back to the area where Ibn Omar lives, two hours away, before darkness or it may draw unwanted attention.

I remind Ahmet to buy something for the child, but nothing that will draw undue notice. "I'll call you later to discuss with you," Ahmet hurriedly says before signing off.

"Anne, just got home," Ahmet e-mails a few hours later. "You should have seen the kid smiling after the goods he got. I guess it was a good deed." He encloses a photo of the purchases —a warm grey winter jacket and strong work boots. It's the best we can do for a boy living as a refugee, spending long days picking cotton for far below Turkish minimum wage, while in daily fear for his life. Now at least he can be warm.

The next morning I hear from Ahmet again. "Ibn Omar," he writes, "stayed with our [Syrian] friend at his home because it was too late to take him all the way to his home. In the morning, when our friend was asking him to wake up, the kid started to scream, 'I'm sorry!' and was holding his hands up in the air. Our friend tried to calm him down, but it took at least five minutes before he could calm him. He thought ISIS had come to get him."

It takes my breath away and I wonder if we should be interviewing minors at all. But then I remember the hundreds of so-called "Cubs of the Caliphate" and I feel renewed urgency to give voice to even just one child if he can warn others about what ISIS is doing to these poor, innocent and impressionable children who have no idea what they've signed on for.

Chapter Four - Meeting an ISIS *Emir*

"I stayed alone, at home. I was very afraid." Umm Amira is explaining how ISIS also abuses women and how she was one of them. When ISIS took away her husband, Abu Walid, some of their cadres told her that he was dead, hoping to take advantage of her as a widow. "Every day they told me that he has been killed. My family was already killed and now my husband," Umm Amira sighs heavily. Only later she learned it wasn't true—that ISIS instead imprisoned him. "I was at home, alone as a woman, and had bad news about my husband every day." Like Ibn Omar, her voice is dull from the traumas she's endured. "They told me, 'You don't go out alone.' You must live like in a prison at home. Nobody from ISIS comes to bother me, but I don't like these people. I'm afraid that they will come," she says as she takes a long pause and then continues, "and I think it's better I stay at home alone. I stayed alone for ten months."

Umm Amira (her name means mother of Amira) is one of the first batch of ISIS defectors that Ahmet and I interviewed. I remained in Istanbul for these first six interviews which included Umm Amira.

Right now, I'm present in these interviews via Skype—and worried and frustrated about it—unsure how my distance from the interview subjects can possibly work. It means I'll be relying on Ahmet's interviewing skills to keep our subjects open and talking, and I won't be able to help by using my psychologist skills as I usually would in a face-to-face setting. My computer keyboard is my only means to provide real-time feedback to Ahmet about what I think I'm hearing during the interviews. I can't even watch because his weak Internet connection relegates me to audio only. I can't see the nuances of body language—how they fidget, stiffen up, and so forth. I have to rely on Ahmet to tell me via chat and I can only gauge emotions from their voices as they travel over the Internet to Istanbul. It's maddening.

As I sit in my hotel room overlooking the mighty Bosphorus, taking in the gleaming, blue water sparkling in the sunlight, and as I watch the large ships calmly moving back and forth from the harbors, I feel agitated and aggravated and jumpy, and wish so much to be in the same room with them—taking in every detail of these people and their riveting stories. But I am grateful. At least we managed to make this unlikely project a go!

Umm Amira is the twenty-two-year-old wife of twenty-four-year-old Abu Walid, a former ISIS cadre. I'm fascinated to meet a woman married to an ISIS fighter. Husband and wife have come together to today's designated interview location to tell their stories of life under ISIS. Our fixer privately informed Ahmet that ISIS cadres sexually "mistreated" her, but we don't know whether or not she'll be willing to discuss it in any detail or even admit abuse occurred. Her story of staying alone in her home for ten months is likely her cover story, to hide her shame and degradation and how ISIS hurt her when she believed her husband was dead and she had no protection.

It's early in our process. They've agreed to come for an interview—but they aren't going to lay all their cards on the table—not yet. Not until they can see that it's safe to do so. It's not a simple game we are playing—their lives, and maybe even ours, are at stake.

Despite not being able to see her covered face, Ahmet can tell that Umm Amira is more comfortable than her husband who appears very nervous about giving this interview. He often rewords his sentences and alters what he says—seemingly fearful that ISIS could somehow discover what is being revealed to us and by whom.

Ahmet describes the scene to me later. Umm Amira is a petite woman dressed in a black *abaya*, her hair and neck wrapped in a headscarf with a *niqab* covering her face so that only her eyes show. The couple has a one-year-old baby that she is holding on her lap. Mother and child both appear frail.

Umm Amira keeps her eyes downcast as she lets her husband do most of the talking, although she is comfortable enough to guide his descriptions and speaks quietly to him from time to time. Abu Walid is tall and scruffy. He's dressed in workman's clothing and looks scrawny to Ahmet—like he doesn't get enough to eat. He's wearing cheap, dirty, brown, rubber sandals instead of the work boots most better paid farm laborers would have. Abu Walid's hair is dark black and he sports a beard, although it's neatly trimmed around his jawline and shorter than most ISIS men wear. His skin is suntanned reflecting the long hours he works in the fields as a day laborer.

As I sit at my desk, behind my laptop monitor in my room on the seventh floor of the Intercontinental Hotel, listening to the two of them tell their story, I have only their voices to lock onto, so I turn back to the Bosphorus winding through the city of Istanbul below to form a boundary and connection; the continental boundary between Europe and Asia, and connection of East to West, the Black Sea with the Sea of Marmara. On either side of the river, the rolling hills of Istanbul are covered with hundreds of thousands of red-roofed buildings and the high-rises that make up the homes of Istanbul's seventeen million inhabitants. My eye catches four minarets of a large mosque glinting in the sunlight, the mosque's domed roof rising amidst the buildings. From time to time I hear the call to prayer. It's a haunting sound and I like the way it stirs something spiritual deep inside me.

"In November of 2013, *ad-Dawlah* took Raqqa," Abu Walid explains. "When *ad-Dawlah* entered the area, they told us, 'You are not Muslim, you are *kafir* [an unbeliever/rejecter of Islam]. You are infidels.'"

Abu Walid was a farmer from a small village near Raqqa—the capital of ISIS's so-called "Caliphate". When the uprising first started in Syria, Abu Walid was part of it. He joined *Jabhat al-Nusra*, a local militia to protect his family and land from the pro-Bashar Assad forces who were trying to violently squelch the uprising. *Jabhat al-Nusra* has since been designated a terrorist group affiliated with al-Qaeda by the U.S., but at the time Abu Walid joined, it was a rag-tag group of men who agreed with the revolt against the Syrian dictator and were trying to protect themselves from being killed, and their wives and daughters from being raped by the pro-Assad forces. In 2013, however, circumstances changed. ISIS took over the area and overpowered *Jabhat al-Nusra* and the Free Syrian Army who had controlled the area previously.

Abu Walid sounds deeply depressed, "*Jaysh al-Hur* [the Free Syrian Army] began to realize it was too late to fight against *ad-Dawla*h. So *Jaysh al-Hur* fighters left with hardly any fighting."

"Someone told ISIS I was not a good person for them," Abu Walid begins to tell us details of his own early encounters with ISIS. "They asked me to come to the police station [where I was arrested]. I spent three days in prison, alone—in solitary. In the morning they came to bring food and then left. After three days they told me, 'We are sending you to Tell Abyad' [a Syrian town on the border with Turkey]. My hands were cuffed and I was taken by car to Tell Abyad to a big court there. It was a *shariah* court. I saw many people and I felt very happy to finally see something. I drank tea and I waited for two hours until they called me and took me by hand in iron cuffs—to torture me. They spread my arms wide and hung me by my forearms and wrists held in iron cuffs from a steel bar. They didn't tell me anything about why they were doing this. They left me there for around two hours. I had so much pain, and started to cry out many things from the pain in my hands and my body. I cried and shouted. They did this again the next day and I cried and shouted again, through the day and night. The next day they took me again, this time they blindfolded me. They told me, 'You know where we take you now.'"

"I answered, 'No I don't know!'" His voice is filled with fear.

"They said, 'Now we take you out to kill you.' After, they added, 'The chief of security wants to speak with you.'" So after torturing him, they threatened to execute him before giving him another chance to "talk."

"They took me to him and he asked me, 'What do you have at home?'"

"I have an AK 47 and a car."

The torture continued but they never asked him again about his car and weapon. What Abu Walid is likely not admitting to us is that he was also being interrogated about the other fighters in *Jabhat al-Nusra* from his unit. Soldiers, even those in Special Forces, tell me that it's impossible to withstand heavy torture for most, and that nearly everyone breaks down. Likely Abu Walid is no exception, but he doesn't want to admit that to us. Instead he focuses on the other questions they asked him—about himself and his possessions.

"During this time while I was in prison, every day they told my wife that I died," Abu Walid tells us, echoing the pain his wife lived through both while he was in prison and later—when he ran away to escape ISIS.

"I stayed in interrogation for thirteen days. On the last day I was fasting and praying that I will get freed. Just before I broke my fast they sent me home. I felt Allah saved me. They told me, 'You are free, go home.' They sent me home with two persons who took the keys to my car. Then they took my car and my weapon."

After a few days, they sent again for me and asked, 'Why you don't come for *dawah* [sharing Islamic teaching] with us, and for our training?'

Abu Walid, like many of the Syrian men who joined ISIS, says he was a reluctant joiner. "I agreed because I knew they will kill me if I don't." He further explains, "I answered, '*Inshallah,* after some time.' I knew if I said no, they will kill me, so instead I said, '*Inshallah.*'"

ISIS began keeping watch over Abu Walid. "Someone from ISIS comes and takes many photos of me. He writes report of where I go and stay. They do this every one to three months." Abu Walid says he continued to delay joining, claiming family responsibilities. "For one year ISIS invited me, but I did not accept their offer. They warned me not to leave the village. After some time, I escaped on a motorcycle."

"I knew that eventually if I didn't work with them they would put me in a prison in Raqqa," Abu Walid explains. "They tried to force me into a two week long *shariah* course. I didn't go to it. I was afraid. After two months of them inviting me, I decided to escape. I knew the area very well, so I took a motorcycle and came [with my wife] across the border to Turkey."

What Abu Walid is skipping over here is that he did join ISIS and fought for them. We know this from a fixer we have helping us, but for now, he refers to it indirectly, leaving his storyline and the time his wife was left alone in their home, murky. They are the first of our informants and we are still working out the best ways to win confidence. Later a former ISIS defector will become our sole fixer, and he will help build trust between us and the defectors.

We later learn, in fact from another defector that not only did Abu Walid not immediately escape, he went to the *shariah* and military training, and he wasn't just an ordinary fighter under ISIS, he rose up to become an *emir* [leader] in the field. It's during those ten months when his wife was left alone at home and repeatedly told by ISIS cadres that her husband had been killed. We only later learn the truth from Abu Said, the ISIS defector who will later become our key fixer and informant.

"How do they get people to join them?" Ahmet asks.

"When ISIS came to Raqqa all the people don't have work. Some join immediately for free food," Abu Walid explains. "The ISIS guys speak with the youth about what they are doing to build an Islamic state."

"Most of the jobless youth joined. They were told, 'Come here and take this *shariah* course for ten days. We'll give you a car, house and money.' In Syria, a youth having a car is impossible, so this is an amazing promise. And they cannot marry without a house and money, and then suddenly, with *ad-Dawlah*, they can. [Syrian] girls also marry ISIS fighters to help their families. They said to the people, 'All people, come with us. We can give you a gun for fighting. Some of you don't have a wife—you can come with us. We will give you money, so you can marry. We will give you about two thousand dollars, so you can marry and a salary every month of two to three hundred U.S. dollars per month. You need not be afraid. You are guaranteed if you die, we will take care of your family with money and food.' They also tell their recruits, 'Now you will be important.'"

Indeed, the "sex now" reward for jihad is one that people often overlook about militant groups like ISIS. Many believe that 'martyrs' are motivated to kill themselves and others for the rewards of Paradise—especially the sexual rewards—the promised *houris* or virgins that await the 'martyr's' arrival. But a young man who is not ready to sacrifice his life for an uncertain, ethereal reward can be even more strongly motivated by the promise of "sex now". With ISIS in charge of morality rules in conservative societies, that promise is one that is usually delivered in the context of marriage—which ISIS delivers to its young Syrian recruits, and also promises to foreign fighters who come streaming in from afar. Tunisia has the highest representation of foreign fighters from Arab countries and we will find as we carry out this project that many of them came because in their own country they were unemployed and unable to marry; they came at least in part for the promise of a wife.

We know from press reports, and will learn repeatedly from our informants, that former Iraqi Baathists intelligence officers from Saddam Hussein's police state joined ISIS, and lent their support and expertise. Before its establishment as a rogue state, ISIS had already developed a very strong intelligence apparatus with generous help from former Baathists, first reported in April 2015, by *Der Spiegel's* Christopher Reuter. Documents discovered in the residence of an Iraqi national spy chief, Haji Bakr, who had been killed by U.S. forces, showed a carefully organized ISIS security arm that relied upon the same secret intelligence gathering techniques previously used by Saddam Hussein's regime—all meant to instill fear in the targeted local populations.

According to the captured ISIS documents, the ISIS security division employs cadres sent out in advance of invasions to recruit local informants, to quickly collect and apply intelligence to gain local control as soon as it decides to advance into new territory. This process includes identifying the powerful families and individuals in a given area; finding their sources of income; identifying rebel brigades and their leaders by name; and learning about *shariah* violations for blackmail purposes. [21]

Abu Walid confirms this and explains how these ISIS strategies were employed to ease their entry into Raqqa, the current center of ISIS' stronghold. "First, *ad-Dawlah* sent small groups to establish themselves inside the city. Secondly, they sent suicide bombers of young boys, especially to the gates where *Jaysh al-Hur* [the local Free Syrian Army militia in charge] had guards. This was very effective, as everyone feared the suicide bombers, and it was very difficult to distinguish if an approaching child was a suicide bomber or not. Being unwilling to shoot a possibly innocent child, the sentries would run away and *ad-Dawlah* could enter." It's an interesting use of psychology—the cynical use of children as suicide bombers by one group against another that they know will be averse to shoot a child.

Abu Walid continues, "They go talking to the people asking them, 'How come you are living under Shia rule? [They are referencing that Assad is an Alawite Shia.] This is degradation to live under the Shia.' They taught us that all the others are *murtads*, infidels. If you are not with them, you cannot do business."

"They tell the guys, 'If Assad's army comes and you do not fight with us, they will take your car and rape your women.'" Given Assad's brutal regime this is sadly true. "An older guy told us, Bashar's soldiers came to a home and told the father, 'Send your daughter with us.' Then they heard a gunshot. The father killed his own daughter, so they cannot rape her! Everyone knows that Bashar's soldiers will rape anyone they find."

"They [the youth] join for a loaf of bread," now bitterness tinges his voice. "When *ad-Dawlah* took over they said you are either with us or not. They gave no food, no jobs except to people who joined them, so the people got so hungry. *Ad-Dawlah* also began recruiting twelve to seventeen-year-olds to become their soldiers. They provided well for them so they can feed their families. The *shaikhs* also pulled the youth in. It was very easy for ISIS to recruit the youth from inside Raqqa."

Abu Walid begins to draw a picture for us that will become increasingly clearer with subsequent interviews: when ISIS enters an area they take complete control over all the local resources and the economy, making life impossible without joining them. "They come and take your wife or your daughter, your money—they take your life."

Reflecting his current state of disillusionment, Abu Walid states, "After some time, in 2014, people feel that ISIS is not good, but bad. Why? Because what they promised to the people, they did not keep. Where is this freedom they promised us?" His tone is again bitter. "The few people who join now, do so only because they need to eat. They are the ones who don't have work. The rest try to escape to Turkey or Lebanon, or go by sea."

Abu Walid learned, while imprisoned, what ISIS were capable of. He understood he needed to be with them and didn't want to learn how far they would go if he continued to resist. So, finally after a year, he enrolled himself in their *shariah* course.

"In the ten-day *shariah* education course, they teach that all people not in ISIS are *murtad*. All governments who do not support ISIS are *murtad*," Abu Walid tells us. He goes on to explain that in the Sunni part of the country, many people under Assad don't know how to pray properly; they are "not taught religion properly".

"They taught religion to us in Tell Abyad," he continues, speaking of ISIS. "We felt a vacuum filled. We hadn't learned in school our history, so *ad-Dawlah* filled an emptiness in us. We felt joy from this and anger at Assad," Abu Walid concludes. "The people are very grateful to learn how to pray correctly." Later, when I meet Ahmet in person, he notes that he's been repeatedly surprised over the years when he's met Syrian Sunnis. Many of them have shallow knowledge of Islam and don't know how to pray according to custom, additional evidence that formal religious education under Assad was likely limited.

Ahmet is very interested to know what kinds of materials are involved in the *shariah* training courses. Abu Walid lists some of the seven or eight books he says are used: "*Kitab at Tawhid* [*The Book of Monotheism*] by Imam Muhammed ibn Abdul-Wahab and several works of Ibn-I Taymiyyah [Taqi ad-Din Ahmad ibn Taymiyyah]." Taymiyyah wrote during the 13th century during the time of the Mongol invasions and his texts are often used to justify the practice of *takfir*, or declaring other self-professed Muslims as apostates. Wahab, from Arabia, advocated in the 18th century to purify Islam, bringing it back to the practices of the first three generations of Muslims (the *salaf)* and fought against any "innovations" to the religion. He is considered the founder of the Saudi conservative strain of Islam called Wahhabism, or Salafi Islam. The texts are basically *Salafi* [Islamic] scholarly writings that are used by terrorist groups to present distorted and violent extremist versions of Islamic scriptures to extol militant jihad and so-called 'martyrdom' missions. It is no surprise to learn that they are also source material for ISIS.

"Everyone who becomes a fighter takes both *shariah* and military training," Abu Walid tells us.

"During the battle days he follows the orders of the leader. After fighting for three days approximately, he returns home for a week of rest with his family." We learn that the Syrian ISIS fighters, unlike the foreign fighters, are housed at home with their families between battles. However, it appears Abu Walid was not allowed to return home for those ten months during which ISIS cadres allegedly preyed upon his wife.

"What are the fighters equipped with?" Ahmet asks.

"Each fighter has his own rifle. A pistol—a Smith and Wesson, Colt or Glock, and a rifle—a Kalashnikov, AK-47 or a M-16, and at least two hand grenades, a backpack with medical supplies, food and water, and at least five hundred bullets," Abu Walid tells us.

Though we don't yet know that Abu Walid was a high commander in ISIS—an *emir*, it's clear in how he describes military matters inside ISIS that he's knowledgeable about how the group works, from trainings to the daily life of an ISIS fighter.

"What can you tell us about the foreign fighters?" Ahmet asks, referring to the thousands of men and women who have come from around the world to join and fight for ISIS.

"The *ad-Dawlah* leaders are foreigners. There is no difference in how soldiers are treated between locals and foreigners. But Syrians do not like the foreign commanders." He's referring to the tension between the Syrian fighters and the Iraqi foreign commanders. The Syrians who welcomed and supported ISIS are called *ansar* [the helpers] referring to those in Medina who supported Prophet Muhammed during his flight from Mecca; the fighters coming from outside of Syria are referred to as the *mujahideen,* or holy warriors.

"Some of the foreign fighters are corrupt-minded," Abu Walid tells us. "For instance, one Tunisian wanted his two wives to be in bed with him together. His wives took him to [ISIS] court. He was sentenced and put in a truck for twenty days and paraded around town." We will hear about this infamous Tunisian again from others.

The baby is getting fussy and Umm Amira gets up to walk him around. Despite this I can hear him as he fusses in the background.

"Can you tell us about the women in ISIS?" Ahmet asks directing his question to her, hoping that Umm Amira might now chime in and open up a bit.

She continues walking the baby, jiggling him in her arms to quiet him while her husband instead explains, "Under ISIS, women are kept very secluded. She can only see her husband or her brother." This male relative who acts as her chaperone is, according to Islamic traditions, called a *mahram,* and must be a son, husband, uncle, grandfather, or brother—basically a male relative whom she cannot marry. ISIS, just like many Arabic cultures, has very strict rules for their honor system in which the virtue of the entire family—if not community—resides in the purity of the female members of their society; meaning female behavior must be highly controlled to safeguard honor and reputation. ISIS achieves this through the use of morality police called the *hisbah,* who patrol their territories to enforce morality rules. Initially, these police were all men, but due to the unpopularity of men enforcing morals on women outside their families, ISIS decided to also employ women to be female morality police. Their brigade is named the *al-Khansaa* brigade after a 7th century woman considered to be one of the greatest Arab poets, especially famous for her haunting elegies of her four sons who were slain in the Battle of Qadisiyah.[22]

"Three *al-Khansaa* women go out on patrol with a male driver," Abu Walid explains. "They go into the market and into the village. They arrest and fine women who are without veils and take some women even into the prison. According to the ISIS rules, if a woman is out of her home without socks on, or her face is uncovered, they take her to the jail and whip her. They lash her from ten to forty times."

"Where does this happen?" Ahmet asks, concern filling his voice.

"They lash her in public—through her clothes," he answers, then continues with a story, "A neighbor in a small village went to visit his neighbor. The man knocked on the door of a woman whose husband was not there. But he was caught [by the morality police] waiting inside the gate when the husband was absent, so he was arrested. He was lashed forty times, so badly that he could not use the toilet and had to stay in bed for twenty days. After, he was forced to take the *shariah* course for three weeks. The woman inside the house was lashed forty times as well because she opened the door to the yard for him."

"In one case, two women were visiting each other when the one woman's husband was out of the home. The *hisbah* came and asked her, 'Who are you?' She answered, 'I am the neighbor visiting.' They asked her, 'Are you married to the man of this house?' She answered, 'No,' and was then taken and put in jail with other women and lashed forty times." As I listen in horror to these brutal punishments, I try to imagine the fear and constricted lives under which ISIS forces these people to live.

"In 2014, I realized that *ad-Dawlah* were liars," Abu Walid says, his voice filled with anger and disillusionment. "For instance there was an ISIS guy who raped a woman, but got away with it." Sadly, we will hear that complaint many times. Despite the morality police insisting that normal civilians live very constricted and conservative lives, ISIS cadres get away—literally—with rape and murder.

Abu Walid takes out his phone and begins to show Ahmet some pictures on it as he explains how some ISIS killings were carried out. "There is a well by the name of Hute. There, they cover the eyes of the prisoners and tell them, 'You are free, just walk now, but don't open your eyes.' They walk and fall into the well. It smells horrible because of all the corpses inside the well. I know that over one hundred people were thrown into that well.

"Life was better before ISIS," Abu Walid rubs his hand across his brow, his face looking agitated as he falls silent. His arm is thin and Ahmet sees how frail he looks for a man of his tall frame. "I prefer Assad, because life was better. *Ad-Dawlah* does not represent Islam. *Ad-Dawlah* are *kafirs* [unbelievers]. We had to run away from *ad-Dawlah*."

"You can see us now," Umm Amira suddenly jumps in, her voice agitated and angry, as she continues pacing back and forth in the small interview room while jiggling her baby gently on her shoulder. "We escaped from *ad-Dawlah*. We don't have a house. We don't have food. We don't have money. All this we suffer to get away from their rule. There, life is very bad, because ISIS won't let people live freely, to do what they want."

"Can you tell us more about how ISIS treats women under their rule? Maybe you'd like to explain?" Ahmet asks turning to Umm Amira, but after her brief outburst, she doesn't take the bait. Instead Abu Walid continues talking, "If her husband is killed as one of their fighters, after three days a woman comes from ISIS. They come bringing one hundred U.S. dollars to his mother, or two hundred U.S. dollars to his widow. They bring food for the family and check on her regularly—to bring her money and they ask whatever the family needs. By this way they keep the cadres intact, because the ISIS fighters know that their families will be taken care."

We will learn that this social safety net was something the ISIS defectors all appreciated—knowing their family members would be provided for if they were killed—but they didn't appreciate how quickly ISIS wives were pressured to remarry other ISIS cadres.

"When a fighter dies, the widows are married to another fighter. In Islam, there has to be an *iddah*, a waiting period of four months and eight days before she remarries to make sure she is not pregnant from the previous husband," Abu Walid instructs us. Indeed, observing *iddah* is a traditional Islamic practice to ensure that the paternity of any child fathered by the deceased husband is clearly established. "But they [ISIS] do not observe this. This was another hypocrisy with them," Abu Walid's voice is becoming embittered again as he rubs his long, thin fingers through his dark head of hair.

"After the death of a husband, the wife can only go out with her father or brother, or her *mahram* [appropriate chaperone], or with other men's wives also." He seems to be reflecting upon his own situation, when his wife was repeatedly told that he was dead and ended up isolated at home. His voice is serious, "She can end up staying alone at home otherwise. If a woman needed milk for her baby she couldn't go out alone, even if she dies." I try to imagine this ludicrous morality—that a mother and baby could die of starvation at home, while their husband is missing in battle or killed because no one is present to act as her chaperone. *Keeping her at home is more important than feeding her child?*

"Can you tell us anything about the Westerners that come to join ISIS?" Ahmet asks.

"Once a family of ten came from Europe. They were from Denmark and the UK. *Ad-Dawlah* took their men to training for forty-five days. Their women and children were kept in a secure area during this time. The men couldn't see their families for these forty-five days. Then after their training they sent them to the front to fight for four to five months without seeing their children again. They told them, 'Our rules are like this. Your women and children must stay at the guest house while you go and fight.' Probably they were testing them as they arrived without initial contacts. When they returned [from the battleground], most of them fled away."

"Anybody who comes to *ad-Dawlah* are welcomed, but we do not accept them as soon as they arrive," Abu Walid again reflects his former leadership role. "We tested them first. Any person from age fifteen and up, we register you and you become a fighter. You are given a gun. Foreign women who arrive become part of the *hisbah* and get married to a fighter." In March of 2016, the German Federal Police revealed an extensive registry of ISIS "entrance interviews" that were leaked via Turkey. These records appear to have been created by ISIS in 2013, and record the names, identifying details and former combat experience of twenty-two thousand foreign recruits from forty different countries.[23]

"Most of the people who are coming from the West are already indoctrinated in *Salafism* before they arrive," he further explains. Later we will hear again and again that Europeans and other Westerners who arrive to ISIS are the "true believers" who came to ISIS enthusiastically to fight jihad and build the "Caliphate". The Syrian cadres admire their dedication and everything that they gave up to come and join ISIS, but rarely share their naive enthusiasm for jihad—perhaps because it is their country and lives spoiled by these wars.

"Do you know anything about the Western women who come to join ISIS, to become brides? Do you know what happens to them?" Ahmet picks up on questions I've typed to him on chat. I'm intensely interested to know what happens to the so-called brides of ISIS—Western girls who travel long distances, coming from Europe, Canada, Australia and even the United States to marry ISIS fighters. I've studied them and written a book about an American, Shannon Conley, who tried to go to Syria to marry the ISIS fighter she fell in love with over Skype.[24] I want to know what happens to those who arrive to ISIS—are they happy? Well, or mistreated? Married, or gang raped? Satisfied or regretting their choices, or desperate to escape, after making their crazy journeys—sometimes across entire continents to reach ISIS?

Except for a few alleged ISIS brides who tweet and blog about their lives in ISIS, what happens to these young girls is a black hole. They simply disappear. We hope through these interviews we will learn more.

"There is a marriage bureau—services where they register the young women and match them with the men in ISIS," Abu Walid explains. Then he changes the subject. "The prospect of marriage also attracts youth. Turkish youth who are poor sometimes go to ISIS just to marry. They tell us, 'I go there, fight for them and get married.'"

Ahmet picks up on this comment, "When a child joins—from Turkey—can a fifteen-year-old child who becomes a fighter, can he come back and visit the family [in Turkey]?"

"No he cannot," Abu Walid answers firmly, sounding like the high up commander we later learn that he was.

"How about recruiting youth inside Turkey, from the refugee camps and elsewhere, does it happen?" Ahmet asks, now moving to a question we'd planned in advance.

"Some of the youth are approached and offered money. My uncle's son was fifteen and taken to *ad-Dawlah* as a fighter like that. His mother went to them for some days begging, 'Give me my son.' She did this for two months; begging, 'Please return back my son.'"

"[But], they didn't give him back. 'Your son died in Deir ez-Zor, with the other brothers' *ad-Dawlah* leaders informed his father. He died as a suicide bomber. 'He went willingly to the cadres and he died willingly. Your son's cemetery is over there [in Deir ez-Zor]. Go and find him.' Up to now my brother [Abu Walid is referring to his surviving cousin] didn't tell his mother that her son died, or how," Abu Walid explains, sighing heavily. "Many people lost their sons this way." So, we learn, that ISIS recruiters do work among the refugees, picking off the most vulnerable as recruits that they seduce into going back to Syria as fighters, or if they are depressed and desperate enough, convincing them to become suicide bombers.

Abu Walid continues to track the terrorist group in which he once was an *emir* and brings us up-to-date, "In the last ten days ISIS makes court orders," he tells us, "The orders are to any person from age fifteen and older telling them, 'Come to our camp to register. We will give you a gun. All people, even old people will fight, because other countries will come to us.'" It sounds like ISIS is on the defensive—trying to bolster their troops and willing to use anyone. As air strikes over the fall of 2015 and spring of 2016 degrade ISIS, we see more of that—turning to younger and younger conscripts to keep their battalions filled.

The baby is really starting to fuss and we can feel our interview is wrapping up. But before we end, Ahmet asks the same question he asked of Ibn Omar, the fifteen-year-old child soldier: "Do you have anything to say to youth thinking of joining ISIS?" Ahmet asks, hoping for a statement that we can use in our anti-ISIS campaign. Abu Walid doesn't disappoint in this regard.

"*Ad-Dawlah* doesn't have anything to do with Islam or with the Prophet Muhammad. *Ad-Dawlah* picks only parts of the verses from the Koran and twists their meanings to come to the meanings they want. They do not use the intended meanings; they only use the meanings they want."

"They are the *Khawarij* tribe," Abu Walid says, referring to the renegade tribe in the time of the Prophet Muhammed who practiced *takfir* [excommunication] and believed they could kill other Muslims who did not adhere to their interpretation of Islam. "I believed when they came to Raqqa that they are not good. They kill anybody among us Muslims, just like the *Khawarij* did. They existed during those times the same—with black clothes and black flags. The scriptures warn, 'when you see them don't follow them.'"

Chapter Five - From Rebel Fighter to Believer to Defector

Today is the second day of interviews and I'm still getting used to being stuck in Istanbul, communicating via Skype, while Ahmet is in the room with the ISIS defector. Today he is speaking with Abu Ahmed, a 30-year-old Syrian, married with three children. Abu Ahmed had been a high school teacher in the Syrian city of Deir ez-Zor—that is until the rebellion against the Bashar Assad regime began.

"We created a militia in our village. We were basically part of the uprising against Assad," Abu Ahmed begins by telling us about the early days of conflict. "When the enemy [the Syrian army] came, we went to fight. Our militia—*al Saraya*—was part of *Jaysh al-Hur* [the Free Syrian Army]," he explains. "We were only defending our village from enemies. We were an independent militia. We didn't take any orders from the other militias, but we were tied to the military council." At least in the early years of conflict, many of the Syrian militias were only loosely affiliated through military councils, local endeavors organized by the citizenry to provide weapons and advice to the locals to defend themselves against Assad's army. They were not aligned with major camps like al-Qaeda and ISIS, even though the West tended to lump the militias together.

"I joined *Ahrar ash-Sham* [Army of the Levant] militia two months before *ad-Dawlah* came to our area." [Again we hear the name ISIS forces its followers to use.] "They were better than *ad-Dawlah*. At least they do not steal. They made everything good for the people. I liked them, so I went with my family, and my wife, and ten other people and stayed in the militia for two months. I was living in al-Hasakah with *Ahrar ash-Sham*."

"Then, after two months of fighting with them, *ad-Dawlah* came to al-Hasakah. I went back to my village near Deir ez-Zor and hid out in my home in my village for about four months." Abu Ahmed knew his life was in imminent danger. "Of course *ad-Dawlah* came to al-Hasakah and to my village near Deir ez-Zor, so I had to flee before they arrived, because I had fought with *Ahrar ash-Sham*."

Rubbing his hand nervously through his black head of hair, Abu Ahmed continues. "When *ad-Dawlah* arrived they killed all the militia who had been fighting against them—executed them all," his dark eyes widen with fear as he recounts it. "Anyone who had not fought against them, but who had been a supporter of *Ahrar ash-Sham,* they took to the courts to repent—to make *at-tawba*."

At-tawba in Arabic means repentance. It is the method by which ISIS rehabilitates anyone previously involved in acts they condemn as immoral or un-Islamic. The *at-tawba* process requires going before a *shariah* judge and formally making a statement of confession and desire to repent. In return, a repentance certificate is issued which functions as an official Islamic State pardon.

"When *ad-Dawlah* invaded Deir ez-Zor they already knew who was fighting against them and who had not fought," echoing the words of Abu Walid, the former ISIS *emir* who just yesterday told us about ISIS utilizing former Baathist members and Baathist strategies deployed in Saddam Hussein's government. "*Ad-Dawlah* has spies in every village, even the small ones. They collect information in these villages…about life, people, work, business, everything. They categorize you by who likes *ad-Dawlah* and who does not; who is pro-Assad and who is with *Ahrar ash-Sham*. And they report everything to *ad-Dawlah*. They do this even before they invade an area so they already know everything when they arrive." Abu Ahmed's eyes show his fear. He's very likely worried that ISIS could also have spies in Turkey right now.

"What is life like under ISIS?" Ahmet asks.

"Before *ad-Dawlah* came into our region [in Deir ez-Zor], there were no fences between the homes. But when *ad-Dawlah* came, they forced the people to build fences between their homes for privacy. Before, our women wore only the veil [headscarf], but did not cover their faces. Now they have to wear a full *niqab* [face, neck and shoulder-covering]."

Abu Ahmed is not speaking of a normal *niqab*. According to a UK press report from women who escaped from the ISIS stronghold of Raqqa, ISIS imposes a uniquely strict dress code on all women from puberty upwards which forces them, "to wear two gowns to hide their body shape, black gloves to cover their hands, and three veils so their faces cannot be seen, even in direct sunlight."[25] Later we will talk to a female member of the *hisbah* [morality police] who violently enforced this dress code, making sure that *abayas* [long Islamic gowns] were not too body hugging and *niqabs* not too transparent.

"If they refuse, they are taken to *shariah* court and punished," Abu Ahmed tells us.

"What is the punishment?"

"In the first offense for failing to wear the required *niqab* they must take a course in *shariah*. In the case of a second offense, they must pay a fine. In the third offense, their *mahram*, or responsible male relative, and the woman who has not complied, are taken to court and afterward they are each lashed forty times," Abu Ahmed says, confirming the punishment others describe.

"The *hisbah* include female policewomen as enforcers and they lash the other women."

"How does this take place?"

"When they lash a woman they do so in public, but they don't remove her clothing. All the executions and lashings are done in public so that people will see it." Later we hear from female *hisbah* members that some of these lashings also take place in the female side of an ISIS prison, where the woman is disrobed down to her underwear and mercilessly lashed and then also bitten with metal teeth on the fleshy parts of her body—sometimes so hard that she passes out or bleeds to death afterward.

"In Raqqa, one girl was walking on the street with her face uncovered," Abu Ahmed tells us. "The policewoman took her to court. The judge ordered, 'Either we lash you forty times or the *hisbah* bites your breast. The woman chose the latter as her punishment, but the *hisbah* [using these metal teeth] bit her breast so violently that she died."

As unreal as it sounds, human bites can be lead to deadly bacterial infections, and Abu Ahmed's words again echo the July 2015 UK press report based upon testimony from women who escaped out of Raqqa. In it a woman described being punished, "They said my eyes were visible through my veil. I was tortured. They lashed me. Now some of them punish women by biting. They give you the option between getting bitten or lashed."[26] According to the press report over sixty British women are thought to be serving in Islamic State's *hisbah*.[27] Some apparently, are extremely vicious.

I've listened to many harsh and inhumane stories in my decades of interviewing terrorists, but I'm not used to hearing of women so sadistically attacking other women, or of humans biting each other. It's horrific. As I listen, I look out at the water to calm my nerves and force myself to stay present and not tune out the cruel vision.

Below, cutting through the shimmering blue water, I'm surprised to see a ship belonging to one of our friends, a Greek shipping magnate, its *TEN* logo proudly displayed on its side. Life was so beautiful during our time in Greece, when my husband was U.S. Ambassador. No three-year-old Syrian boys washing up on its shore to become the photograph that begs the world to pay attention to the Syrian refugee crisis. I turn back to listening again, after the brief mental distraction.

Abu Ahmed explains how he wound up in Turkey, "I didn't meet anyone from *ad-Dawlah*, but when I heard they are asking about me, I escaped. I now live in Akçakale [a Turkish town near the border]."

We know that his quick escape from ISIS is likely untrue—just like Abu Walid the day before. Our fixer confirmed that both of these men had been ISIS fighters who defected. However, true to our pre-agreed upon ethic, we don't ask them directly about being ISIS fighters. Instead, we wait to see what we can learn from them. If they are knowledgeable about being inside ISIS, it's highly likely they were fighters but are not willing, or too scared, to directly admit it. This is how our research starts—circling around each other, gaining knowledge to enable us to ask more insightful questions and slowly win trust.

"When *ad-Dawlah* arrived in the area, all the people who don't have work, and the youth between ages fifteen to eighteen, liked to work with *ad-Dawlah* immediately because they paid," Abu Ahmed continues. "After some time the people who lost their jobs and had no food and no money also needed to work, and they also begin to go with *ad-Dawlah*. It got so that even adults, for a loaf of bread, would work for *ad-Dawlah*. All of the services in a village are controlled by *ad-Dawlah*—electricity, water, health services, etc."

"The Sunni tribe, *al-Sheitaat* did not accept *ad-Dawlah* and fought against them," referring to a Sunni tribe that refused to surrender to ISIS rule.[28] "So afterwards, they had a big problem. *Ad-Dawlah* collected them and executed seven hundred men in one day. They basically vanquished their tribe. Very few of them stayed alive, only a few youths who chose to fight with *ad-Dawlah*, or help them. All the young men from their village ran to Turkey, to Urfa, and areas nearby [he lists them]. Now some of them work with *ad-Dawlah*, and others do not," Abu Ahmed tells us, his face becoming clouded. Later, we will hear in much greater detail about this ISIS massacre of the *al-Sheitaat* tribe.

"How does *ad-Dawlah* train?" This is Ahmet's way of not asking Abu Ahmed directly if he fought for ISIS—only a fighter would likely know in any detail.

"During the training the trainers don't use their real names, they use aliases, probably because there could be spies," Abu Ahmed answers without missing a beat. He doesn't seem to mind sharing what he knows from having been on the inside when not pressed to confess to it. "They also train in *shariah*."

"What texts do they use?" Ahmet asks. I feel as if I know the answer before he speaks. As the *emir* reported yesterday, and from my years of study of militant jihadi groups like ISIS, and al-Qaeda, and all its offshoots, I know that they generally rely upon the original *Salafi* writers who were justifying jihad and glorifying martyrdom at the time of the Prophet and in the ensuing centuries. Today's violent extremists distort these writings to try to justify modern-day suicide attacks and terror operations, as if their battles and terror attacks of today are the same jihad and martyrdom operations of old.

Abu Ahmed recites a list of the usual texts that al-Qaeda also uses.

"Did they also use videos?" Ahmet asks. I know there are so many militant jihadi videos out there and ISIS is producing them in the hundreds. I wonder if they also use them for training.

"I didn't see any videos during training, only books," he answers. So ISIS' social media sophistication, with its slickly constructed videos and memes, appears to be reserved for the Internet; on the ground they rely on the old methods of *shariah* teachers instructing their pupils in person without the assistance of modern technology.

"Is *ad-Dawlah* recruiting in the Turkish refugee camps?" Ahmet asks. This is a particularly important question to us because there is a polarizing debate going on in the U.S. and many Western countries about whether or not to take in Syrian refugees. Are they a security risk? I've argued in the press that leaving them to waste away in refugee camps is leaving them open to becoming a security risk. Young boys, in particular, get picked-off by terrorist recruiters who play upon their despair, boredom, lack of positive identity, dashed hopes and dreams, and wish to do something significant with their lives as they languish in camps; leaving terrorist recruiters to appear as role models offering false visions of manhood and mission for those who are vulnerable enough to fall into it.[29]

The *emir* yesterday told us that young boys, like his nephew, fell victim.

"After I arrived in Akçakale, no one from *ad-Dawlah* came to speak with our Syrian people to try to bring them back to fight for *ad-Dawlah*," Abu Ahmed answers. "But I do know of a case in *Harran Camp* near Akçakale. I saw one woman crying. I learned that her thirteen-year-old son willingly ran away to *ad-Dawlah*. He called his father after thirty days, from Tabaq [a city in Iraq] to say, 'I am a *mujahid* now. I have power. I am a strong man. I became a man. Don't be afraid [for me],' and then he shut down the phone. A few weeks later his parents learned that he became a truck suicide bomber in Iraq."

Listening to this I let my eyes skim over the blue water of the Bosphorus once again. It's so peaceful and beautiful and I let my soul take a momentary respite.

"There is another story from a Turkish shopkeeper I know," Abu Ahmed continues, as sadness suddenly fills his deep brown eyes. "There was a young Syrian boy working in his shop, providing for his family. One day I asked the shopkeeper, 'Where is this boy? I don't see him?' "The shopkeeper told me, 'We heard that he became a suicide bomber.'" Abu Ahmed lowers his head for a moment, staring down at his plastic sandals. *Perhaps he is ashamed that, as a teacher of youth, he wasn't able to protect a child from his own country being sucked into the ISIS suicide machine?* I wonder, *or am I projecting too much?*

"*Ad-Dawlah* tries to attract the thirteen to fifteen-year-old boys to join," Abu Ahmed continues. "They can easily manipulate them because they are very emotional and their families are hungry. We don't have food, and they cut our water and electricity at night, so these families become desperate. If the young kids join, they can bring home money to their families. When a youth comes to training, *ad-Dawlah* sends food to their families regularly."

"*Ad-Dawlah* also tries to steer the young ones into 'martyrdom' operations. During *shariah* trainings they observe the youth and look for those who are vulnerable in order to select them for 'martyrdom'. The rest they send to fight."

"How do they motivate them?" I type, and Ahmet gives voice to my question.

"Those that they select for 'martyrdom' are motivated by targeting their emotions. They don't let them think, but excite them, and get them to decide [on 'martyrdom'] without thinking."

"*Ad-Dawlah* is getting help in psychologically manipulating the youth from the teachers who come from Saudi Arabia and the Emirates," Abu Ahmed explains. "They are very clever in manipulating these young boys into *shariah* thinking. They can manipulate up to fifty students in one month, or forty days. They are specialists in identifying the vulnerable ones." As we listen, Ahmet and I are both keenly aware that these observations come from a high school teacher who knows this age group well. He knows how children can be influenced and has now seen it done to the extreme.

"Sometimes they chose leaders from among the youth, for example, fifteen-year-old boys to be *emirs* of small groups of men. They do this to test the [adult] trainees in that group because obeying orders is a must. They want to see that they will obey without question—even obey a youth," Abu Ahmed explains. "*Ad-Dawlah* choses the very best trainees and extends their trainings. The rest are sent to fight after three weeks, but they keep the best ones for additional training."

"In our area all our people were fighting Bashar," Abu Ahmed says, referring to the uprising against Bashar Assad's dictatorial regime. His voice fills with irony as he continues, "But *ad-Dawlah* came and killed almost all people from our area. Now no one is fighting Bashar. So who is the enemy of Bashar—we, or *ad-Dawlah*?" We will hear this a lot—that the Free Syrian Army fought the regime, but ISIS fights the Free Syrian Army rather than fighting Assad.

Unlikely alliances have sprung up during the rise of ISIS. "Some former Baath party members are in *ad-Dawlah*," Abu Ahmed explains. Baathists are pan-Arab nationalists, hardly individuals one would expect to find in ISIS.

"*Ad-Dawlah* does an investigation of anyone who had a place in the Baath party, to learn what he wrote, what he did. The primary enemy of *ad-Dawlah* is *al Nusra* [al-Qaeda's affiliate] and *Ahrar ash Sham* [Army of the Levant], but the secondary enemy is the Baathists, yet in secret, some are involved with *ad-Dawlah*," reiterating, "The mentors and strategy guys in *ad-Dawlah* were from the Baathists."

This information corroborates what was found in Haji Bakr's documents, the former Iraqi Baathist intelligence chief who served in ISIS until he was killed, which detail how the Baathist cadres working with ISIS built the current Islamic State's intelligence procedures, basing them upon the previous intelligence operations of Saddam Hussein.[30] If the Iraqi Baathists wished to retake power, they were going to use ISIS to do it and begin in Syria—taking advantage of the chaos of the uprising there.

As I reflect on these alliances, I recall being in Amman, Jordan, in 2007 and stumbling into an interview with Saddam Hussein's former cabinet. The former Iraqi cabinet members heard, through the grapevine, that I was interviewing former extremists and invited me to come meet with them. They were living in refuge in Amman. All of Saddam's former cabinet was there, except for former Foreign Minister, Tariq Aziz, who had already been captured and imprisoned by the Coalition forces. When I entered the room with my translator, ten or more of them were seated around a board table and chain-smoking furiously. After some nervous laughter about meeting the wife of a U.S. Ambassador, they explained to me how they had formed a coalition with the Sunni *sheikhs* in Anbar province and were planning to retake power in Iraq after having fallen from power during the 2003 U.S. led Coalition invasion of Iraq. They were adamant that Iraq would not remain in Shia led hands and that Sunnis would again ascend to power. They asked if I could set up a meeting for them with General Petraeus. Afterward, I did ask the General for the meeting—out of courtesy for their time meeting with me—but the General's staff laughed them off. However, it may have been Saddam's cabinet that got the last laugh as we now learn that after U.S. forces departed Iraq, former Saddam Hussein government leaders, disillusioned by events in Iraq, joined forces with ISIS. They brought all their military and intelligence expertise to bear and helped ISIS take over significant parts of Syria and Iraq. Former Colonel, Haji Bakr, was one of them.

"Do you know anything about how ISIS finances itself?" Ahmet asks.

"*Ad-Dawlah* sells oil without any problem, even to Bashar. In al-Hasakah they have a pipeline to Bashar," Abu Ahmed states. We will hear about this again in more detail—how ISIS and Bashar Assad's regime have come to a "devil's alliance" over oil sales.

"*Ad-Dawlah* also sells oil to the Kurds by trucks," Abu Ahmed continues, telling us information that is well-confirmed in press reports.[31] "They assigned an *emir* to be in charge of the oil wells," he tells us. "He was tired of counting, so he decided that a kilo of dollars equals so much, and that's how he counted the cash. Finally, he ran away with the money, but *ad-Dawlah* covered it up and assigned another *emir* in his place."

Later Abu Ahmed shows Ahmet a wealth of incriminating photos still stored on his phone that he took while serving in ISIS. Among them is a photo of two bearded ISIS cadres lounging on the grass together, laughing as they hold up wads of hundred dollar bills while other wads of hundred dollar bills are piled up on one of their bodies. Obviously intoxicated—with the corrupt wealth of ISIS.

Ahmet moves on to the subject of women.

"They are married to the fighters," he answers, and then explains the Islamic custom of the required waiting period before a widow can re-marry. "This is called *iddah*, but when a fighter in *ad-Dawlah* dies they don't worry about it for his widow. She simply remarries another fighter immediately. They either don't know to follow this practice, or don't care." Disgust laces his voice. "For the women, they are hungry and through marriage to the fighters they find food. *Ad-Dawlah* makes the people hungry so that they have to come to *ad-Dawlah* for food."

"What about the foreign women who come as brides?" Ahmet asks. My ears prick up.

"When foreign women arrive it can take as little as eight days to put her in a family," then he turns to an infamous story from his area, "Abu Usamah, from Iraq, the previous *emir* of *ad-Dawlah* in Syria, wanted to get married to the daughter of a very prominent person in our region of Deir ez-Zor—to a princess. He paid two hundred thousand dollars in dowry to the father of the princess and they got married. However, after fifteen days he died in battle. The family wanted to take her back home. Instead, *ad-Dawlah* refused and tried to marry her to another fighter, but the family fought it. *Ad-Dawlah* took the girl to Raqqa to take her away from her family but eventually the family took their daughter back before she got married to another ISIS member. Maybe they paid for her, I don't know."

"Are there forced marriages between the locals and *ad-Dawlah* fighters?" Ahmet asks.

"No, the Syrian women marry the *ad-Dawlah* fighters willingly, because *ad-Dawlah* starves the people," Abu Ahmed reiterates. "They have no bread, no nothing, so finally the families allow their daughters to marry the *ad-Dawlah* fighters for a small amount of money so they can survive. But it is the daughters who agree to it, not their families selling them to *ad-Dawlah*. The daughters want their families to survive."

This is an important point, repeated by other informants, because it again refutes slick propaganda circulated by the Syrian regime and by Russians to discredit the uprising against Assad and hurt the rebel cause, by claiming that foreign women who come to join ISIS take part in *jihad al-nikah*, the practice of marrying these wannabe "brides of ISIS" to multiple fighters over a short time period, basically turning them into prostitutes.

Other ISIS defectors we will speak to have also heard this rumor and take pains to tell us it simply is not true. However, slaves, we will learn *are* sexually abused by multiple ISIS cadres, but not the foreigners who come to be brides—other than they are pressured to remarry if their husband is killed in battle.

Hypocrisy with ISIS is a recurrent theme. And we will later learn from others that many Syrian fathers are heavily coerced to give their daughters to ISIS fighters in marriages—some last only a short time, others evolve into real marriages.

Abu Ahmed continues, "Many of the lowest parts of society jumped to join *ad-Dawlah* [ISIS] in the first days. For instance, a woman who was running a whorehouse and who had men coming to her home to meet with her joined *ad-Dawlah*. After, she became the *emir* of the *hisbah*. These types go to the *shariah* court and make *at-tawba* [repentance] and then swear their *bayat* [allegiance] to *ad-Dawlah* and start a new life. They understand how to rise up in the new system." Perhaps connected to maintaining strict allegiance and control, he also notes that "under *ad-Dawlah*, the girls don't go to school. There is no education for them. Only their *mahrams* [chaperones] can educate them."

"When *ad-Dawlah* fighters are walking on the street, if they see someone smoking he is lashed forty times because he is smoking," Abu Ahmed continues along this theme of hypocrisy. "Yet, they walk away, one or two hundred meters, and then take out their cigarettes and smoke. No one can smuggle in cigarettes but *ad-Dawlah* fighters are selling them secretly. I have even seen *ad-Dawlah* bringing in marijuana. There are many in *ad-Dawlah* who use marijuana, even some who are *emirs*."

He also tells of sexual abuse. "In al-Mayadin hospital in Syria [a city in eastern Syria, part of the Deir ez-Zor governate], two *ad-Dawlah* fighters took one girl who was working near there and raped her. People saw this and killed the *ad-Dawlah* fighters. *Ad-Dawlah*, however, closed this incident and did not go after the locals who killed their fighters because they wanted to keep the rape quiet." We will unfortunately hear such rape stories time and again from defectors—ISIS fighters sexually molest women and cover it up.

But Abu Ahmed also tells us that some, especially foreign Arabs, join ISIS not for the spoils but to "cleanse themselves of their previous sins".

"There was a Tunisian fighter that I asked, 'Why are you here in our country? Do your own jihad in Tunis.' He answered, 'I cannot bring *shariah* to my country, so I bring it here.' He felt he had many sins to repay. He told me, 'We had girls in our family and we would go to the beach and to the sea. They went in bikinis and I made a lot of sins. All my life I drank alcohol. I did drugs and alcohol. But now, in October, I came here in Syria for this bad thing I made with my religion. I went to *at-tawba* [repentance]. I came here to cleanse myself.'"

The story of joining militant jihad and even desiring to 'martyr' oneself is a story I've heard many times from Islamic extremists who fear the everlasting repercussions of their sins. For example, in 2008 I interviewed a Briton of Kashmiri descent who told me that he wanted to die as a 'martyr', admitting it was because of sins he didn't wish to share with me, but for which he feared punishment.[32] The vision of hell in Islam is fiery and horrific and there is no way, aside from relying on Allah's compassion, to guarantee on the final Day of Judgment that one's good deeds will outweigh the bad—except by dying as a 'martyr' and ensuring everlasting salvation.

"There are many young men like him—from Egypt, Tunis, Algeria. They have a bad story with their family. They smoke marijuana. Maybe even they have been with a girl or a boy, and they come here. They want to clean their sins," Abu Ahmed continues.

The foreign fighters also perform another notorious role for ISIS.

"Many foreign fighters act as executioners," Abu Ahmed tells us, and adds, "They always cover their faces with black, and wear long beards. They don't want others to see their faces." Later when Ahmet and I meet in person, he theorizes that the foreign fighters carrying out executions likely cover their faces so they can't be identified in the many photos and videos ISIS distributes to recruit, terrorize and memorialize its barbaric acts, fearing someday they may be called to account for their actions.

"What other things have you seen with ISIS?" Ahmet prompts. Abu Ahmed's eyes are burning with anger as he moves onto another topic we will hear about from more than one defector. It seems ISIS leaders are adept at trading territory and resources they've won on the battlefield, even with the groups they are at war with, in order to strategically gain advantage or money.

"Tell Abyad was sold by *ad-Dawlah* to the PKK [Kurdish rebels] for money," Abu Ahmed tells us. Tell Abyad is the Syrian city that ISIS captured in June 2014 but then lost back to the Kurds and Free Syrian Army in June 2015. In that battle, Abu Ahmed states, "No bullet was fired. *Ad-Dawlah* were strong, but they just left."

Abu Ahmed turns to the story of an ISIS fighter he calls a close friend, who told him that he'd re-captured the border gate of the predominantly Kurdish Syrian city of Kobanî ten times. "'Each time I told the *ad-Dawlah* fighters I took over the border gate,'" he reports his friend telling him, "'but each time they told me to retreat. I couldn't ask anyone [why they would tell me to retreat].'" Abu Ahmed says his friend told him he was thinking of quitting, but "before he ran away [from ISIS], the Coalition forces killed him." As he speaks, his eyes fill with sadness at the corrupt practices that let his friend fight and die over territory ISIS willingly traded away.

"What happens to people who try to escape from ISIS?" Ahmet asks.

"If someone runs away from *ad-Dawlah*, their homes are

bulldozed. *Ad-Dawlah* takes away all their animals and all their furniture first, and then gives away their land."

"How did you escape?"

"I paid a smuggler two hundred Turkish lira [per person] to help me pass the border." Later Ahmet tells me that a Turkish high school teacher would make three thousand Turkish lira a month and an unskilled laborer only twelve hundred a month, so for himself, his wife and three children, he paid nearly a month's salary as a laborer in Turkey to get across the border. "When I arrived in Akçakale, there was no problem, I could settle down."

Turkey is currently the world's largest recipient of refugees from the conflict in Syria and Iraq. Neighboring Lebanon and Jordan have restricted access for refugees, but Turkey has maintained an open-door policy so far, welcoming refugees to live as "guests" until the conflicts are over. Now with over two million registered refugees, Turkey is spending nearly six billion dollars in refugee support. Only ten percent of the refugees live in government-run camps.[33] The majority, like Abu Ahmed and his family, choose instead to live on the local economy, residing in cities scattered along the Syrian border, although some also migrate deeper into Turkey.

As we will do with every defector, we ask what their message is for those considering joining ISIS. "If you could make a statement to the youth in Syria and also in the West about joining ISIS, what would you tell them?" Ahmet asks.

"*Ad-Dawlah* or Bashar, it makes no difference," he responds. "They work for each other. If *ad-Dawlah* continues to stay, they will brainwash all of our children. Now there are many people who don't like *ad-Dawlah* and who want to fight *ad-Dawlah*. Anyone who wants to fight *them,* give him freedom, a gun, and food." It's not exactly the anti-ISIS statement that I had hoped for, but it's his honest sentiment.

As we finish our interview, I reflect on something Abu Ahmed had said to us: "Only twenty meters from my home [in Akçakale, Turkey] I can see *ad-Dawlah*." He's literally looking homeward, across the border of Turkey into Syria, and seeing ISIS holding his home hostage. He cannot return home.

Chapter Six - Life Under ISIS Rule

On the last day of my stay in Istanbul, we interview three more former ISIS fighters, all also Syrian. Due to how far away they live, they have traveled together to our makeshift studio to be interviewed as a group. They are twenty-seven-year old Abu Abdur Rahman—a former law student; twenty-seven-year old Abu Zar—a former high school teacher; and twenty-year-old Ibn Nasir whose education was interrupted by the war.

Ibn Nasir, it turns out, was married just four days ago. He's beaming with pleasure and blushes deeply as the translator teases him. Even Ahmet chuckles knowingly, before asking them to begin telling us about life under ISIS.

The tone in the room instantly changes and Ibn Nasir's face darkens as he recalls ISIS imprisoning him after he crossed the Turkish border to earn extra money as a smuggler. "*Ad-Dawlah* members beat me very badly," he begins. "One day I made a mistake with the *sheikh* from *ad-Dawlah* at the border gate [to Turkey]. The *sheikh* had ordered us, 'Don't go to Turkey today. We are finished with Turkey.' But Ibn Nasir disobeyed and found himself facing ISIS prison upon his return.

"They lashed me twenty times—ten when I entered, and ten inside. There were about twenty persons in the prison. One was from Raqqa. He was there because he drank wine. Another was there because the *hisbah* was walking by the houses and saw his wife through the crack of their outer door. One man was there because he didn't close his shop at prayer time. Another was lashed three hundred times because he had a [forbidden] prayer book. That book makes them crazy—it came from Gabriel."

The book Ibn Nasir is referring to is the *Jawshan al-Kabir*, which is made up of a lengthy prayer that recites the names of God and is believed by many Muslims to have been revealed directly by the Archangel Gabriel to the Prophet Muhammed as an armor to protect against evil. ISIS, however, sees its existence as an apostasy and claims it is not the authentic words of Allah.

"After my time in prison I was not allowed to go to the [Turkish border] gate for about one week," Ibn Nasir continues. "After two days, *ad-Dawlah* took me from home to the court and the judge said, 'You made a big mistake.' The judge accused me of taking foreign fighters [defectors] to Turkey. He said, 'We will come and take you at any hour. We can take you and do what we want.' They made me a prisoner in the area near my home. They said, 'Don't go to the border gate with Turkey.' But after one month they forgot me and I did take someone else across the border," Ibn Nasir smiles with youthful bravado at how he managed to continue in the people-smuggling trade even while being a fighter in ISIS. Apparently he's a resilient, as well as illicit, businessman!

Since Ibn Nasir is talking about smuggling people we ask what these men know about the slave trade. "*Ad-Dawlah* have *sabaya* [female sex slaves]," Abu Zar, the former high school teacher, answers. "They tell the locals, 'If you fight us we will kill your men and take your women as our wives.'" Indeed, we will learn from many of our informants that this is exactly what happens. ISIS captures their enemy's wives and daughters and young men, who are then forced into slavery. The male slaves, Abu Abdur Rahman, the law student explains, are useful for military training in ISIS. "*Ad-Dawlah* took male slaves so they could cut their heads off during training."

My stomach flips as he explains this offhandedly—it's sadly become a kind of "normal" for these former ISIS cadres—but for me it remains sickening.

"You can buy them—the *sabaya*," young Ibn Nasir continues, turning to the subject of the female slaves. "When you have one, it's like your wife. Although unlike wives, there is no limitation on the number you can have. If you are with her and have a child with her and she becomes a Muslim, she can then become your wife."

"There are special places in Raqqa where they sell slaves in the government palace— the Market *Nihase* is in the building that was the previous governor's compound. It is in the center of the city. It is only for *ad-Dawlah*. There they have the *hisbah al-Khansaa* [the female morality police]. They are in charge of everything about the slaves." While it's shocking to learn that women are in charge of selling their "sisters" into sexual slavery, it makes a sick kind of sense in terms of ISIS morality that women—even those destined into sexual slavery—should be sequestered from men.

"Only a fighter can buy a slave woman. He needs documents from the *hisbah* and then he can come to the slave market to buy. They are sold by dollars. The minimum price is one thousand U.S. dollars and the maximum is three thousand dollars. And there are rules," Abu Zar adds, "Like you cannot have a mother and daughter sexually at once," and "if I am a [foreign] fighter, I can sell my slave, but I can sell only to other *mujahideen*,"

Ibn Nasir, and many of the others refer to the foreign fighters as the *mujahideen* (holy warriors) who they distinguish from the local Syrian fighters who they call the *ansar*—the helpers. (In Islamic history, the *ansar* were the citizens of Medina who helped the Prophet Muhammad when he fled there to escape persecution in Mecca.) We will learn that the *mujahideen,* or foreign fighters, are granted many more privileges— including sex slaves—than what the local fighters receive. Ahmet asks about the extent to which a slave girl can be viewed before purchase, if she can be unclothed and viewed naked. He's testing them to see if they will exaggerate, as he is sure this is something ISIS will not allow.

"In the slave market, if I am allowed to buy one, I can sit with her and speak to her," Ibn Nasir explains. "If she has a *hijab* I can remove it to see her face, but a buyer is not allowed to see her body. If the man wants to marry his slave he can and [unlike other Muslim women] she can come in the presence of other men to serve chai, coffee. She does not require a *mahram* [chaperone]. The slave women also have different rules in terms of covering themselves."

"When he buys the slave she is like his wife. He can do as he wants with her. A man who buys a slave can also free her if she becomes Muslim. Maybe she will have a child, so there is also an *iddah* period observed for her when she is sold. It is four months and ten days, but the sale contract is in place while her new owner waits to be sure she is not carrying someone else's child."

"If a slave girl has a boy or girl and the owner says, 'Yes, I am father of this boy or girl,' then they are legitimate children," Abu Zar further explains, adding that all is not calm in this seemingly well-organized slave trade. "A Saudi man bought a slave but she tried to kill him with a gun, but was not successful." I frown listening—wishing she had succeeded.

We ask about male slaves and specifically what happens to the Yazidi boys whose fathers are killed while their women and children are taken. Yazidis are an ancient, monotheistic pre-Islamic religious sect residing in parts of Turkey, Syria and Iraq. ISIS leaders accuse the Yazidis of devil worship and have as a result captured and killed most—enslaving the rest.

The Islamic State is particularly harsh on the Yazidis, differentiating them from other believers who follow "the Book"—those of other Abrahamic faith traditions. "In Syria there are Kurds and so on, but *ad-Dawlah* takes mainly the Yazidis as slaves. They believe that they have Satan as their God," Abu Zar explains. "The Yazidi boys are taken at thirteen to fourteen-years-old. They are given the choice to convert to Islam or be killed. The Yazidi boys convert and fight for *ad-Dawlah*. They are very fierce and good fighters. The *ad-Dawlah* army from Raqqa has them. They also go on suicide missions."

"I saw three Yazidi young men at the *shariah* court who had just converted to Islam. They wanted to go to battle and 'martyr' themselves," Ibn Nasir tells us. "Once they convert and go to *shariah* training these Yazidi boys get so brainwashed that they say, 'My mother and father were wrong. They deserved to die.'"

We are consistently hearing that the power and influence of the ISIS *shariah* trainers is overpowering for young boys. I swallow hard, reflecting on the horror of a child who later embraces the group that murdered his parents.

When we ask how the Yazidi boys are indoctrinated so quickly to become 'martyrs', Abu Zar, the former teacher, tells us: "They have a special school and imam for these boys where they are indoctrinated. They memorize all the Koran."

Yazidi youth who are forced into *shariah* training may likely see no alternative to being killed by ISIS, other than renouncing their parents. They may also be coming to terms with traumatic grief by embracing the 'martyrdom' missions that ISIS offers. Strange as it seems, suicide can be a rational choice for traumatically bereaved individuals who believe in an afterlife; they see death as a comfort and a means of rejoining those family members or loved ones who have been murdered or killed suddenly.

I interviewed would-be suicide bomber, Arin Ahmed, a young Palestinian woman in an Israeli prison in 2005, who described volunteering for a suicide mission in 2002 shortly after Israelis killed her fiancé. Activated very quickly into the role of 'martyr' by *al-Aqsa Martyrs Brigade*, a Palestinian terrorist group, Arin told me that she and a young boy were dispatched together into Israel wearing suicide bombs they were to detonate sequentially in a crowd of Israelis. The youth exploded himself, but Arin, already harboring doubts, came to her senses upon seeing a young baby and realized she had no right to take the lives of innocents. Afterward, in prison reflecting on the reasons she volunteered herself as a 'martyr' and about how quickly she'd been activated—under a month's time after her fiancé's death—Arin complained about the terrorist leaders who sent her while she was still grieving, "They definitely used me! They exploited me at a very vulnerable time. I would never have done that at any other point in my life."[34]

ISIS also manipulates vulnerable individuals into 'martyrdom' though in different ways. Abu Abdur Rahman, who lived away from home while studying law before ISIS rose to power, explains the charismatic power of the *shariah* trainers and how they deeply affected even him, despite his advanced legal education. "I was a [law] student in *al-Furat* University, [close to] graduating. It was 2014. I came to Tell Abyad to visit my family for the Ramadan festival and saw many things different and strange. At the borders of the city area I met border patrol soldiers from *ad-Dawlah*. One asked who I am and where I'm going. I told him I am a last year law student coming home to visit my family. When I told him my university is in al-Hasakah they didn't like it. They don't like al-Hasakah. [ISIS lost battles there to Kurdish militias.] They took my documents and took me and they told me, 'You don't leave Tell Abyad.'"

"They made me very sad because I lost my studies. Since I couldn't return, I couldn't finish my course in university. My psychological state was very bad as a result. I needed only six months to finish. They took and made me a prisoner at home. I couldn't go out because I didn't have an ID card anymore. If I tried to leave Tell Abyad, Bashar's soldiers were there also, and they will need my ID as well, so I could not pass."

"'You need *dawah* [Islamic study]' *ad-Dawlah* told me, and I must repent. So I took their *shariah* course for one week. *Dawah* for me was special because I had already studied law. But the more you study with them, you must deny what you learned before and say you now believe in *shariah* law." (Abu Abdur Rahman repeats again the names of the books used and describes the face-to-face *shariah* instruction similar to what we've heard from others.)

"We had fifteen persons in our class between the ages of twenty to thirty. Actually we also had two persons, ages fifteen and seventeen. The *sheikh* was very kind and spoke wisely. He was from Jordan. I liked him very much. His words were wise. After two days we all liked him very much. We weren't afraid of him at all. In comparison to my Syrian professors there was no one like this *sheikh*. They were very good teachers. They were foreigners—Saudi and Jordanian. *Ad-Dawlah* chooses very high-level teachers who are well educated in *shariah*. They also have very good characters. This *sheikh* even had a doctorate in the English language and was [formerly] an English professor at a Jordanian university."

"You are a law student and used to asking questions of your professors," Ahmet chides him. "But with this training, you submitted?"

"The teacher was very charismatic and he gave examples from the Qur'an so we couldn't challenge him on this—because it was the Holy Qur'an. The Jordanian *sheikh* asked us when he taught our course, 'Why don't you make prayer? Why do you shave? Why don't you dress with a long *thobe* [male Islamic robe]? Why do your brothers come [to your home] and see your wife? And so many things about Islam. But he said the most important subject is that we are not living as proper Muslims. He told us why we shouldn't let my brother see my wife, why I should be growing a beard. The teacher explained and we believed him. We all liked him and enjoyed the course very much. I took everything in the course very seriously. He taught us from our religion—things we didn't know before. He taught us basically the rules of our religion. The *sheikh* told us this is the real learning. What we teach you is based on the Qur'an. When we finished they gave us the books and I read them in my home—those four books."

True for all of our subjects, Ahmet and I must keep in mind that as former fighters for other militias, or simply encountering the brutality of ISIS, they were constantly made aware that life under ISIS is cheap. They could be accused of treason and killed at any moment, and on any pretext. When facing that kind of anxiety from near daily encounters with brutality and death, to be taught that there is certainty and truth in Islam would certainly be very comforting.

Abu Zar, the former high school teacher, started as a fighter for *Jabhat al-Nusra,* the group that later affiliated with al-Qaeda, although in 2013 it was likely still just a local militia taking part in the uprising against Bashar Assad. His story is one that illustrates the complexity of alliances within the region. When ISIS came and took their territory, he and his fellow cadres fled their posts and left their arms with *Jaysh al-Hur,* the Free Syrian Army. "They told us our guns will be safe if we leave them with *Jaysh al-Hur.* We left seventy percent with them and took thirty percent with us. It was guns, bazookas, etc. After one day we heard that *Jaysh al-Hur* joined *ad-Dawlah* with our weapons! They made their *bayat* to *ad-Dawlah!*" A look of incredulity crosses Abu Zar's face.

"*Ad-Dawlah* captured the [Syrian Army's] 93rd tank division from the area the next day. Before *ad-Dawlah* came, the regime's helicopters cannot land because there is firing at them, but after *ad-Dawlah* arrived, every day there comes helicopters from Assad's forces, coming with no problem. So in 2013 it's clear that *ad-Dawlah* and Assad are not fighting each other," Abu Zar informs us, shaking his head in cynical disbelief. We will hear this again—that ISIS appears to make many compromises with the Syrian regime when it is to their advantage to do so.

Many of our informants are suspicious of, or actually have knowledge of, ISIS making deals over the sale of oil or trades for territory with Bashar Assad as well as the other factions that ISIS is battling. Ibn Nasir harbors the same suspicions. "I don't believe that the PKK and *ad-Dawlah* are really fighting each other. Wherever *ad-Dawlah* pulls out, PKK invades without fighting. And I don't believe it was *ad-Dawlah* who attacked in Ankara," referencing an October 2015 suicide attack in Turkey's capital that made international headlines. (In Syria, the YPG is the Kurdish militia and the PYD is the political authority, but ISIS members often refer to the Kurdish militia as the PKK.)

He doesn't trust the PKK either. "No Arab wants any Kurd to take his home of course, which happened in Tell Abyad. The PKK told my uncle, 'We have forgiven you. Come back and claim your house [in Tell Abyad].' But when he went with his children and they opened the door it was booby trapped and his two children were killed!"

"When we come back to Tell Abyad we saw how *ad-Dawlah* operates," Abu Zar, the teacher picks up from here, and again we hear about the totalitarian intelligence prowess of ISIS that they were taught well by their Baathist members. "*Ad-Dawlah* has good intelligence and military. They sent spies inside *Jaysh al-Hur* so they already knew who was who when they invaded. The people were shocked because *ad-Dawlah* killed anyone they saw as resistance. Any officer, any *sheikh*, any important person was killed."

Abu Zar and his men fled when ISIS first came to their area. "There is a small village named Melluh. We stayed hidden there. Suddenly we have a phone call from our friends in the military council. They warned us to go out from our place because *ad-Dawlah* is coming in a few minutes. So we came out and went to Tell Abyad where we fought *ad-Dawlah* for about seven days. This was nearly the first month [January] of 2014. When we quit fighting, we all came to Turkey. We gave our guns into the Turkish military [what they hadn't already given to *Jaysh al-Hur*]. We stayed for about six months, in Turkey."

But twenty-seven year old Abu Zar desperately missed home and decided to return to Syria and accept ISIS rule. "I told my friend and family that I want to return to Syria to join *ad-Dawlah* and make *dawah* [study Islam with them]—if they won't hurt me. I know I need to make repentance to *ad-Dawlah* so they won't kill me. I asked them if it's possible for me to return."

"I really missed my family. I could see my house and village from the [Turkish] border. I was crying. I really wanted to go back home. It was just days before Ramadan [when all families gather each night for the meal that breaks their fast]. At that time al-Baghdadi [the leader of ISIS] issued a letter to everyone and asked all former *mujahideen* to make *at-tawba* [repentance] in the *shariah* court and it would be like an amnesty."

"The answer to my request came, 'Even if you killed one thousand soldiers from *ad-Dawlah* we are going to forgive you. Come back to your country.'"

"When I went back I was in a very bad emotional condition. When I saw my city I cried. I thought to myself, 'I will go there—even if they kill me, it's okay.' It was two days before Ramadan. I took my holy Qur'an and went from Akçakale Border Gate across Tell Abyad and went inside. Inside they took my documents. They told me, 'Go home. Tomorrow we'll call you.'"

"On Saturday morning a microbus came with many persons sitting in it. They came to my home and they took me. There were some *shariah* offices where they took us and in one of them there was a *shariah* judge sitting on a chair. We were three men—me, and two others who also came back from Turkey. 'Place your hand on the Qur'an and say the *at-tawba,*' the judge told us. We did it—we said this pledge to the *ad-Dawlah* judge.

"'You will go to *shariah* camp after this,' the judge ordered. And we were sent directly. We stood in the mosque for the training. In the *jamaat* [brotherhood] there were about fifty or sixty persons. In this *jamaat,* our teachers were Abu Hamza, al-Jazrawi, and Abu Cerir. [*Sheikh* al-Jazrawi is a name we hear frequently and is likely an alias meaning he's from Saudi Arabia.] We study these books: Kitabu't Tevhid - Muhammed Bin Abdulvehhab and Al 'Aqidah as-Sahiha vel Usulessalah," the list we keep hearing of the *Salafi* and *Wahhabi* authors. "After all this studying they took us home."

He also told us, 'We are free here, and we don't force anyone to fight the enemy Bashar.'" Meaning, ISIS soldiers were supposedly free to volunteer for battle. "When our *sheikh* says this everyone cried because they fear how evil the regime soldiers are." While the focus of this book is ISIS defectors stories and the atrocities committed by ISIS, it's important to keep in mind the context in which all this was occurring. Assad's soldiers were raping, torturing and mistreating all who opposed them, so much so, that some Syrian Sunnis preferred living under ISIS.

"The *sheikh* who taught was from Saudi Arabia. I liked very much *sheikh* al-Jazrawi. He put me into a good psychological condition. The *sheikh's* face was smiling. He made us very comfortable. I liked them [the *shariah* trainers] very much." Abu Zar echoes what we will hear repeatedly—that the *shariah* teachers are carefully picked to be warm, attractive, charismatic and knowledgeable about the ISIS version of Islam. "I liked what he was teaching. He talked about the hereafter, our brothers that are in prison, that we need to save them. He talked so powerfully that the students cried. After three or four lessons [with him], I felt I was ready to become a 'martyr'."

While it may seem strange that a battle-hardened man could be moved to considering 'martyrdom', after only a few lessons, these men were well aware of the atrocities that were occurring under Assad. Like other soldiers, some became willing to sacrifice their lives to fight this evil—especially when they were being taught that this "ultimate sacrifice" was a holy one that would result in Paradise.

"For example, he taught, 'Subhan'Allah [Praise to Allah] Prophet Muhammed was revealed to humanity for good through his sword.' I know now that this is not in the Qur'an, but he said it was. And he put in our mind that these are the last days [End Times] and that they are good."

"This is what the *sheikh* said, 'Heaven is our bride. The dowry of this bride is giving up your life.' He gave verses from the Qur'an. After ten courses from this *sheikh,* I started to see everyone else as infidels, and I believed that any government that does not rule by *shariah* law is *kufr* [denying the truth of Islam]. Our *sheikh* told us that we will go to Paradise.

This makes us willing to go to jihad and die. He makes us happy to go to Paradise. The *sheikh* also told us, 'If you want to go to Paradise you will kill a life in your hand.'" Abu Zar is likely referring to the required practice to behead a prisoner at the end of the training to graduate into an ISIS fighter. Following our research ethic, we do not ask if he killed a prisoner and let him continue.

"He told us that what he taught is from the Qur'an. He taught us the following verse: Those who leave their homes in the cause of Allah, and are then slain or die, on them will Allah bestow verily a goodly provision.[35] After this training I was deeply affected."

"Now, I know that the *sheikh* was very clever and gave only the first parts of the verses and then changed the end of it, or vice versa. They take only small parts from the Qur'an in order to deceive their students. Suicide is forbidden in Islam but they convinced us that dying as a suicide bomber is jihad and ordained by Islam. They gave a new meaning to the verses by twisting the words to apply their beliefs."

"Everybody in this training had a gun against *ad-Dawlah* before. All in this group were from the same area. They all became convinced, and after the course we all gave our *bayat* to *ad-Dawlah*. We gave our *bayat* to al-Baghdadi as well, as the *Caliph*."

"The training took fifteen days. When we finished the course, many of the people, about forty-five of us went to fight with *ad-Dawlah*. Before that we didn't really know Islam very well: *tasattur* [proper Islamic dress for men and women], prayer, and fasting. They taught us the real Islam that we didn't know. We liked very much to go pray in *masjid* [the mosque]. It was Ramadan. Everyone fasts. No one can eat or smoke during this time. Life was serious, with a real Islamic atmosphere."

"They also taught us the *bayat* of *al wala' wal bara'*." Abu Zar is referring to the Islamic concept of loyalty and disavowal—or of loving Islam and hating and disavowing everything that is not Islam. Groups like ISIS take this to the extreme, demanding one hate, kill, and destroy anyone and anything that opposes their extremist version of Islam. "They don't believe our people in Syria are Muslim. Only those who make *bayat* to them are Muslim."

As is often the case, the *shariah* trainers and their words don't match the brutal realities of ISIS. In short time, Abu Zar began to doubt. "After my *bayat* I began not to believe them. I asked my father, my best friend and my wife, 'What should I do?' They told me, 'Don't go to *ad-Dawlah*. Stay near them but don't go to fight with them.'"

We turn next to ask about marriage under ISIS.

"We heard about *jihad al nikah* [marital or sexual holy war]. Muslim girls coming and giving their body as prostitutes for the *mujahideen*. It is absolutely not true," Abu Zar immediately volunteers in a cynical voice.

In September 2013, I'd seen this claim written all over Russian government-sponsored news sites, including the English speaking ones. In addition, giving credence to it, Tunisian Interior Minister, Lotfi ben Jeddou, announced to his National Constituent Assembly that an alarming number of Tunisian women have gone to aid rebel militants in Syria and were having "sexual relations with 20, 30, 100 militants" and that "after the sexual liaisons they have there in the name of *jihad al-nikah*, they come home pregnant."

The Tunisian minister's claim that in Syria, Tunisian girls were being subjected to multiple "marriages," abusing the Shia tradition of *muta* marriage seemed strange to me. *Muta* marriage allows a traveling Muslim man to make a suitable material offering to a woman for a temporary marriage contract. I noted on a piece I wrote at the time, given that *muta* marriage is a Shia tradition, whereas ISIS is Sunni, it seemed rather unlikely that a conservative Islamic group like ISIS would engage in such practices.[36] Later, many human rights advocates and those who had a lot of contact with Syrian refugees also refuted these stories. Even though they were no defenders of groups like ISIS, these human rights workers said there was absolutely no evidence of truth in these allegations of sexual or serial "marriage" abuse. It appeared to be pure and simple Russian propaganda.

"So if ISIS marriages are normal marriages, why do girls marry the fighters?" we ask.

"The situation in Syria under ISIS is so bad," Abu Zar states, his voice again sounds heavy with sorrow as we again hear how girls sacrifice themselves for their families. I get the feeling from how sad he sounds that Abu Zar sees this as the ultimate family tragedy—to have to trade your daughter, or to have her trade herself into marriage, to help keep her family members alive.

He answers, "Someone comes from *ad-Dawlah* and wants to marry. He asks, 'Please I want to marry your daughter', like we do usually. But in Raqqa, all of Raqqa—all people have problems of money. They don't have food. For this reason, many young women think, *if I marry, maybe I'll help my family*. The girl herself thinks this. This is not her father selling her. There is no food—no work—nothing." Abu Zar rubs his forehead, clearly pained by this thought of girls marrying ISIS fighters out of financial need.

"All the people of Raqqa don't want their women to go and be with ISIS," Abu Abdur Rahman, the one-time law student explains. "Poor people come to fight from the areas of Palmera and Aleppo. They join ISIS because they have no money. Their women come also and marry ISIS fighters out of poverty."

When we ask about the foreign girls who come to marry into ISIS, Ibn Nasir tells us, "There are also many women coming from Tunis, Algeria etc. and they also want to marry. The *hisbah al-Khansaa* arranges it."

I have learned from talking to security professionals in the UK that young girls lured into ISIS are shown pictures of fine homes, swimming pools, good food and that one thirteen-year-old girl who was saved before embarking on this "one way trip to hell" later remarked that from the pictures they'd sent her, she thought she was agreeing to go to "Islamic Disney World". As I listen, I think that it's likely the Tunisian and Algerian girls have also been lured by the promise of adventure, marriage, building a "Caliphate", and the material rewards of having a nice house, etc., along with perhaps agreeing with the hope of building a Utopian Islamic "Caliphate".

"If any girl comes to Syria from another place, the first step is they take her to reception, after one week the police ask her many things," Abu Abdur Rahman confirms the suspicion that ISIS has of all outsiders until they can verify that the newcomers are committed to the cause, and not spies. "After, she is cleared no problem."

"But many of the foreign girls don't want to marry a Syrian fighter," Abu Zar adds. "They usually want to marry from their own nationalities. For instance, the Europeans want to marry Europeans. There is a special marriage bureau that gives an order yes or no about marrying. A German for instance comes and says, 'I want to get married.' He goes first to the bureau to get permission. The women go to the *hisbah al-Khansaa*. She writes her name that she wants a husband. Then it is arranged between them. When they come to the marriage bureau it takes time. The young man is studied for four to six months by the bureau. They also make a study about the girl before they marry."

"The *hisbah* runs a hotel for the women who come as marriage partners, the brides." We'll later learn more about this "sisters' house" in greater detail from a European woman who stayed in one of them while her husband went off for his *shariah* and military training before swearing his *bayat* to ISIS.

"What do you know about the European brides?" Ahmet prompts.

"There is a group of European girls—twenty-five of them," Ibn Nasir tells us. "They live very comfortably in Raqqa. They have houses and cars. Their sole job is sitting on the Internet recruiting other European women. During the daytime they come to this nice place and write on the Internet. All these girls are married to *mujahideen*."

Sex scandals happen in ISIS as elsewhere. "There was a *sheikh* with two wives," Abu Zar re-tells the story of the foreign fighter from Tunisia who married two Syrian women. "His wives went to the *hisbah* to complain that he wants to come in bed, taking the two at the same time. The judge had him lashed. Then he was put in a pick-up truck and paraded around town with a sign telling what he did. He was held twenty days. Many people saw him. The *ad-Dawlah* court said, 'We have justice. If anyone does this, we punish him.'"

"All [Syrian] women married to *mujahideen* have bad psychology," Abu Zar bemoans. I wonder if the idea of a foreigner coming to claim one of their Syrian women as a bride is, for him, beyond belief. "These women can only go out with their *mahram* [chaperone], but two can go together." I ask if the European brides who come are also unhappy and am surprised to hear his answer.

"Some Western women are very happy. They go and wander around outside with their weapons. After their husbands die, they remarry," Abu Zar is saying this from observation, as we begin to learn that it's rare that the Syrian fighters like the three we are speaking to today, ever communicate directly with the Western brides. Aside from the likely language barrier, ISIS forbids it.

But not all are content.

"Many European girls don't like to stay in Raqqa," Abu Zar tells us. "They want to return home."

"Do any of the foreign fighters try to escape?" we ask. "Do you know of any Westerners who tried to leave?"

Ibn Nasir chimes in. "I know the story of one European girl who wanted to escape. Someone tried to help her go back to Urfa, to escape. But they caught and killed him, and took the girl back to Raqqa," Ibn Nasir's big black eyes open wide. "An Irish husband and wife also tried to escape ISIS but they were stopped. This Irish couple was caught while they were fleeing. The man was killed at the scene. They cut his throat. His wife was brought back to Raqqa. I was at the gate (to Turkey) at that time and I saw it all."

As I listen, I marvel at the fact that these men took the chance to smuggle themselves across the border—and made it. Something gave them the courage to flee despite the life or death odds of getting caught. *Their disgust with ISIS? Disdain for bloodying their hands further on behalf of the brutal group? Fear of their own imminent demise?* I wonder.

The killing of this Irish defector starts a discussion between Ahmet and the men about Westerners who have come to Syria to join ISIS— would they be able to pass back through Turkish borders again? They agree that if the Westerners had managed to keep their passports and had them stamped, (which might not be the case if they were smuggled into Syria), they could legally cross back into Turkey. However, most ISIS cadres are required to destroy or surrender, their passports when they join.

Ahmet asks about the make-up of these foreign fighters—how many there are and where are they from.

"In Tell Abyad there are fifty Americans," Abu Abdur Rahman responds and Ibn Nasir confirms, "I saw at least fifty Americans in Tell Abyad. They were very big guys, blonde, and in black clothes like the Pakistanis used to wear."

"What are they like?" we ask.

"When you see Western *ad-Dawlah* members, they smile at you. Their faces are clean. You are not afraid of them. They are trustworthy. When they see a child they do not spread fear to the child. They hide their guns [in front of children]. Syrian *ad-Dawlah* are not trustworthy. They are like animals."

Ibn Nasir tells us that he knows firsthand how ISIS treats foreign fighters when they first enter Syria via Turkey. "There is a special place [along the border] when a man comes to join ISIS from Turkey, through which he is led. Anybody that comes from that gate, I take him to reception, serve him food and so on. He is put in good conditions—but for security reasons, I watch him. Maybe he is a spy, police, or who? This is the first step. Then we take him to Raqqa and give him money to rent or buy a house."

But once in ISIS it's impossible to leave, Ibn Nasir states, "If anyone tries to leave they will be made prisoner. If they get caught at the border trying to escape they will immediately be killed. Anyone [from ISIS] who is stopped at the gate without documentation from *ad-Dawlah* to go to Turkey is killed. Their throats are slit."

Ibn Nasir turns to the *kassas*. "*Kassas* is what they call their executioner. The man who executed the most people is from Serbia. During trainings they [the *shariah* trainers] watch and figure out who among the trainees are the cruelest and then assign them as *kassas*. Sometimes they give drugs to the people who are going to be executed so they are passive. And they make movies of what they do."

I think of the ghastly video of American journalist James Foley and how calm he seemed as he was going to his death. *Was he drugged?* I've spoken to his parents and listened to their grief and saw their unspeakable shock that their beautiful son was beheaded. Indeed, Mr. Foley's father has publicly questioned if perhaps our country is wrong to stand in the way of paying to recover hostages from groups like ISIS. Hearing this father's grief, I couldn't help but wonder as well, if there isn't some way to consistently recover hostages—perhaps using middle countries like Bahrain to negotiate, as has been done in some cases in the past.

My mind returns from the Foley family's horror and grief as Ibn Nassir continues, "In one of the training camps near Tabqa they train the *mujahideen* and teach them that there are spies among them. If they catch a spy, they put him in front of a judge and then cut his head at the training centers." I realize these are likely the prisoners who get beheaded at graduation from *shariah* training.

Again, we want to know if these men saw positives in being in ISIS.

Our teacher is the first to respond. *"Ad-Dawlah* never [systematically] rapes," Abu Zar answers. "They never take war booty. They never touch it. When they wage a battle for an area, they give three days for anyone who wants to leave. They say, 'Leave now. We are not going to touch anyone who stays at home and does not fight.' And they are sincere in this. People in Syria are saying the fire of *ad-Dawlah* is better than PKK's heaven. It's true, the PKK rape when they come. So a regional woman will prefer *ad-Dawlah,"* Abu Zar explains.

"Ad-Dawlah taught me Islam, and *salah* [Muslim prayer]," Ibn Nasir reflects and then wrinkling his nose adds, "However, I don't want their ideology." He continues, "They helped people who don't have money. They distribute alms, and under *ad-Dawlah* everybody pays their debts."

"The foreigners don't want to go back," Ibn Nasir adds, pointing out that ISIS has an enduring appeal to the foreign fighters despite all the corruption and brutality. *Perhaps the foreign fighters like all the material benefits?* I wonder. And many Westerners would face prosecution if they returned home.

Ibn Nasir also lists ISIS commanders that he admires: "Emir Shishani [Abu Omar al-Shishani] took all the tough places—Aleppo, the Menagh Airbase. He is well-known, strong and tough. Khattab Kurdi [a Kurdish ISIS commander] was also tough," Ibn Nasir says with more than a trace of admiration in his young voice. *I guess if you fought with these men, you would admire that they're tough and strong commanders,* I think, even as I am a bit sickened by this continued admiration in his listing their names.

We ask what prompted them to risk their lives to finally leave ISIS.

"Even though I know now that I was right to leave *ad-Dawlah,* I could not at first leave them. After taking their *shariah* training and becoming convinced, I felt that I must live one year under *ad-Dawlah*. When the PKK took Tell Abayd I went willingly to Raqqa, even though I could have left them then," Ibn Nasir says. "Later we saw that these *ad-Dawlah* people say something, but they do the opposite. Then, I understood that they are very bad."

"A lot of people in *ad-Dawlah* are not good, and life is very hard," Abu Abdur Rahman seconds Ibn Nasir's opinion.

"I guess *ad-Dawlah* is trying to ruin our Sunni roots," Abu Zar interrupts. "They keep sending our children to the camps. Then the Coalition planes bomb the camps and our Syrian teenagers die." Indeed, it's the consensus in this group that the Coalition intel often leads to bombing civilians, or camps where there are teens, more often than actual ISIS strongholds, and they wonder why. We will hear this again and it's confusing for us as well. We too, wonder about all the conflicting actors and their interests in Syria and the intelligence wars among them that often seem to end in the wrongful killing of civilians.

Ahmet turns the conversation to an area of particular interest to him. "Can you tell us about how they conduct military training?"

"For those who train as fighters they have military training during the day time and at night continue on with *shariah* training," Ibn Nasir is echoing what we have heard before. "Trusted fighters from Turkey are sent back at least every six months to Turkey to see their families. This is a rule of Islam." So once again we hear how easily ISIS cadres cross the borders to and from Turkey. Although to hear that Turkish ISIS members cross the border for home leave, is quite surreal. Something so normal—home leave, practiced by a terrorist group with the possible complicity of a NATO member state.

"There are military courses for [male] fighters. They are very hard," Abu Abdur Rahman tells us. "In military training there are three courses. First is sport—something like football [soccer]; second is military tactics; and third is fighting. And some learn bombs, gas, etc. and other special techniques."

"Are the suicide bombers trained with the rest?" we ask.

"For the jihadi special course they have only the Qu'ran and *Hadiths* and prayer," Abu Abdur Rahman explains. "They don't see any other fighters—*ad-Dawlah* separates and isolates them. They eat and sleep together and they practice fasting for one to two days to be hungry for a long time [in case their mission requires this]. Both Syrians and foreigners can become martyrs." Ibn Nasir refers to a Turkish man who 'martyred' himself for ISIS. "He killed twenty-three people!" Later we will learn about the many different ways that these 'martyrs' are equipped to kill themselves and others.

"*Ad-Dawlah* commanders in different regions don't know each other," Ibn Nasir continues, detailing military training. "Our commander was Abu Ahmet. He was a [former] Baathist. All the important commanders are from Iraq, and are former Baathists," he adds. Apparently Saddam's former cabinet wasn't so far off the mark when they said the Iraqi Sunnis would return to power.

"How is life under ISIS for the regular civilians?" Ahmet asks the group.

"Everyone wakes for *fajr* [dawn prayers] at the mosque. If the air force attacks, we don't go to prayer." Abu Abdur Rahman answers. "If you don't go to the mosque during prayer time you are punished. But it is dangerous if a person prays regularly at mosque and doesn't come one day, they come check on him. The *hisbah* comes and asks, 'Where is he? Is he sick? Or left the area? What happened with him? Did he go to a job, or his farm, or battle?'"

"For *salat* [obligatory prayers] anyone who does not go to *masjid* [the mosque] is taken to *shariah* court. He is fined and his shop is closed for ten days. If anyone closes the door of his shop but stays inside it [during prayer time]—if they find him inside—they close his shop forever."

"Then everyone sleeps again for two to three hours," he continues. "Then they go to their jobs or work in the markets."

We hear again about the restrictions on women. "The *hisbah* patrol the town. Any woman who doesn't wear *hijab*, they take her and she gets punished. If a woman wants to go by taxi she must have a *mahram* who must sit in the first seat by the driver with the woman in back. There are no *shariah* courses for women. The males teach their family members at home. Other women can only sell women's items in the market."

And in a funny twist that only war-torn events can provide, Abu Abdur Rahman explains that there are no longer any mannequins in the shops. "They are all used to deceive the jets. They put clothes on them to make them look like *mujahideen*!" I can't help but laugh at the image of female mannequins dressed in ISIS garb.

"How is the intelligence of ISIS? Are you afraid now in Turkey?" Ahmet asks the group.

"Every village in Syria has spies. If they ask me in *shariah* training, 'Do you have a family member in *Jaysh al-Hur,* or *Jabhat al-Nusra?'* if I say yes, I die, because I'm seen as a spy," Abu Abdur Rahman continues. "They have a lot of money to pay informants and pay money to collect intelligence at the mosque and everywhere else. There are spies in Turkey as well. The Turkish government requires us to register and give our name, address and phone. This information can later be purchased by *ad-Dawlah.*"

"*Ad-Dawlah* intelligence is very strong wherever you are," Ibn Nasir agrees. "One of my friends was talking to someone from Syria who was against *ad-Dawlah*. They were together in Urfa in a café. Somehow an *ad-Dawlah* intel agent took their picture. When my friend went back to Syria, I learned that *ad-Dawlah* asked him why they were talking. They showed him the picture and then killed him." His eyes widen in fear. "Here, I am trying not to upset anyone—neither *ad-Dawlah* or *Jaysh al-Hur*. If I want to live I must not make them upset."

"The *hisbah* is in everything. They don't let you be. They pay money to young children age ten and so on to give information, even from inside their families. I could not be myself in front of my little nieces, because maybe, they are paid informants," Ibn Nasir grimaces as he rubs his hands nervously through his black head of hair.

"When they say, 'Take him and kill him,' I wonder, *Why* do you kill him? Did you open his heart and see?" Abu Abdur Rahman's voice now fills with disgust and indignation over the way ISIS accuses people of being traitors and executes without trials or evidence brought to prove their guilt.

"I don't see any locals who are fighting for ISIS willingly in Syria anymore. Those who fight willingly are foreigners," Abu Abdur Rahman continues. "When I work with these *ad-Dawlah* guys in business I see how bad they are—they take bribes. Nobody right now likes *ad-Dawlah*. They hate him in the market, in the street, in his home. They don't visit him. One guy even said to me, 'I have been praying in the mosque without *wudu* [mandatory ablution] because I am being forced and I don't like being forced.'"

"In Islam there are some *Hadiths* that are true and others that are less trusted," Abu Abdur Rahman says, "but ISIS twists any of them to their own purposes. And *ad-Dawlah* limits the promises of the Qur'an only to Muslims—not to all humans."

"Right now we don't see *ad-Dawlah* dealing with the United States and Europe because they are very busy with Syria and Iraq, but if it was a benefit to them they would carry out attacks," Ibn Nasir states and adds, "They sent many ISIS men among the refugees who went to Europe." When we ask the men more about this significant allegation—ISIS infiltration into the refugee population—it's clear that Ibn Nasir is relying more on hearsay than actual knowledge, although there is no doubt that ISIS does send its cadres back and forth through Turkey, into Greece, and on into Europe. We will soon see that the ISIS cadres involved in the

December 2015 Paris attacks did exactly this and we will see it once again in 2016.

The call to prayer sounds in Istanbul, where I am in my hotel looking out over the water and typing notes, and in Şanlıurfa where Ahmet and these men are gathered. It's a haunting call that spreads out over the water and throughout the city, calling all to stop whatever they are doing and pray. These three men are hungry and anticipating the kabob lunch that Ahmet has promised them—meat that they rarely eat anymore now that they are refugees—and they need to go and pray. Ahmet tells me that we need to end the interview. We ask our last question: "What would you say to anyone thinking of joining ISIS?"

"They are not related to Islam in any way. They are the *Khawarij* that the Prophet Muhammed talked about—those he told about who would come with black clothes and black flags," Ibn Nasir answers, and we hear another reference to that reviled tribe that rose up during the Prophet's time to name other Muslims as apostates and kill them.

Ahmet rises and thanks them and goes with them to pray as I sit listening to the *muezzin* calling everyone to prayer. Later we find that Ahmet's act—of proclaiming his faith as an important part of his life, and taking them out to a nice lunch afterward—opens the door for continued interviews.

"We've never seen a professor pray before," they tell him, still speaking through their Arabic interpreter that the smuggler sent along with them. And as they eat their Turkish kabobs, one of these three men speaks up in broken English and quietly tells Ahmet, "We don't trust this interpreter. We're not sure about him."

Ahmet asks this Syrian for his phone number. Later, when things become even more dangerous, this will turn out to have been a prescient move. This defector will become our main fixer. We will no longer work through the smuggler or involve any outside interpreters. We'll tighten down our security entirely. While they've opened up and shared a lot, it's clear these battle-hardened men still fear the long arm of ISIS and soon, we will as well.

Chapter Seven - A Surprise Visit

I know that the long arm of ISIS wishes to extinguish all of Western civilization. Yet on my last morning in Istanbul, the shimmer of the Bosporus once again pulls me. Gazing out over the vast expanse—the history of Istanbul laid out below—I imagine Sultans and hundreds of years of a very different Caliphate that was once centered here, and I can't help but feel that the horror stories we've been hearing dim in the face of the eternal. This peaceful blue water will still be here long after ISIS has come and gone, just as it flows here now, nearly one hundred years after the Ottoman Empire. I turn back to packing as I think back over the first seven interviews we've completed this week and meeting Ahmet face-to-face for the first time the night before.

I never dreamed we'd get this close to ISIS, hearing first-person narratives about its inner workings, and I know that it is really due to Ahmet's courage. He's reached out among former ISIS cadres living in southern Turkey and they have taken us inside ISIS. Ahmet is just like his e-mails and the gentle voice that resonated over Skype—a handsome, physically trim, fit and good man. Meeting him, I immediately sense warmth, intellect and a sense of humor.

When Ahmet arrived at the hotel in Istanbul, he agreed with a big smile that, "the view is amazing!" and later told me that he'd taken a few photos as he settled into his room, to send to his wife. I hope she hasn't feel left out or worried about him visiting a female professor in a hotel without her being present. *I'm in a conservative Muslim country,* I remind myself.

A former State Department colleague had warned me before this trip to not leave the hotel or go to the Grand Bazaar as ISIS cadres, now active inside Turkey, rendered it no longer safe for tourism. Indeed, the October 2015 explosion in Ankara strangely blamed by Turkish authorities on *both* ISIS and the PKK had rocked the Turkish capital only a week before I arrived.[37] I'd been in Turkey so many times though, and knew the lay of the land well enough, that I decided not to heed her advice. I did, however, take more care to dress each morning like a local in long jackets and sweaters that hung well past my backside, and a big scarf wrapped around my neck and shoulders. It was always good to blend in and keep a low profile—not proclaiming myself by dress, or otherwise, as an American—and I returned to the hotel earlier each night, before darkness fell. I could see that Istanbul is changed—and I could feel it.

As I walked around during the past week, going to the Grand Bazaar and other familiar haunts that I know well, I met and chatted with Syrian refugees who were trying to rebuild. I read in the local English newspaper that the police had just uncovered an alleged ISIS-run training school for Uzbek and Tajik immigrant children inside the city.[38] Now, in a taxi on the way to the airport, I read that Turkish intelligence had uncovered an alleged ISIS plot to run four undercover operatives into the country to try to carry out terrorist attacks.[39] Their fake passport pictures, somehow captured by Turkish intel, are published in the paper and I see that one of the ISIS suspects is a European-looking woman dressed in a simple headscarf. She looks like many of the Turkish women I've encountered on the street, if not more Caucasian than the rest. *I wouldn't have suspected her,* I think, as the taxi speeds toward the airport.

From here I'm headed to Madrid, to present my terrorism and radicalization research at the *Club de Madrid* conference, a gathering of former heads of state, and to (hopefully) do more interviews with former terrorists elsewhere in Europe. The driver chats with me in broken English about Istanbul. When we pass a bridge with a man pushing a tall and rickety cart piled high with old stained mattresses, he tells me that they are rented at night to Syrians who have fled their homes and who presently live on the streets of Istanbul, many overnighting under this bridge. My heart hurts imagining the scene here at night. Like the rest of Turkey,

Istanbul has opened its arms to the fleeing Syrians. This city currently houses three hundred and sixty-six thousand Syrian refugees, more than all the Syrian refugees currently sheltering across Europe.[40]

Ahmet and I spent our day together going over our interviews with this first group of former ISIS fighters. Each first-hand account has been fascinating; each one revealing and confirming new and different aspects of life under ISIS. We corrected things I'd missed when the Internet connection failed. We talked over our respective pasts in the counter-terrorism field, and discussed how we hoped to continue working together. "I'd like to finish my career as a professor in a university in the United States," Ahmet informed me. He asked for my advice—whether it would be wise to begin his American job search now or wait until we had a chance to write up our results. "I still have two more years to earn my full retirement," he explained, "And my son will graduate university then, so maybe it's better to wait?"

"I wouldn't rush it," I told him, thinking these new publications we'd write together would fill out his academic C.V. He was, after all, still a new professor with limited academic publications because he'd spent the bulk of his career in counter-terrorism as a police officer, culminating his law enforcement career as the Chief of Police in Şanlıurfa. In his policing capacity, he'd worked side-by-side through the U.S. Embassy in Ankara with experts from the FBI, U.S. Drug Enforcement Agency, Department of State, and Department of Defense, as well as with NATO and EU officials, when they were together chasing international terrorists. He had built quite a portfolio of experts he knew personally, but he still had the academic writing to fill out if he wanted to land a good job in American academia. We plotted out the next year's work together, the luxury of time on our side.

Ahmet had brought with him the transcript of Abu Jamal, an ISIS defector interview he had conducted just before we started working together. Abu Jamal is a thirty-five-year-old former ISIS commander, so his access and knowledge of ISIS is particularly intriguing for us. As we sat at dinner in the elegant top-floor dining room of our hotel, we dug into that transcript. We discussed Ahmet's very first question to him, one that for me was such an important question "Do you think there are ISIS fighters in the refugee camps in Turkey?"[41]

"There are thirty thousand refugees in Akçakale camp, most of whom are Arabs. In the Kobanî fight, many killed ISIS members were carrying Akçakale Camp IDs on them," Abu Jamal answered. This means that even refugee camp members were moving back and forth across the Turkish borders, into and back out of ISIS ranks—an extremely disturbing thought. Although, given that ISIS cadres move back and forth across the Turkish border anyway, we shouldn't be surprised that some would also infiltrate the camps. As we discussed it, Ahmet pointed out that the government requires the camp authorities to lock their gates in the evenings and monitor travel, letting only those working in the fields move in and out of the camp early in the mornings, and return in the evenings before the gates are closed. It appears that ISIS, however, manages to move about more freely.

"There are around twenty quarters in Akçakale camp," Abu Jamal had explained. "Every quarter has a *masjid* [a mosque]. There are Arabic-speaking *sheikhs* who are imams leading the prayers and carrying out the sermons. Some of those *sheikhs*, or other undeclared preachers who are called *sheikhs*, preach to recruit for ISIS. They gather people around, either in *masjids* or tents to preach. There are many youngsters who flee the camps to join *ad-Dawlah* after being recruited through those *sheikhs*. The *sheikhs* preach that jihad is *fard al-ayn* [an obligatory Islamic duty] for all Syrian men because Syria is in war."

That militant jihad is an obligatory duty of Islam is a claim that nearly all militant jihadi groups make. Anwar al-Awlaki, the American and Yemeni English-speaking preacher who the U.S. killed by drone in 2011, can still be found preaching this call-to-duty on his audio and video sermons circulating on the Internet. He has, even in death, convinced nearly every Western kid involved in militant jihadi terrorism that he or she had to either come to the battlefield or bring the battlefield to where they are—making a strong argument for homegrown terrorism. Shannon Conley, an American who left her Catholic roots to convert to Islam, found Anwar al-Awlaki on the Internet and as a result began downloading urban guerilla jihadi manuals from al-Qaeda, studying how to bring jihad to where she lived in Denver, Colorado. She studied how to carry out a VIP convoy attack and contemplated it until her plans got diverted to becoming a bride of ISIS when she fell in love—via Skype—with an ISIS Tunisian fighter.[42] Sadly, there are hundreds like her in the West, radicalized via the Internet, who become convinced that to be a Muslim means the duty to fight jihad is obligatory, even if that means bringing the battleground to their home countries in the West.

"In the camp, it is like a mafia," Abu Jamal continued. "The *ad-Dawlah* people force and threaten you, but the camp authorities don't know about it. And they promise, 'if you die [for ISIS], we will take care of your family.' But if you don't want to join *ad-Dawlah* than you have to flee. They will not let you alone." Others told us that recruiters talk to young kids, both those living in the camps and living outside in the local economy, to seduce them into leaving their families in Turkey to return to Syria to fight for ISIS, but Abu Jamal is the only former ISIS member to tell us of an organized and actual presence, or "mafia," of ISIS cadres living inside the Akçakale refugee camp among the Syrians. That he was the only one to say it doesn't mean he's incorrect.

"[Once in ISIS] whoever wants to return, gets killed," Abu Jamal continued, echoing what everyone else has said about joining ISIS—it's a one-way ticket to hell with no return. "I have seen a boy in *ad-Dawlah* who was from Turkey," Abu Jamal shared with Ahmet. "He met with his Turkish father at the border gate in Akçakale. His father did not want him to go back [into ISIS] but crying he said to his father, 'They will kill me here—right now—if I don't turn back now.' And suddenly there were around fifteen ISIS fighters who came out of nowhere, showing themselves, to ensure that he was not going home with his father."

"There is no fleeing," Abu Jamal continued. "All the smugglers are forced and paid to inform on any *ad-Dawlah* members who are fleeing. The only way to ensure safe passage is to bribe the smuggler in high amounts, or he will inform *ad-Dawlah* and you will be immediately killed. Also, there are several *ad-Dawlah* checkpoints. If you are caught at the checkpoints, you also get killed."

Which begged the question, "How is the border with Turkey, for ISIS members?" Ahmet had asked.

"Passing the border for *ad-Dawlah*, is as easy as eating cheese," Abu Jamal replied. The smugglers are doing this for money. They charge usually two hundred U.S. dollars per person, but as I told you, it depends on the situation. There is a coffee shop close to the border in Akçakale. Anyone who wants to pass the border goes there to meet with the smugglers. You can see the PKK and *ad-Dawlah* members sitting there together. In Akçakale at the Tell Abyad border gate, there is a middleman called the *alligator*. He handles everything in the name of *ad-Dawlah*. He is a very scary man. He works with *ad-Dawlah* intelligence. *Ad-Dawlah* has very strong intel in Turkey as well. They knew who I befriended even while I was here in Akçakale. *Ad-Dawlah* members have a lot of money, so it's easy for them. They can come to Turkey and rent a house and use it for maximum ten days, let it go, and then return and rent another."

During his time policing, Ahmet told me that when the Turkish National Police would radio into headquarters that they had detained a foreign fighter heading to ISIS at the Şanlıurfa bus station or airport, the officers would receive orders back over their phones to "Let them go. Let them pass unimpeded." Likewise, several times police officers at the bus station would capture ISIS members at the bus station barber shops where they were having their beards shaved off and shortening their hair—

probably in order to re-enter Europe. But again they would be ordered not to intervene in accordance with unwritten official Turkish government policy. In fact, their seniors harassed some officers for stopping suspected ISIS members. Ahmet has found it extremely frustrating that the Turkish government has a supportive view of ISIS. There are however, a number of strategic advantages for Turkey to overtly or subtly support ISIS, among them, ISIS keeps the PKK engaged in battles, thus relieving the Turkish government of this longtime threat.

It isn't just people who can pass the border, according to Abu Jamal. Turkish authorities have also turned a blind eye to smuggling weapons and supplies for several years now. Ahmet also knows this from his time policing and it is well known among security analysts as well—much of it funded from wealthy donors in Qatar, Kuwait and Saudi Arabia.[43]

Abu Jamal says, he's seen this with his own eyes. "Through Akçakale border gate, *ad-Dawlah* acquired long, strong pipes and a lot of fertilizer. Those pipes and fertilizer were used to make a kind of rocket in Raqqa with LPG [liquid petroleum gas] tanks. Those are named *hell fireballs* and they are more powerful than normal rockets. We [ISIS] produced and used thousands of them. I know that the number is over eight thousand, as we had that many LPG tanks when we captured the LPG tank factory. I don't know how they brought more LPG tanks into Syria after that."

"The weapons are coming from everywhere," he adds. "But mostly we take the weapons from other groups and from the fights we win. We obtained a lot from capturing Bashar's army warehouses as well. Bashar left all his weapons including the tanks to the PKK and PYD. We also took some of them."

"What was your ISIS training like?" Ahmet asked.

"I was fighting for the Free Syrian Army before *ad-Dawlah* captured Tell Abyad [the Syrian town just across from the Turkish city of

Akçakale]. When they captured Tell Abyad, I fled to Turkey, but I didn't
stay long." In Turkey, Abu Jamal felt as Abu Zar, the former high school
teacher had—homesick and he wanted to return home. "I had people I
knew talk to them [ISIS] and I asked forgiveness so that I could go back to
my village and family. They said they would forgive me on the condition
that I fight for them. So I went back."

"They detained me at the border. They blindfolded my eyes and
brought me before the judge for my trial, only then opening my eyes. The
judge said 'You helped the infidels and because of this you are considered
an infidel as well. Now, ask forgiveness from Allah. And promise us that
you will never draw a weapon to the Muslims, and pledge allegiance to
the Caliph Baghdadi so that we can forgive you. Also, you have to help us
whenever we need your assistance.' I agreed and I was freed."

"However, this did not end here. They started to ask me to join the
ISIS ideology classes [*shariah*]. I was forced to attend those classes for
three months. This is the ideological preparation stage. At the third class, I
declared that I was ready to be a suicide bomber as I was really affected by
the preaching of the teacher. So you can understand how well they choose
their teachers. *Ad-Dawlah* preachers are well-educated and impressive."

"There were three hundred students like me. The [*shariah*] classes
lasted around two hours per day."

"What kind of things did they cover in these classes?"

"*Sheikh* Khalid Rashid is one of the preachers that they force
their people to listen to his recorded speeches. He is imprisoned in Saudi
Arabia. His son became a suicide bomber." So ISIS does use some
technology in their trainings. (We later find more evidence of this when
Ahmet penetrates ISIS chat rooms on Telegram.)

"They usually mentioned about the political problems that
Muslims are facing around the world, how the Muslims were assimilated
[by other powers] and their lands and wealth were imperialized. How
Bashar's soldiers were raping our sisters. They said we should be sending

birth control pills to our sisters if we choose not to fight Bashar and others. Also of course, we had the ideological education."

Aside from personalizing the conflict to the Syrian scene, this is the typical militant jihadi ideology common to al-Qaeda, al-Shabaab, ISIS and the others—preaching that the West overtook Muslims lands during colonization and has propped up dictators that oppress the people; and that Islamic people, nations, and even Islam itself, are now under attack by the West. Therefore, a defensive jihad is called for. In the case of Syria and Iraq, it makes more sense because these people are actually at war. The Russians are helping Bashar Assad; and to many Sunnis it seemed that the U.S. Coalition had helped put the Shia Iraqis into power.

Of course this ideology completely misses the misdeeds of corrupt Islamic tyrants themselves who took Western aid provided to help their people and pocketed it. It blames most problems of bad governance on the West, and more importantly it misses the times that the West had come directly to the aid of Muslims—in Kosovo for instance. According to these *sharia* teachers of ISIS, since the fall of the latest Muslim Caliphate (the Ottoman Empire which fell after World War I), the West has only been evil; it's necessary to rebuild the Caliphate and overtake the world with true Muslim governance. Never mind that the regime ISIS is building is as bloodthirsty, if not far more, than any Western-supported Muslim dictator has ever been.

"Graduation only happens when they feel that a student is ready and at that point they would ask the student to cut off the head of a detainee to demonstrate that he is ready to pass the ideological training," said Abu Jamal, making my point. He's not the only defector to make this disturbing assertion. Again, I feel my stomach flip in horror. Choices for Syrians living under ISIS rule are seriously constrained—basically consisting of choice-less choices. "If you don't fight for ISIS, you die of hunger as they would not feed, nor support you, or let you work. So, eventually, you either fight for them or die. I withstood them for six months before I was out of money and then I had to join."

"Prisoners who were released by *ad-Dawlah* mostly joined them," Abu Jamal recounted. "When you go around the country, you do not see youth anymore in the villages. They are either fighting for *ad-Dawlah*, dead, or fled not to fight for *ad-Dawlah*."

"If you fight for them, they give you two hundred U.S. dollars per month, in addition to supplying all your needs. So, you don't need to spend any money. Two hundred dollars is a lot more than a high-ranking judge can make in Syria today and equals to over sixty thousand Syrian pounds. They told me I needed to go to fight in Ramadi for a year and then I will be free to go anywhere in the Caliphate. They also give you a free house, furniture and all your needs in a house—even the money to purchase slave girls." It's unclear if Abu Jamal is referring to foreign fighters being given these benefits, or that even some Syrians receive these rewards, although he is clear about how the slave girls are used. "Our teacher, whom we called our *sheikh*, had two slave girls. They are called *sabaya* in the ISIS tradition. Only the foreign fighters would have slaves who are captured from the enemies."

One topic that was not often brought up by ISIS defectors was the subject of Israel. Abu Jamal was one of the few who did. "Once I asked our *sheikh*, 'Why don't we fight against Israel?' The *sheikh* answered, 'We have to fight first with the hypocrites and pretenders. Otherwise they will backstab us when we fight Israel.'" While al-Qaeda's ideology often focused on the plight of Palestinians and strongly condemned Israel, ISIS being rooted in the Sunni/Shia power struggle in Iraq, seems less focused on Israel—at least for now.

According to Abu Jamal, his *sheikh* told them, 'The last war will be in Dabiq—once we win over the hypocrites.'"

This last statement is very important. It refers to an Islamic prophesy in one of the *Hadiths* about an End Times battle taking place in the Syrian town of Dabiq. ISIS was very careful to capture Dabiq early in order to ultimately claim this prophecy. They also named their online propaganda journal *Dabiq* and frequently refer to the final apocalyptic battle in their online propaganda. As we know, this online propaganda is an important tool in recruiting foreign fighters. Ahmet asked Abu Jamal what he could tell us about foreign fighters.

"ISIS usually recruits from the West over the Internet. The foreign fighters train near Tabqa Dam—it is an area around twenty-five miles away from Raqqa. ISIS has the control of this dam. The foreigners' training camp is in this area. All the foreigners arriving in Syria are transferred to the camp there. Based on the language of the foreign fighters, ISIS sends *sheikhs* to this camp. After their ideological training, the trainees are sent to military training for another two months." Because our informants tell us different lengths of time for military and *shariah* training, we gather that these can change depending upon the military needs of ISIS and how fast they need to mobilize fighters.

"The military training camps names are: *al-Hasakah Osama bin Laden Camp*, *Raqqa Zarqawi Camp*, *Raqqa 17th Battalion Camp* and for the children between eight to seventeen-years-old, *al-Sheb of the Khalifa Camp* [The Youth of the Caliphate Camp]. The children stay at this camp for three months for indoctrination," Abu Jamal explained. "Children mostly become preachers for ISIS. However, they also receive military training. In order to graduate from this children's camp, you also have to cut the throat of a prisoner. ISIS prisoners are kept in the Tabqa Dam area for precisely these purposes."

I want to retch thinking of a child being coerced into cutting off the head of a prisoner—although I know it's true—ISIS made sure of that with the release of their July 2015 video of a young boy, looking to be around ten-years-old, beheading a prisoner. ISIS also has videos of young children preaching jihad, mouthing brutal words at an age when it's hard to believe they even know what they are saying. I wonder how any child can recover from such horrors. I think back to our interview with fifteen-year-old Ibn

Omar and wonder if he, too, was forced to behead a prisoner. All we were able to do for him was listen, witness his horrific story, and buy a pair of shoes and a coat for him—such small gestures after what he has been through.

We learned that the foreign ISIS fighters were not mixed in with the Syrians, but Abu Jamal was an exception due to his high rank within the ISIS command structure. When Ahmet asked, "Did you have interactions with the foreign fighters?" Abu Jamal shared several instructive experiences and observations.

"Yes, once I took a French ISIS member to our truck while he was fleeing from the Kobanî battle. The French ISIS fighter called the Arab ISIS fighters hypocrites and told me that they [the Arab ISIS fighters] would not pray as they are obligated [their five times daily prayers]. 'They are after money, not jihad,' he told me."

"The French fighter converted to Islam with his wife and two children and then flew with his entire family to Istanbul as a tourist. From Istanbul, they traveled to the Syrian border where he was instructed to meet his handler. They were then taken to a border village and from that village they passed the border with the assistance of a smuggler. After their arrival and settling down, he was given *shariah* courses for two months. His passport and phone were taken and destroyed. There is no Internet inside *ad-Dawlah* and it is not allowed [except for at their 'post offices']. After *shariah* training, he received military training for around a month and became a fighter."

"Some people join ISIS in order to become 'martyrs' so their past sins are forgiven," Abu Jamal further explained. "I spoke to our *sheikh*. He told me, 'I am from Saudi Arabia. I was very rich and I committed most of the serious sins. I thought that I had to do something big to have myself forgiven so I left everything behind to fight here to cleanse my soul.'"

"As far as foreign fighters in ISIS," Abu Jamal recounted, "I have seen people from the United States, the UK, Germany, France, Russia,

Chechnya, China, Indonesia, Sri Lanka, Malaysia, Tunisia, Algeria, Egypt, Palestine (but only some), Lebanon, China, Azerbaijan and Uzbekistan. There is an *ad-Dawlah* Chinese village where the people speak fluent Qur'anic Arabic," Abu Jamal also shared with Ahmet. "There are around five hundred of them with their families. They are settled in a big village. I do not know how, but they speak fluent Fusha Arabic, as they are genuine Chinese people!"

"We would talk among our group, about the Russian *ad-Dawlah* members because we thought they must be foreign agents [spies]. They were blonde and real Russian-blooded people [versus Muslims from the Caucuses] and we didn't trust them."

While there are Russian white converts among these rebels, it wouldn't be the first time that Russia has sent agents inside other militias. They had done so during the Ukrainian uprisings in 2013 and earlier in Afghanistan. Indeed, I had interviewed one such KGB agent in 2005 in Tashkent, Uzbekistan, who told me how crazy it made him to pretend for years to be an Uzbek jihadi living among al-Qaeda operatives in Afghanistan. It took him over a year after returning from his undercover mission to not still rise for all the Islamic calls to prayer, and to shed all the Islamic practices he had taken on during his undercover work.

But many fighters from the Caucuses have joined ISIS. The Islamic Caucuses Emirates, an umbrella group of approximately fifteen thousand members from rebel militias in Chechnya, Dagestan, Ingushetia and the surrounding areas (that grew out of the Chechen rebel independence movement against Russia) made a *fatwa* [Islamic religious ruling] giving permission for their cadres to leave their group to join the Islamic State. They also more recently pledged their allegiance as a group to ISIS.[44] Thus, ISIS includes many Chechen, Ingush and Dagestani cadres who joined early on in the Syrian uprising, having decided with the rise of ISIS that they should leave their jihad on behalf of independence for the Russian Caucuses and go to Syria to build the Muslim "Caliphate" with ISIS. The Chechens, many of them already battle hardened, have distinguished themselves as particularly brutal fighters for ISIS. Our defectors reported that the different nationalities of the foreign fighters color how they act within the ISIS structure, something Abu Jamal knew a lot about. "The worst of *ad-Dawlah* are the Saudi fighters; they are very brutal. Once during a campaign, there was a group of one hundred Saudi fighters. An American F-16 bombed them and around fifty died. They called for help during the airstrike and were told to wait and not leave their stronghold. However, they left. The commander learned of it when they sent ten men back to their ISIS command center. These ten were immediately killed as they had not listened to orders. Afterwards, the other Saudis, with their commanders, fled and joined *al-Nusra*."

We will hear this repeatedly—that abject obedience to authority is a requirement inside ISIS, and that failure to obey ends in an immediate death sentence. Within ISIS, the hand of justice is deadly. Abu Jamal told us that when corruption is found, *"Ad-Dawlah* investigations should be carried out by *shariah* judges. However, they claim that because they are at war, they don't need to make a trial. So they execute instantly without waiting and consulting."

Abu Jamal also had more insight into ISIS military strategy.

"The strategy of ISIS before their battles is to watch the group being targeted. They usually try to kill the top commander in an ambush before they attack so that the group that they are attacking will be without an experienced commander. *Ad-Dawlah* members also support each other to death—the other militias are not like that. For instance, during the Battle of al-Tabqa Air Base, the top Syrian commanders fled by helicopter at night. After they fled, *ad-Dawlah* captured and killed almost seven hundred of the remaining soldiers there. Almost all were killed via beheading."

As we dine elegantly, Ahmet taps on his phone explaining, "Abu Jamal showed me the videos and pictures of it and I have them now on

my phone!" I take a brief look but feel disgusted and don't want to see
such horror right now, so incompatible with our tasteful meal, served on
fine china, overlooking the twinkling lights of one of the world's most
beautiful cities. I shudder to think that normal people are carrying such
photos and videos on their mobile devices—even someone as kind as
Ahmet.

Humanitarian aid is another topic on which Abu Jamal shed some
unfortunate light. Aid meant to help internally displaced Syrians often
does not reach its intended target, he told us, and highlighted two thousand
trucks of aid that went to the embattled city of Kobanî . "There were very
few people living in Kobanî , and the people did not go back, after the
battles. So, all those truckloads of relief were mostly passed to *ad-Dawlah*.
And, in some trucks explosives were hidden and transported under the
cement bags [sent for rebuilding]."

Our waiter brings an assortment of Turkish sweets—honey and
nut filled baklava, creamy rice pudding and a pistachio-covered gelatinous
sweet. As we enjoy them, Ahmet addresses one of the risks that has been
hanging over our heads. "I think we should drop the smuggler and his
Arabic translator now and begin to work through this Syrian defector we
interviewed yesterday who spoke privately to me."

Ahmet feels the Syrian's circumstances help make him a more
trustworthy fixer and he recounts what the former defector told him the
day before during the meal with the three defectors, "He told me quietly
that the others didn't fully trust the interpreter that smuggler sent, so they
wouldn't open up as much."

Ahmet continued, "The Syrian is an insider, a defector just like
them—they know him and trust him. And he can be killed—just like them.
So the trust will be stronger—and I trust him, too. He was one of their
commanders and I feel he's a decent man, despite having served in ISIS.
Although it means you would need to get an Arabic-to- English translator
on your side instead of on our side. But then we leave outsiders out

completely."

What a choice. Trust a shady smuggler or a former ISIS commander? I asked myself, but reminding myself how much they all now hate ISIS, it seemed the former defector is the better choice.

We discuss logistics and decide that I don't need to return to Istanbul to keep Skyping into the interviews. The time difference in Washington D.C. will mean I'll rise early to join an interview but my Internet connection at home should be better than what I have here in the hotel. The sketchy connection has meant I am missing bits and pieces of the interviews—pieces Ahmet has now filled in for me during our day together.

As we part late at night saying our farewells, I can see I have a great research partner in Ahmet. He has an early morning departure back to Şanlıurfa and I am headed to Madrid. We may have the chance to meet again soon in Washington, D.C., in November, when Ahmet will come to give a talk at a criminology conference, although I'm supposed to be traveling to Denmark during that time to give a talk based on my experience designing the prison de-radicalization program in Iraq for twenty thousand detainees and eight hundred juveniles. It seems all over the West, we are all searching to understand the motivations for entering the terrorist trajectory and what might keep people from doing so, as well as ways to get them off this path. While in Denmark, I also hope to interview people who have gone through a unique, early intervention program run by the police in Aarhus, and also interview some additional ISIS defectors there—if they will agree to talk to me.

Still I offer, "I hope I can arrange to welcome you in Washington!" as we say our goodbyes. "Otherwise we'll continue on by Skype and e-mail!"

"*Inshallah* [God willing]," Ahmet answers, smiling warmly.

Little do I realize just how crucial his trust in God's providence is going to become in the next months—when Ahmet and his family learn that they, too, will need to flee the long arm of ISIS.

"*Inshallah*," I respond in kind.

Chapter Eight - The Long Arm of ISIS

But for now, Ahmet has safely returned home to Şanlıurfa. It's four days since I left Istanbul. I'm now in Madrid giving my talk on the radicalization of female terrorists to the former heads of state at the *Club de Madrid* conference.

But just days later, there is frightening news. Two anti-ISIS Syrian activists have been murdered. They'd been exposing ISIS' deeds in the press, and were found shot dead, their throats cut in their apartment in the center of Şanlıurfa—Ahmet's town. Ibrahim Abdul Qader and Fares Hamadi, both Syrian refugees, were activists with *Raqqa is Being Slaughtered Silently* (RBSS). The crime scene photos soon emerge—two men lying in pools of blood on their apartment floor, nearly beheaded.

Two days after the double murder, an ISIS video emerges claiming responsibility, saying the men had been targeted "after they conspired with the Crusaders against the Islamic State." It was a clear threat to the other members of *Raqqa is Being Slaughtered Silently (RBSS)* as the announcer intoned, "May every apostate know that he will be *slaughtered silently*". The video showed a montage of news reports about *RBSS* and it's anti-ISIS activities and closed with grisly footage, apparently taken by the murderer, showing the slaughtered body of Fares Hamadi, his throat freshly slit.[45]

Fares Hamadi and Ibrahim Qader were two of *RBSS'* twenty-six activists who on a daily basis risk their lives to smuggle news out of the Islamic State and into the hands of journalists throughout the world. One of its members is in Madrid at the same conference as me, his presentation about how ISIS has overtaken their city and is brutally murdering its inhabitants daily. But as we give our talks, neither of us has any idea of what has just taken place to his compatriots in Şanlıurfa, so near to Ahmet and his family.

In Raqqa, ISIS had previously executed several *RBSS* members and their families when they were discovered dispatching reports, pictures and videos via their mobile phones to RBSS members living in Turkey and elsewhere. Those members would in turn distribute the footage to international journalists. The members of *RBSS*, like Ibrahim Qader who lived in Turkey, were careful and certainly feared ISIS, but they also believed they were basically safe once in Turkey. But no longer. [46]

For Ahmet and me, that ISIS was a threat inside Turkey suddenly moved beyond academic. Here was proof that ISIS cadres, just as our informants have been telling us, pass with impunity across ISIS-controlled portions of Turkey's five hundred sixty-six mile (nine hundred and eleven kilometer) frontier with Syria and can attack anyone.

The day of the murders, I was traveling back to the U.S. and Ahmet had kindly written, "Dear Anne, Have you made it back safely?" Then within hours, while I was still waking up, a bit jet-lagged from the long flights, he was sending me the grisly news. With his report, he included the pictures of the crime scene. They were gruesome and bloody. "Do you remember," Ahmet wrote, "During the interviews they said how strong ISIS intel was inside Turkey and how they were scared to talk to us?"

Of course I remembered as thoughts came rushing at me – *Are Ahmet and his family safe? How can we continue this research if this is what happens to those who publicize the horror of ISIS? Can they do this to Ahmet, also?* But then I reminded myself: *He's the former Chief of Police for Şanlıurfa; certainly he knows how to protect himself...*

In fact, Ahmet didn't seem worried and offered to quickly co-author a report on the murders for our new *International Center for the Study of Violent Extremism (www.ICSVE.org)*—where I had asked him to serve as Research Fellow.

Sounding all police-like and academic, his response was analytic,

"A few thoughts to consider. This happened at the heart of the city, just behind Şanlıurfa municipality building, seven meters across from it. Also, if you remember one of the subjects told us this story about one Syrian man meeting with an anti-ISIS Syrian at a cafe and ISIS intel taking his picture at that café. When this guy returned to Syria, ISIS showed him the picture and killed him because he had met with that anti-ISIS person. Two important elements here—that cafe is nearby the same municipality building at the city center and may be one hundred meters to the house where this incident happened. Second, ISIS intel is precisely collected and used for end results. Our subject gave this example to explain why they were still scared of ISIS inside Turkey, and he was right, as we can see from the example."

How can he be so calm? I thought.

We continued to discuss the murders by e-mail as well as the logistics of our project and how to tighten up security even further. I admitted to him, "I couldn't stop thinking about those murders and about the pictures of your family and wondering—are you all safe doing this project?" and asked, "Do you have any worries about your own safety?"

Ahmet wrote back addressing our logistical issues, and telling me that we would have an opportunity to meet in Washington, D.C. in November at the international criminology conference where he'd be speaking about his counter-terrorism policing work. Only toward the end of his e-mail did he finally answer my question about his safety:

Thank you very much for asking and I really appreciate your thoughtfulness. I have my handgun and a shotgun at home. I am praying that the situation does not come to that. Though, my biggest concern is my children, so I am trying to be more careful in regards to them. Moreover, I am very grateful to Allah that we crossed each other's road on such an important mission to counter one of the world's greatest problems. And, I know from my heart that everything in this world has a reason and I guess we were brought together for an important purpose. I love it and am willing to work very hard for it.

I agreed with his sentiment. In all my work on terrorism, I've "fallen" into unexpected partnerships and gained access to interviews of people I thought would be impossible to obtain. These relationships often came together in ways that were hard to explain. I was once again on another research "journey" and no one knew where it would lead. I just hoped Ahmet and his family would be safe.

As Ahmet and I corresponded about the murders, our new translator/fixer, Abu Said, the former ISIS defector, was also running his calculus on the situation. He contacted Ahmet by phone, just as Ahmet was arranging camera equipment at the new temporary studio he was setting up, in order to capture our next round of interviews on videotape. Abu Said had just arranged for more defectors to be interviewed, this time on video, though they all insisted their faces be covered and turned away from the camera in order not to be identified.

But Abu Said had come to a different conclusion, "Given what just happened, I think it's too risky to continue. I'm really afraid of them!"

"Come to the city," Ahmet calmly replied. "We can talk it over and discuss our options."

After about an hour, Ahmet got into his car to drive to the bus station to pick him up. Abu Said, like most of the Syrian refugees we were interviewing, lived an hour away from Şanlıurfa. He had taken a mini-bus into the city. At the station, Ahmet watched as Abu Said stepped out of the mini-van accompanied by another Syrian, a serious and hardened individual who looked to be in his mid-to-late-forties. He had expected Abu Said to be alone.

"Merhaba [hello]," Ahmet said as he drove up to their arranged meeting spot just beyond the bus station and opened the passenger door for Abu Said. The two men looked nervously about as they quickly got in the car. The stranger got in the back seat and Ahmet wondered what was going on.

It was a short drive to their makeshift studio and when they arrived, Abu Said and the man walked quickly from Ahmet's car to seek cover inside the building, each glancing furtively around to see if anyone noticed their entering. But it was after hours and no one was present.

"What's up?" Ahmet finally asked once they were inside as he sized up the muscular and tan stranger whose dark eyes bored holes into him. The stranger looked around as he, too, sized up the studio and Ahmet. Ahmet felt a quiver of alarm creeping up his spine. This was a man who could easily take him down with just a few blows.

"This is Abu Zafir," Abu Said said, interrupting their staring match and introducing the two. "We need to talk about the risk of continuing these interviews," Abu Said continued, fear lacing his voice and his eyebrows knit in anxiety. "I'm really worried. What if *ad-Dawlah* learns that defectors are talking? They'll kill anyone who dares to tell the truth about them! I'm the person driving everyone here. I'll be killed for sure," adding, "You know how they do things!" In Turkey, murder could happen via a large truck hired to run him off the road or crash into his car to kill him, and no one would question anything.

"I don't think anyone can learn what we are doing," Ahmet answered coolly. He was used to undercover operations and felt he had thought through all the possibilities of leaks. "The only people who know about this are your guys [the informants], my colleague who I've known for years, myself and my American psychologist colleague of course, but she's in the U.S. and she's not talking to anyone on the ground here. So there *cannot be* any leaks—unless you picked someone who hasn't really defected. Then we have an issue," Ahmet continued, his voice serious and firm.

"No, I vet people really well," Abu Said answered, his voice becoming more confident. "The guys I'm bringing to be interviewed are all people I know personally from *ad-Dawlah*. They're done with *ad-Dawlah* and they are too afraid to talk to anyone else about having given an interview," Abu Said conceded. "But *ad-Dawlah* has spies everywhere. What if they see us coming and going and figure it out on their own?" he asked, fear again overtaking his voice.

"We change the locations each time and we aren't letting anyone come in groups. They come one-by-one and they don't know about each other," Ahmet answered evenly. "You are the only person who knows everyone. We don't even know their names. I don't think their spies can figure it out."

All the time Ahmet spoke, Abu Zafir's dark eyes stared at Ahmet, watching and evaluating him, though his face revealed nothing. Abu Said clearly respected this stranger and was acting deferential to him—yet Ahmet had no clue who he was, or how he related to the project—although Ahmet had a strong feeling his decision about it would deeply affect the future of our project.

"Come, let's drink tea," Ahmet offered as he lead the two men into the office next to our makeshift studio as they continued to talk. Putting the hotpot to boil he turned and saw that Abu Zafir's demeanor had changed completely. Ahmet had won his trust and was about to learn just how valuable that would be.

"I have so much knowledge on ISIS hypocrisy and how they operate—it would be very useful for the people who are fighting against it," Abu Zafir began. "In order to counter *ad-Dawlah,* what I tell you must be put out in the public so that we can stop others from coming to join them."

Shocked, Ahmet suddenly realized that Abu Zafir was not just an ordinary informant. This man was surely a former high-level ISIS commander.

"Hold on," Ahmet said, holding up his hand for Abu Zafir to stop.

"Let's go back into the studio. If you are here to talk, I want to capture this on film." This would be our first video interview and Ahmet nervously hoped he could operate the video camera correctly and get the microphone to work, even though he'd prepared ahead of time and pre-tested all the equipment.

"Here, wrap your head in this *keffiyeh* so no one can see your face, and you can turn and face the corner," Ahmet offered. "Let me get the tea and sweets." As he did, he saw that Abu Zafir was carefully considering anything that might identify him. He removed his wristwatch and placed it on the desk nearby.

Ahmet returned with a tray of baklava and steaming hot glasses of tea, surprised to see how quickly and skillfully Abu Zafir had wrapped the checkered *keffiyeh* tightly around his entire face and head, completely obscuring his identity. Ahmet hooked up his microphone and switched on the camera and signaled for Abu Zafir to begin.

"I was a high school teacher before the rebellion," Abu Zafir started. "But in *ad-Dawlah* I was the Security Commander at the Central Military Base in Raqqa. Before that I was in the field, as a soldier's commander. I'm forty-six-years-old and I pray to Allah that what I am telling you here will be useful to save people from this evil terrorist organization."

"How did you join?" Ahmet asked, as he tried to keep his voice calm in the face of this remarkable opportunity. The Security Commander of the Central Military Base in Raqqa![47]

"While I was fighting in *Jaysh al-Hur* [the Free Syrian Army] I met with an *ad-Dawlah* member named Abu Hamza. We talked and chatted and became close. 'We are in Allah's way,' Abu Hamza told me about *ad-Dawlah*. 'This is the correct way and we will, *inshallah*, establish the Caliphate.' I believed and trusted him and as a result joined *ad-Dawlah*. Also, what persuaded me was the fact that when I looked at *ad-Dawlah*, I could see that they were practicing Islam better than

Jaysh al-Hur and the foreign fighters who came to join *ad-Dawlah* from all around the world were for sure better Muslims than we were, which prompted me to join them.

"How did they accept you?"

"It was November 2013 when I joined. Since I had been fighting as comrades with Abu Hamza and the others while they were in *Jaysh al-Hur,* we knew each other very well. So, there was not a trust issue, and because of that I was not taken into a training camp initially. 'I would like to join and fight with you,' I told Abu Hamza, and there I was in *ad-Dawlah*—as I really liked their intentions at the time. I looked at the *mujahideen* and saw them as heroes, as they looked very sincere. I was thinking that they were like the companions of the Prophet Muhammad. Some of the *mujahideen* were even fighting barefoot without shoes or boots. I asked them why and they answered, 'We are going in Allah's way and we will die anyway, so why should we go to Allah with shoes?' They were very spiritual, sincere and deep in their beliefs, which really affected me profoundly."

"Since I was educated, I knew Islam. But I was not a radical. I was a practicing Sunni Muslim. I knew how to pray and I was praying. The difference between *ad-Dawlah* and *Jaysh al-Hur* is that *ad-Dawlah* wanted to establish an Islamic state and rule by *shariah* whereas *Jaysh al-Hur* wanted democracy. That is the reason *ad-Dawlah* calls *Jaysh al-Hur* infidels. That's the main difference. Also *ad-Dawlah* goes to war with Islamic practices: with *wudu* [Islamic ablutions], praying the *salats*, reading the Qur'an and basically with the religion. *Jaysh al-Hur* fighters go to battle without *wudu*—of course not all of them—but the religious preparations for battle are less than in *ad-Dawlah*."

"So basically I liked *ad-Dawlah* better because of two reasons: They weren't out there to fight for just land. They were really fighting sincerely for Allah—to build the Caliphate. They knew Islam very well, a lot more than many *Jaysh al-Hur* members. And they were practicing it."

"Overtime, I realized there were two types of people in *ad-*

Dawlah. Some were real and genuine Muslims, who are really good people. And others were bloody-thirsty people, who joined *ad-Dawlah* as if to degrade the religion of Islam. They love to kill brutally."

"Is that why you left *ad-Dawlah?"* Ahmet asks.

"When I realized that some things were fishy and they had under-the-table dealings and cooperation with some of our enemies, I left them. Actually, I had to leave them. I decided to leave during the Raqqa war, in April 2014, when I saw they were killing Sunni Syrians without any reason. I was with them, but could not accept the fact that they were killing our own innocent people without any reason, so I had to leave. I saw that, if you are against them, even though you are a good practitioner and believer of Islam, you are killed."

"Some of *ad-Dawlah* members are very bloodthirsty. One of their *emirs,* for example, invaded a place unnecessarily so that he could spread fear and so that he could torture and oppress people."

"Why are they so brutal?"

"Very few of the blood-thirsty murderers are from Syria. Most of them are Saudis and Iraqis, who are very bloodthirsty. Some of the Iraqis are from Saddam's Baathist party," Abu Zafir says, bringing with them not just the intelligence aspects of Saddam's totalitarian regime, but also the sadistic.

"Iranian Shias have also infiltrated *ad-Dawlah,*" Abu Zafir says in an interesting twist we have not heard from others. "There are a lot of Shias in *ad-Dawlah.* They conceal themselves and claim that they are Sunnis. There are two to three percent of concealed Shias in *ad-Dawlah.* Most of them are *emirs* and they decide what *ad-Dawlah* will do. I can understand who is Shia among the ISIS fighters based on my experience and have seen many of them operating as ISIS commanders and fighters. ISIS kills mainly Syrians, Sunni Syrians, and they are also behind the killings of the Sunni populations." It seems Abu Zafir has tried to figure out why ISIS would kill other Sunnis in such large numbers and has come to an explanation that makes sense to him—that the Shia are really behind it all.

In his logic, Abu Zafir is referring to the Shia/Sunni divide brutally playing out across the entire Middle East, and particularly so in Iraq. When the U.S. Coalition invasion of Iraq destabilized the old power structures, it unbridled sectarian conflict. When the precursor to ISIS—al-Qaeda in Iraq—arose, they named the Shia as their number one enemy and called for all Shia to be killed as apostates. This unleashed bombings of Shia shrines, mosques, marketplace bombings and bloody civilian murders. These were retaliated in kind by Shia militias killing Sunnis in a similarly brutal and indiscriminate manner. That Abu Zafir would blame mass killings of Sunnis in Syria as a plot backed by the Shia would fit with his experience and knowledge of the region. Most experts concede that the Shia took positions of power in Iraq as the U.S. withdrew, and that Iran was involved and tried to exert influence and control inside Iraq through Shia leaders, like former Iraqi Prime Minister Maliki, for instance. Abu Zafir sees the actions of ISIS playing out these sectarian divides. He fears that ISIS may have been infiltrated and is being manipulated by Shia against non-ISIS Sunnis, despite ISIS being a Sunni rebel group.

"For example, Naed Samir, Bashar's commander in al-Hasakah, told the PKK, 'If you do not behave, I will leave the land where you are to *ad-Dawlah* so that they could take care of you,'" Abu Zafir continues. "This alone showed me that they [ISIS and Assad's regime] were cooperating behind closed doors."

"How can it be that ISIS accepts Shia members?" Ahmet asks, incredulous at this suspicion, though it does provide a bizarre—but not totally implausible—explanation as to why ISIS kills so many Sunnis.

"They enter *ad-Dawlah* for political reasons. They do not say that they are Shias. They cover themselves. They say they are Sunnis. They say they are advocating for the Sunnis, but they actually brutally kill Sunni Muslims only. They are there to finish up the Sunnis. Those Shia are from

Iraq. They are coordinated from the outside. I am not for sure," Abu Zafir admits. "However, I know that Iran has a hand in it and Maliki."

Now we are hearing that the Iranians and the Shia led government of Maliki in Iraq may also have placed their agents inside ISIS. For a group that takes all comers, it seems that anything is possible for those willing to risk it and convince ISIS that they are true believers. Why wouldn't Russian, Iranians, and even Assad's regime try to place false plants among the ISIS cadres? We cannot dismiss Abu Zafir's thoughts as mere conspiracy ramblings.

To us, ISIS is beginning to appear as a different kind of 'weapon of mass destruction' and it may be that everyone wants to use it to their own advantage. It's true that if Iran had the possibility to place its agents in ISIS they probably would do so, and for those sectarian haters seeking to destroy each other, some Shia may want to use ISIS or any other means, to destroy Sunni populations. When we later read through Ahmet's notes from this interview, we marvel at the convoluted intrigues that may be operating in the Middle East—that even Iran may be attempting to use and control ISIS by secretly placing Iraqi Shia agents inside it.

Thus far we have heard and will hear from others that ISIS, when it benefits them, cuts deals with Assad's government, even going so far to offer safe passage for Assad's oil engineers to come and repair oil wells and refineries and selling oil to Assad afterward that then—in a bizarre twist of events—turns up in barrel bombs that Assad's air force unleashes back on ISIS territory. These oil sales between ISIS and the regime were subsequently confirmed in April 2016 press reports of captured ISIS documents.[48] We also learn from the defectors, that at times ISIS conceded hard won territory to the Kurdish rebel PKK group, as it did when it withdrew without much resistance from Tell Abyad. Some ISIS defectors are also convinced that Russian soldiers had infiltrated their ranks and may have been placing GPS chips to guide Assad's planes for where to bomb. The depth of conspiracy and intrigue when it comes to ISIS starts to look like a web without limits.

"*Ad-Dawlah* consists of five types," Abu Zafir continues. "First, there are foreign countries which are behind *ad-Dawlah* and their agents present in the group. I cannot tell you exactly who they are, but overtime I realized that there are foreign intelligence agents in *ad-Dawlah*. Second, there are the bloodthirsty ones [sadistic psychopaths] who are there to spread fear. Third, there are the traders of *ad-Dawlah* who are made up of two types: some to make money for *ad-Dawlah*, but most to make money for themselves. They joined *ad-Dawlah* to get rich. Fourth, there are the *mujahideen*. Those are the real Muslims who believe that they are just like the companions of Prophet Muhammad. However, most of the time they do not know who they are fighting and they are mainly told they are fighting against Assad's soldiers, even though they are not. Lastly, there are the *ansar*, the local Syrians. Many of them who are inside *ad-Dawlah* are bad people. They are there for theft and looting."

This is a good analysis of who ISIS attracts. Psychopaths—people Abu Zafir refers to as bloodthirsty, come to ISIS from around the world knowing that here they can indulge in the extreme brutality that their sickness thrives upon. Likewise, the "true believers" coming from the West hoping to build a utopian "Caliphate" have no idea when they are sent to slaughter enemies of ISIS that they are Sunnis, because they cannot speak Arabic, nor discern between who ISIS leaders tell them are Assad's forces and the local militias who are themselves fighting Assad.

"How are decisions made in *ad-Dawlah?*" Ahmet asks.

"The bloodthirsty make the plans. But their decisions and the intelligence come through the *emirs*. The bloodthirsty ones take care of the rest."

"So what is the real objective of ISIS?" Ahmet asks.

"I can say for sure that it is not the establishment of a real Islamic State. The utmost real reason is to save Bashar, to stop the uprising in Syria. Bashar supported them to finish Sunni Islam. He told the world,

'If I do not exist, they will exist' [meaning if Assad falls, ISIS will rise into power]. I am eighty percent sure, the command of *ad-Dawlah* have connections with Bashar. Although many are not aware of the fact of what is going on. Of course, if there is Bashar, then there is also Iran and Russia involved."

"For example, I was seeing that there was real support flowing to *ad-Dawlah* from Bashar, and though Bashar was supporting *ad-Dawlah*, they were killing Bashar's soldiers. I was confused with that at first," Abu Zafir admits. "Later, I realized that the soldiers *ad-Dawlah* were killing were Sunni Muslims, even though they were in Bashar's army," Abu Zafir explains, horror filling his voice as he recalls when he realized that Assad might be willing to sacrifice his own soldiers who were not from his Alawite (Shia) sect for the sake of pretending to fight ISIS.

"Take for example, in Ayn-el Isa, there is this 93rd tank battalion. *Jaysh al-Hur* fought for months and could not take it. This battalion is constructed on vertical land, so they can see over five kilometers away without any problem, which means no enemy can approach. They also have many armored vehicles, tanks, anti-air missiles etc. Nobody could approach, period."

"However, *ad-Dawlah* took this battalion in two hours without any difficulties. Why? Because of hidden cooperation with Bashar. When *ad-Dawlah* arrived, there was no decision-making commander available in the battalion. Helicopters had taken them all out. The soldiers left there could not make up their minds to fight as they did not have orders to fight against *ad-Dawlah*, so they could not fight. They simply surrendered—around seven to nine hundreds of them. And all of them were slaughtered—some at the battalion and some [were taken to be executed publicly] inside the cities to spread fear to the people. *All* of them were Sunni Muslims. There were very few poor, unimportant Alawites [Shia]. Later on, *ad-Dawlah* handed over this same captured battalion area to the PKK, and again without any fight."

Many of our informants also questioned this battle—how ISIS could so easily have taken over the highly fortified and well positioned 93rd tank battalion and capture their troops and their entire weapons arsenal, and how Assad's forces would flee without taking or at least destroying their weapons arsenal, leaving it all for ISIS to capture and equip themselves. To many of our informants, it smacked of cooperation with the regime, and now we are having a high-up commander tell us about this again, but in so much more detail that it's difficult to believe there is not some level of cooperation between ISIS and Assad's regime—at a minimum—in that battle, as we now know for sure in trade.[49]

"When we were fighting in Tell Abyad with *Jaysh al-Hur, ad-Dawlah* was still a small group. They sent their people to Tell Abyad to live among us so that they could do prodding, instigation, incitement, stirring up and provocation, which they succeeded in doing. The Kurdish Muslims and *Jaysh al-Hur* were getting along well, however *ad-Dawlah* ruined that. A year passed, and *ad-Dawlah* cleared *Jaysh al-Hur* from Tell Abyad. Many died at the hands of *ad-Dawlah* and many also fled out of fear for their lives."

"So, there is now no *Jaysh al-Hur* left in Tell Abyad. And, later on *ad-Dawlah* left the city to the PKK/PYD and there was no one from *Jaysh al-Hur* or from the local population to say no. Of course, the PKK/PYD is part of the Nizam [Bashar's regime] and *ad-Dawlah* is also a part of Bashar's order, so *ad-Dawlah* left Tell Abyad without fighting. So what happened: *ad-Dawlah* cleaned *Jaysh al-Hur* from Tell Abyad and left it to the PKK/PYD on a golden plate."

Again this echoes stories from other defectors who questioned how ISIS decimated *Jaysh al-Hur* and left Tell Abyad to the PYD after conquering it. They say *Jaysh al-Hur* are the only rebels who really are fighting for the Syrian uprising against Assad; and ISIS, it appears to them, is cooperating with the regime rather than fighting it.

"So, *ad-Dawlah* is winning, Bashar is winning, the PKK is

winning and of course Israel is winning, as they can use Northern Syria to transfer its natural gas to the Mediterranean Sea. Now what happens when the Kurds decide to establish their state in and around Tell Abyad? There are two important and big Sunni tribes: the *al Baggara* tribe made up of two million people and the *al Aqeedat* tribe made up of three million people. Those two tribes will not leave the region to the Kurds, as the land was theirs for over five hundred years. So, they will fight to the death to get rid of the Kurds and will have the manpower and the means to do so. They are only waiting to see what is going to happen."

While Abu Zafir may be completely correct about the plethora of powers and actors involved with ISIS, each with its own political objective, it's impossible to know if his suppositions are true—although his observations are as a high-level operative and many of them make sense, however conspiratorial—and chilling—they are.

Abu Zafir turns to the subject of daily life in Raqqa.

"They have big screen TVs in Raqqa [outdoors] where they show videos [to the public] explaining that whenever your sins are too much, the easiest way to cleanse your soul is to become a 'martyr'," Abu Zafir tells us. "Their women follow the rules of Islam more than any others. They have to be covered; even their face cannot be open. They cannot show and reveal any colored clothing. If they follow those rules, *ad-Dawlah* members behave very well and politely toward them. Otherwise, they would be very bad."

"*Al Khansaa* is the women's *hisbah,* made up entirely of women. In the past, male *hisbah* would bring the women and lash them in front of the people. The woman would be in her clothes and they would lash them furiously. This disturbed people very deeply and also steered them away from Islam. *Ad-Dawlah* would say that we have to apply these rules to ensure that the men would not look at the women, to ensure that there will not be adultery."

"Some *hisbah* members would also go into homes unannounced

and look at the girls if they are covered or not. If they would see you uncovered through a door, or window, or a balcony, they would punish the woman and would call her father, husband, or brothers to the *hisbah*. You cannot be yourself as you wish, even inside your own home."

Again the issue of forced marriage between ISIS cadres and local Syrian girls comes up. "They force girls to get married. There was this man, who was a very good hearted and clean, ordinary man, like an angel. He had like three daughters. When he went to get some bread from the bakery, a Tunisian *mujahid* [foreign fighter] saw him and asked him how he was and if he needed anything, and then asked him if he had children. He said three girls and two boys. He asked how old the girls were because he would like to get married with them. This is how bad they are. They would look for girls to get married with, by force or tricks."

"In a village, there was this girl, she was a little bit cognitively underdeveloped. They also wanted to get married with her but her family said that she is not well. However, they took her anyway. Twenty days later, they dropped her back at her family home saying this girl was retarded, which the family had said since the beginning."

Ahmet turns back to the all-female morality police—*al-Khansaa*. "Which women work for *al-Khansaa?*"

"Usually the locals from Raqqa who are the wives of the *ansar* [local Syrian] fighters. Some of the women in *al-Khansaa* carry AK-47's. There is also like a federal *al-Khansaa* consisting of *mujahideen's* wives. They have more power and authority. *Ansar* and *mujahideen* wives are not mixed in *al-Khansaa*."

"*Al-Khansaa* brigades get their orders from the *emir* of the *hisbah*. However, the *mujahideen's al-Khansaa* does not get orders from anyone. They are independent and act by themselves." This is an interesting comment and explains what many others have told us—that the European female *hisbah* members walk around with great authority and are often sadistically brutal. They appear to act with impunity—perhaps as a reward for having come to join ISIS from abroad. This may explain why foreign females attracted to ISIS accept ISIS's misogynistic behaviors—they at least, attain positions at the top of the pecking order.

"Other women [not serving in the *hisbah*] stay at home with their husbands," Abu Zafir continues. "Not all of the *mujahideen* women from Europe are married. *Mujahideen* women are not required to go out with *mahrams* [chaperones]. There is a *fatwa* [religious ruling] for that. And *al-Khansaa mujahideen* can also go to war to fight with men. There are many *mujahideen* from European countries like France, Italian, Belgium and even Americans. They get married with other *mujahideen.* You can see them walking on the streets. *Mujahideen* women can carry their weapons when they are out. They also reach out [over the Internet] to younger girls in their countries to bring them to Raqqa. Also, ISIS's people in those countries deceive their people to go to Raqqa."

"Some doctor *mujahideen* came to Raqqa with their wives to work as doctors and so that their wives would treat the women." Abu Zafir is referring to the policy of the Islamic State that prevents male doctors from seeing female patients. "In the city of Mayadin [a city in eastern Syria, in the Deir ez-Zor Governate], a gynecologist was killed because he operated on a woman *mujahideen*. Because of that many of the gynecology clinics were shut down. Now midwives do deliveries at the pregnant women's homes. ISIS asks doctors for their *bayat.* If they do not give it, they close their clinics. There is also a guard posted at the office of each doctor in Raqqa to ensure that he or she will not flee and to ensure that the wrong people are not treated."

As we hear more stories of the European and foreign women who come to ISIS it becomes clear that despite the danger of living in a war zone, the foreign fighters enjoy many privileges. They live in large homes, enjoy relatively large salaries, enjoy good food while others around them go hungry, and unlike all the other women living under ISIS, the females can walk about freely without a chaperone. For those in the *hisbah,* if they have a sadistic streak, or any stored anger inside, they can take it out with apparent license on other women—mercilessly flogging them on the streets. The downside to privilege is, of course, that if their husbands are killed, they may be heavily coerced and even forced to remarry. Later we hear from a defector about one ISIS woman who remarried thirteen times. One might also presume that witnessing the barbarity of ISIS is psychologically damaging if not traumatic, but for someone with a psychopathic tendency, this might be appealing.

"ISIS is like a state, so they control and provide everything," Abu Zafir continues. "Everybody has a duty. I do not get involved in your duty and you do not get into mine. If you make a mistake, I do not tell you anything, but I go to your immediate *emir*. This is the reason you cannot break up their bureaucracy easily. They are taught to obey and be ordered. The first thing in *shariah* training they teach is *to listen and obey*. The *emir* tells, and you do." We have heard this more than once now and it explains, along with the brutal punishments for disobedience, the zombie-like obedience that ISIS instills in its cadres. The ideal "Caliphate" under ISIS is nothing more than a brutal totalitarian regime whose efficacy might impress history's best tyrants.

"It's important to understand that *ad-Dawlah* took all of the grain warehouses when they arrived. They confiscated all of the goods inside the city. They acquired the oil wells. Now they own everything. If you are with *ad-Dawlah*, everything is free to you: bread, LPG tank [cooking fuel], food, etc. However, if not, you need to pay, and without them you don't have any means to pay. This is the policy of *ad-Dawlah*. They force you into hunger. After a while people would start to think *if only I join ad-Dawlah, I could feed myself and my family*. So, people start to join *ad-Dawlah* to be able to survive. For example, before *ad-Dawlah* took over a city, every day ten truckloads of vegetables would arrive. After *ad-Dawlah*, it was diminished to five trucks and they gradually diminished it more. Now, with that little shipment, only real *ad-Dawlah* members can get vegetables and the rest cannot," he adds, "This is from the Baathist policy. Hafiz Assad [the former Syrian dictator and father of Bashar Assad] used to say, 'Have your dog stay hungry, it will follow you.'"

"How do they actively recruit and teach their ideology?" Ahmet asks.

"They usually use the notion of jihad. They would come to you and talk to you saying that as Muslims we are oppressed; our rights are taken. They would behave toward you very nicely and they would persuade you. They also use family and friendship ties to recruit people. One time they persuaded one of the tribe's leader's sons to join *ad-Dawlah*. After that many of that tribe's youth joined *ad-Dawlah* taking him as an example. Now, once a tribe starts to join, rival tribes feel like they have to join because of jealousy and because of the fact that a tribe with *ad-Dawlah* gets stronger, so their rivals being stronger disturbs them. Some others join because they would have the opportunities and the goods, and the possibilities they would otherwise not have in their civilian lives such as cars, weapons, authority, female slaves, etc."

As for recruiting from abroad, "Some *mujahideen* are solely assigned to work on the Internet to recruit people from abroad. There are around twenty-five of them. The females and males work separately there. They also have post offices where you can reach and connect with everywhere in the world." These "post offices" we learn are really ISIS controlled satellite Internet and cell phone service providers where ISIS members go to get online and reach others around the "Caliphate"—and beyond. Having all the Internet access organized in this manner, ISIS is able to also control and limit the communication of its people. Indeed, in an interview with a parent in Belgium of an ISIS commander, the woman stated that her son was only allowed to call home at certain times and often appeared to be monitored by "minders" and had to end the calls when his minder said to stop. There is also a recent report from *Raqqa is Silently Being Slaughtered* of an ISIS member in Raqqa who followed orders to kill his own mother after he reported her to ISIS for wanting him to quit the organization. The killing was reported (*by RSBS*) to have taken place in front of the Raqqa "post office building" where she worked as an employee[50].

"Do you know anything about the *mujahideen* traveling home again?" Ahmet asks, curious about foreign fighters moving back and forth out of Syria and Iraq to their homelands.

"The *mujahideen* are sent back to their countries for two reasons: so that they could recruit and so that they could carry out and facilitate new attacks." As we know, this is exactly what happened in the Paris attacks and in subsequent interviews, we'll learn this tactic is not isolated.[51] In fact, I'll be witness to one of these attacks.

Abu Zafir's assertion leads Ahmet to ask an extremely sensitive question with a potentially disturbing answer. "Do you know about the Suruç and Ankara bombings?" For *every other* attack around the world, the Islamic State loudly takes credit, but for all three bombings thus far in Turkey, the Turks blamed ISIS, including the January 2016 Istanbul bombings that killed fifteen German tourists, the Islamic State is uncustomarily silent. Ahmet is asking if the Turkish government's claim is true—that ISIS was behind these bombings or if something more sinister is going on. Alternative explanations abound about who else might have carried out these bombings—ranging from false flag attacks made by some renegade Turkish intel; to terror attacks carried out by the PKK—many of its leaders were freed by Erdogan in his bid for re-election; or even elements of the Syrian regime angered by Turkish support of ISIS and rebel groups. The German intelligence chief, Hans-Georg Maassen, also questioned ISIS' involvement.[52]

Abu Zafir remains silent and apparently does not want to reply. But then, after some hesitation, he decides to offer his opinion. "I don't think *ad-Dawlah* carried out those attacks. Turkey has not harmed them, instead always helped, why would they want to harm Turkey?"

"How have you seen Turkey helping ISIS?" Ahmet follows up.

"Of course, there is always flow of weapons and ammunition coming from Turkey secretly now. *Ad-Dawlah* also did not blow up Suleyman Shah shrine [an Ottoman tomb in Syria] even though it could, and they sent back the Mosul Turkish consulate personnel without harming them," Abu Zafir points out that ISIS has destroyed many other shrines but they left this one that is guarded by Turkish soldiers and considered to be Turkish territory (based on an accord signed by France and Turkey in 1921) despite it actually being located inside Syria.[53] And though ISIS took forty-nine Turkish consulate personnel hostage when they overtook Mosul, and held them for three months, they eventually sent them home unharmed. In both cases it appears there were trades made. Turkey appears to have returned some ISIS fighters and foreign jihadists, as well as brokered for some ISIS prisoners held by other groups, to be released, for trades with Turkey.[54] Experts on the region also report that Turkish officials appear to willingly bargain with ISIS.[55]

"What can you tell about the Turkish border crossings?" Ahmet asks.

"Now it's more difficult," Abu Zafir says. "The Turkish soldiers do not allow free passage anymore. However, the smugglers know how to pass the border and they make good money." Since we have heard so much about how easily ISIS cadres cross the Turkish border, Ahmet does not pursue this point further.

"Tell about their military training," Ahmet returns to his particular interest.

"They would divide the trainees into age groups: seven-year-olds, fifteen-year-olds, twenty, thirty and up. The training starts with early Morning Prayer, then two hours of running and sports, physical activity. Then there is breakfast—but they give very little food, to encourage patience. Then we have military training AK-47; Bixi [a Soviet produced automatic machine gun]; anti-air artilleries, bombs; etc. For the younger kids they learn to dismantle and reassemble an AK-47; hand grenade throwing; physical training and driving skills; and later on RPG [rocket propelled grenade launcher] and other heavier equipment. If you had served in the military, the training would be less, like two to three weeks; otherwise it was longer—one to two months."

Military training is one thing; 'martyrdom' is another. "How does ISIS justify suicide bombings?" Ahmet asks.

"They see it as *istishadi*—becoming a 'self-martyr'. There is this *fatwa* from Ibn Taymiyyah that says, 'If there are good deeds at the end of the actions you are taking, if there is support to Islam with what you are doing—it is permissible—and if you die, you go to Paradise.'" Ibn Taymiyyah is a thirteenth century Islamic scholar. During the times of the Mongol invasions he ruled that jihad was a compulsory duty of all Muslims—a writing that today's jihadis love to quote. His writings, in which he justified attacking the Mongol rulers who claimed to be converted Muslims, are also the basis for modern day jihadis to practice "Takfir"—naming other Muslims as apostates worthy of death.

"Before they send someone on a suicide mission, they would preach to them specially. They would tell them that all of the targets are infidels, that they work for the enemy, they need to be killed, and it is right to kill them, etc."

"How are they chosen?"

"Many of those children that they send are very poor, their parents are dead, and they are not educated. They take those children and behave toward them very well and politely. The children are happy with this approach and they feel love and passion. Then they start to teach their ideology and once they feel that the child is ready, they will use that child as a suicide bomber." I feel sickened. To think of using children, even orphans, in this way—it's so cold-hearted and cynical. But in this regard, ISIS is not alone. This manipulation is similar to al-Qaeda recruiters who over the last decades took children from poor families in Pakistan and central Asia, and other groups that have recruited children, and manipulated them into becoming terrorists, suicide bombers and child soldiers.[56]

"I saw children at the ages of nine and ten who were being prepared for suicide missions. At this special camp, there are children between the ages of five to sixteen. Whoever they easily persuade, they take that child and make him a suicide bomber. Their *sheikhs* are like magicians. They affect the children very deeply. It is as if they are hypnotizing them with their speeches. Also, they would drug some of the children before the attacks."

"Twenty days ago in Tal Asamin village they distributed gifts to the children, like balloons, so that they deceive them easier and so that the children feel close to them. This is also a way they recruit among those children." Abu Zafir has a video of this event that he shares with Ahmet.

"Do they give the soldiers drugs also?"

"Yes. When we were fighting against the *nizam* [Assad's army] in Ras al-Ayn, there were loud sounds exploding all over around me and I was very scared. There was this guy from *ad-Dawlah* near me. He looked at me and realized that I was scared. He even asked if I was afraid, and I answered, 'Yes, I'm really scared!' He gave me a tablet. It was very bitter, brown in color. I swallowed it. In thirty minutes, I became a different man—as if I am a hero. I went after this into the battle very bravely alone to the very fronts. My friends told me to come back, but instead, I kept moving forward, and answered them saying, 'No I want to die!' I became so brave. After, I didn't sleep for three days. It gave me so much power. I felt as if I am indestructible and unbeatable."

"After this tablet, I went back home on the fourth day without sleeping. I sat together with my family. Then I lay down for three to four minutes and I felt like I hadn't slept for years. At that moment, I could not move my arm and couldn't speak. I realized that it was because of the drug, so I didn't take it again. They told me later that I would not become addicted if I kept using this drug, but I didn't. Many of the ISIS members use it. There are different varieties of it, some yellowish, some light brown."

When I later go in search of information, I find news articles about Islamic State fighter's use of amphetamines and in particular, a pill known by the brand name *Captagon* that fighters pop before going into battle. Soldiers call it the "Super Soldier Pill". The description of *Captagon* fits precisely with Abu Zafir's description of a tablet brownish in color, with the effect of conveying feelings of extreme confidence and strength. The *Washington Post* called it "the tiny pill fueling Syria's war and turning fighters into superhuman soldiers", and the *BBC* referred to it as "the drug fueling conflict in Syria".[57] The role of drugs in this war cannot be underestimated.

"What can you say about Islamic State's logic and psychology?" Ahmet asks.

"Whenever they talk, they always talk about Allah, Prophet Muhammed, and jihad. They do not talk about themselves—but the life hereafter and more divine things." As example, Abu Zafir volunteers a personal story about a man, who after slapping an *ad-Dawlah* member on the face, was brought to court in Raqqa where Abu Zafir was also present that day helping out with the security of ISIS central court. "I brought this man in front of the judge. Meanwhile, he wanted to talk, and I told him to stop talking. Later on, when I was taking him back to the prison, he told me something which I will not forget until I die: 'You tyrannized me,' he said. 'You did not let my heart speak. I am going to make a complaint to Allah about you, after Morning Prayer.'"

"I was so upset with what he said that I went upstairs from the prison cells. I knew he was right. The first court was on duty and the judge of the court was my friend. I told him about the man and asked him to please allow me to free him. The judge answered yes, and I went to free the man. Later on, my friend, the judge, asked me, 'Why did you want to free him?' I answered that I was scared of his malediction and curse during the Morning Prayer prostration, which I believed would be accepted by Allah, as this man was right; and added that he was innocent so I wanted to free him."

It's interesting that Abu Zafir could be such a battle-hardened soldier and yet so fearful of a curse offered in prayer that an innocent man was about to make against him.

"The reason I tell you this," Abu Zafir explains, "is there are a lot of people in ISIS who are really out there for the acceptance (of the will of) Allah. Of course there are others who are there for money and booty. Many ISIS members live their lives very richly. They have money and authority. I know Abu Usama al-Iraqi. He was one of the senior leaders of ISIS. He was married to four women and he had three *sabayahs*—all Yazidi women. He was from the Baath party. He had gone and stayed in Afghanistan for eight years to fight the Russians. He lost one of his eyes there, so he was using his one eye only. He would not go into battle because of that. *Al-Nusra* commanders called him the 'one eyed devil.'"

"Was there any good in ISIS?" Ahmet asks.

"Yes, there was no theft," Abu Zafir answers. "Women were [properly] covered. *Malayinat* [unnecessary things which take people away from Allah's way] were swept away. Alcohol, gambling, vices, were all banned and the places where those things were being carried out were also closed down. If you dropped money on the street, you can go back there one day later and find your money," Abu Zafir states, perhaps exaggerating the point.

But there was also corruption and cover-ups he tells Ahmet, "In 2015, there were two hundred car thefts in Raqqa in the first four months. The thief was caught and we realized that he was working for one of the *emirs*. They said they killed that *emir*, however, we later realized that he was sent somewhere else to work and only the thief who was working for him was imprisoned. There was also this police chief in charge of traffic.

He was seen sitting with a woman in lingerie [i.e. this meeting looked like adultery]. We were told that he was killed. But when I had business in Talafar, Iraq, I saw that man there in a checkpoint, alive, working for *ad-Dawlah*. Later on, he was brought back to Raqqa and he was forgiven as he had relatives high up in the *ad-Dawlah* bureaucracy."

Ahmet informs me that under *shariah* law, adultery can only legally be prosecuted when there are four witnesses to the actual sexual act—which makes it nearly impossible to prosecute. Clearly Islamic law is not interested in prosecuting adultery, yet groups like ISIS are overly interested in keeping sexual relations under strict governance and willingly prosecute and punish transgressors without the four witnesses.

"Tell us about the media arm of ISIS and their online magazine *Dabiq*" Ahmet asks, referring to the mechanisms by which ISIS has put out thousands of slick, high quality, and bone chilling videos and an online magazine encouraging the steady flow of foreign fighters into ISIS. As we go over this part of Ahmet's interview with Abu Zafir, I feel frustrated that we are struggling on a shoestring to collect these video interviews of insiders and have very little funding to professionally produce a product to fight ISIS propaganda in the social media space—yet that is exactly what we remain committed to doing. Later, a Syrian video editor pursing asylum in the United States, informs us that prior to the uprising, Syrians already had high quality equipment and video production capacities—things ISIS has now capitalized on to recruit so avidly among foreigners. My frustration deepens.

"There are many engineers in *ad-Dawlah*. Many of them are foreigners, but some are also locals. Those engineers are used for the media activities, so the media is done professionally. They have the required equipment. For *Dabiq*, they prepare everything beforehand and send it to the *emir,* and after approval it is distributed. It is prepared professionally just like in the West." The gruesome murders seem to feed its media arm.

"Why do they behead people?"

"Their aim is first to spread utmost fear. They are showing everyone that they need to be scared of them." Showing force and spreading fear is a tactic all totalitarian governments practice, in varying degrees.

"And they also want to stain the religion of Islam, as the leadership is not sincere Muslims. They are showing the whole world that there are different kinds of deaths inside *ad-Dawlah*. This is another way of spreading fear. Normally it is forbidden to burn living matter—including humans, animals, even vegetation. So how do they justify the burning of the Jordanian pilot?" Abu Zafir asks, referring to a Jordanian fighter-bomber pilot burned alive after he was captured.[58] "They found the *fatwa* from Ibn Taymiyyah before they burned him alive." The thirteenth century scholar is one that both ISIS and al-Qaeda heavily rely on to justify militant jihad, the killings of other Muslims, 'martyrdom' operations, and other terrorist acts.

"In his *fatwa*, Ibn Taymiyyah told that you may harm your enemies in the same manner that they harmed you," Abu Zafir explains. "So, this pilot dropped napalm bombs on us, and we can then burn him alive! They always rely on Ibn Taymiyyah *fatwas*. ISIS uses Ibn Taymiyyah as it wishes and sometimes it twists his ideas and *fatwas* for its own objectives. ISIS also uses only half of the many Qur'anic verses to reach a verdict, basically cheating the Qur'an."

"What do you think of Syria and ISIS's future?" Ahmet asks.

Reflecting local views of politics and the reality of all the foreign powers that potentially reap benefits from ISIS, Abu Zafir answers, "If Bashar's government and Israel exist the way they exist now, *ad-Dawlah* will there be for long years as these two powers will not leave this region alone. If some countries have profits, advantages, and expected benefits here in Syria, there will be *ad-Dawlah*." Indeed, many regional players, each with their stake in the outcome, have benefits to gain from the continuation of ISIS, both by the harm ISIS can inflict and the trading to be done with ISIS.

"In truth, *ad-Dawlah* is like a bad virus. It harmed the children the most. They are teaching Islam to the children at school as they wish it to be and brainwashing them. So, our future will also be corrupted. How can we cure those children? The ideas implanted by *ad-Dawlah* will stay there forever simply because they took the love inside children and put evil in its place. There is no cure for that. The girls are not at school. I think *ad-Dawlah* is just like Hitler. *Ad-Dawlah* took all those tyrant's policies and is now applying those policies to us and to our children at their schools."

While Abu Zafir has a point, certainly controlling the children's minds and implanting hateful ideas and prejudices is damaging, but he's not correct that it's impossible to reverse. If ISIS children are freed from the tyranny of the Islamic State and their parents and teachers no longer hold onto its hateful ideas, it is likely these children will, overtime, revert to being more open-minded, tolerant, and even loving. Of greater concern is the grim brutality the children have witnessed that can leave a lasting imprint and to which they have been normalized. Many may be overly fearful or aggressive as a result and that is much harder to change, and may contribute to enduring and unhealthy character formation, and repeated cycles of violence.

"What can the world do to end ISIS?" Ahmet asks.

"Defeating ISIS is not about taking back territory. *Ad-Dawlah* states that, if necessary, they can embed themselves among the civilians. They spread the feeling that they are already inside us with their spies, so even if they are dismantled as a group, we cannot be against them as they might come back or harm us without coming back necessarily as a group. So you can understand the volume of fear they spread."

Abu Zafir sees the answer to ISIS and the conflict in Syria in terms of people finding the humanity, love and truth in their religion and reforming their corrupted selves. "We need a solid and true Islamic belief system—powerful *iman* [beliefs]; and we must bring back the love of our country, and lastly we need to go back to Allah's book and Prophet's way of life. We need to learn our real religion and get a hold of it very tightly." While Abu Zafir clearly means practicing Islam in a more tolerant and loving manner, he is preaching what ISIS also preaches—that it is necessary to learn and get hold of the "true" Islam. Who defines what is "true" Islam, is one of the issues here, as well as whether or not people are forced or can choose to believe and comply as they wish.

When it comes to non-Muslims, he diverges from ISIS completely. "Prophet Muhammad was sent to humanity, according to the Qur'an, not to the Muslims only. So, we cannot misbehave toward other people who are not Muslims. However, *ad-Dawlah* degrades this writing and makes two categories: the *ad-Dawlah* Muslims and considers the rest as infidels. Therefore, we need to better understand the Qur'an and the Prophet and behave accordingly."

"Why do they call everybody else infidels?" Ahmet asks.

"Ad-Dawlah calls anyone who does not join the uprising with them infidels, so as *Jaysh al-Hur* is not with them, they are infidels. Turkey is not ruled with the book of Allah [the Qur'an and *shariah* law], so they are also infidel." To further illustrate his point, Abu Zafir shares yet another gruesome story from the ISIS desire for complete control:

"One time at one checkpoint, they stopped several trucks coming from Lattakia [a port city in Syria]. They asked the drivers simple questions of prayers. Those drivers were Sunni Muslims. Many of them could not reply because they were so afraid. Some replied wrongly as they were shivering and had difficulty in talking, so they were labeled as infidels at the scene, and they were killed. I knew some of them were devout Muslims and would pray five times a day, however they killed them."

But ISIS fully justifies every killing. "They say, we kill and if you are a good Muslim, even if we kill you, you go to heaven. If you are not, you go to hell anyway. This is their approach," his voice is cynical and disappointed. Indeed, he is repeating excuses al-Qaeda in Iraq also gave when criticized about marketplace bombings in which innocent Muslims were killed—good Muslims go to Paradise and the rest are destined for hell.

"What they are doing or saying is not what Islam imposes but rather their own desires and evil wishes. I finally came to believe that they are doing this on purpose—so that the people are steered away from Islam." Abu Zafir strongly believes that Assad and the Shia want to destroy Sunni Islam. "I know a few people who lived under *ad-Dawlah* and fled to Europe or Turkey. They told me that they are so much driven away from Islamic beliefs because of those animals and that now they don't feel like Muslims anymore."

Abu Zafir then mocks Bashar Assad: "Bashar says, you wanted freedom, I gave you everything. If you want Islam, *namaz* [five times praying], *sawm* [Islamic fasting] or if you want other ways—alcohol, women—everything is free. But you wanted more freedom. Now I give you more freedom--with ISIS. Do what you do with it." Under Assad, the Syrian people were free to choose to be religious or not, but they were not free to challenge the regime. Now that they have, they can have their "freedoms" under ISIS and see how they like it. Now the former commander seems sad and weary. Ahmet wants to wrap up the interview.

"What are you happy about the most?"

"When I left them, I realized that the evil in my heart left me. According to them, everybody is infidel but them. Now I live in peace. Now, I am not scared of dreaming bad things—like they are coming after me."

"What would you say to young people thinking of coming to join ISIS?" Ahmet asks, as they finish up their interview.

Abu Zafir sits up straight in his chair. He speaks in a clear, strong voice as he begins to denounce ISIS, "Oh my brothers and sisters, the young people out there: Please do understand and learn the real Islam, not the Islam *ad-Dawlah* teaches us. Islam and jihad are not as *ad-Dawlah* tells you. They will bring the young girls here and get them married three or four times in a very short time against the rules of our religion. They are dragging the youth here to die, or kill. The real jihad is to stand against people who are harming us."

This is the first interview for which I've not been present by Skype and as soon as Ahmet is finished, he emails to tell me what happened, starting with our fixer's security concerns and the unidentified man on the bus—who turned out to be a high-ranking former ISIS leader. "We talked beforehand for about an hour and finally I persuaded them that they are not under threat, as we will never let that happen, and we even will not use Şanlıurfa again as our video recording location to ensure that. After that, we started to interview this guy. That interview came out to be the most beneficial and richest one we had so far." Indeed, it was amazing to hear what this former ISIS *emir* had to say.

"He showed me his pictures with the armed vehicles and during the armed conflicts, etc. I recorded everything from the beginning till the end," Ahmet shared. They spent six hours together, four recording the interview, the first of our video recordings. We both feel excited for what is yet to come.

As always the emotions run strong with this work. Ahmet later wrote of our fixer, Abu Said, "He has a four-year-old daughter. When they were escaping Syria, he and his family were without any food for over four days while they were fleeing. From that time till now, even though his daughter is full, she keeps saying 'Daddy, I am hungry...I'm starving.' Psychologically she could not overcome the trauma." I asked if it was possible to find good Arabic psychologists or social workers to refer these people for help. "It would be too risky. They are still scared, and openly say that the threat is imminent. So we are trying to be very careful. They would never trust someone who is not an insider." Sadly, there is no one on the inside trusted and skilled enough to help. I later meet a Syrian woman, a psychologist, seeking asylum in the United States. She tells me she spends hours volunteering on WhatsApp and Skype, counseling those who have been devastated by these conflicts.

I wish there were more like her.

Chapter Nine - Another *Cub of the Caliphate*

I'm up before the sun for this, our first planned video interview. I have an Arabic-to-English translator by my side. I remain concerned about Ahmet and our fixer's safety, but he insists he's taken every precaution. Ahmet is relying on Abu Said to translate on his end. Ibn Mesud, our ISIS defector today, is an eighteen-year-old former ISIS fighter from al-Hasakah in the northeastern corner of Syria—an area where many Kurds predominate. Like Abu Zafir, yesterday, he's wrapped his head and face in a *keffiyeh* to obscure his face and he turns away from the camera as he begins. The ISIS defectors are all terrified of being discovered and killed here in Turkey, and he is no exception. The recent murders in Ahmet's hometown of Şanlıurfa have heightened everyone's fear. Yet they agree to talk to us because they feel coerced and duped into joining ISIS and carrying out actions they now regret. Each wishes to tell the truth about the "Caliphate".

"There were eight children in our family," Ibn Mesud begins. "I have one brother older than me, all the rest are younger; and there are also five girls." In the typical Arab fashion, he lists the number of children in his family counting only the boys. Syrian families are commonly large—a typical family often having as many as ten children. "My father fell and broke his leg and needed an operation. His surgery didn't succeed so he's now handicapped. I had to go to work and I was working up to the revolution," Ibn Mesud explains, his voice still sounds youthful.

"How did ISIS come to your region?"

"When they first came after winning over *Jaysh al-Hur* [the Free Syrian Army] and they started to talk about Islam, they were pretending that they were good. They took the young men to the camps."

"How old were you at that time?"

"I was sixteen at the time, in December 2013. They called young men to the mosque after evening *isha* or *maghrib* [evening and sunset prayers] to talk with them."

"What did they tell you?"

"We learned about the Islamic State and its presence in Iraq, their battles and fights, things of that sort."

"Was it only about freeing people from a bad regime?" Ahmet asks, trying to draw him out.

"They told us that these people had robbed the country and don't apply Allah's laws. They said we want you to join us to establish Allah's laws and so on. Also that the Islamic State is following the true Islam, and when you go to join us in battle, if you die, you will go to Paradise."

We've found that many of the Sunni Syrians who joined ISIS were illiterate and not well grounded in Islam. Similarly, when I studied the Chechen suicide bombers with Dr. Khapta Ahmedova, an expert from Chechnya, we found that they also often didn't know their religion well and easily accepted *Wahhabi* fundamentalist teachings of the Chechen terrorist groups, including their claim that suicide terrorists were Islamic 'martyrs' and heroes of the faith. Likewise, among Chechen youth, we found that they often looked up to the "brothers" who seemed powerful at a time when their own fathers could not protect them from the Russians.[59] It is the same in Syria—fathers who cannot find work and are cowed by ISIS are sidelined, as the ISIS recruiters move in to snatch their sons and daughters. Likewise, in Belgium, recruiters often discredit fathers and manipulate their mentees, telling them that only those reading the Qur'an in Arabic can divine its true meaning, therefore they should trust the recruiter's violent interpretation of Islam (Chapter Fifteen).[60]

"There was this guy, al-Asawi, who was talking to us about joining," Ibn Mesud continues. "We started at their headquarters and they took us later to their camp. At the camp they put us through athletics and sports classes and taught us about the Qur'an."

"Where was their camp?" Ahmet asks.

"The camp was in Gol [a town in Syria]. When we got to the camp they brought us clothing, something like a uniform. It was black. In the morning at dawn we would go to the morning prayer."

"How did they wake you up?"

"They would come and say, 'Get up young man, go to the morning prayer, because the early morning prayer makes you closer to Allah.' So we would get up and do our ablutions and then go and pray. After we would go for breakfast and for some sport. After that we would learn about the Qur'an and jihad, and learn *ribat* [guarding Muslim frontiers] and those kind of subjects."

"After religious lessons, what were you taught?" Ahmet asks, his voice gentle as he talks to this youth. I always smile listening to how Ahmet immediately changes his tone with young kids—probably talking to them the same way he talks to his own sons.

"They taught us how to handle and use weapons, how to shoot on the various types of weapons, how to shoot a Kalashnikov. They taught us the 12.5, the 23, the Serta, tanks, the 57, and the various kinds of weapons."

"Hand grenades?"

"Yes. After the lesson in weaponry, it would be around one or two p.m. We went back for ablutions and afternoon prayer, and then we went to another lesson. We readied ourselves for combat. Some people would guard others. Some people took more lessons, some went to sleep, but as guards we practiced guarding, then later we got to rest also."

"What about *ribat*?" Ahmet asks.

"They take you to *ribat*," where the youth witnessed, but did not yet take part in, the fighting that was taking place on the borders of ISIS. *Ribat*, it seems is a twisted internship of sort for the *Cubs*—to learn about the battles before they'd be sent to fight in them. "They talked to us about the events in Islamic history. There were one thousand and five hundred youth in the camp—my age, younger and older."

"How did they convince you?"

"They talked about jihad, honor, what the Prophet said, may peace be upon him, that it is an obligation of Muslims to join jihad and things like that. They wanted to unify our ranks in jihad. We spent about a month and half in the camp."

"Did they try to convince you to go and blow yourself up?" Ahmet asks, reflecting on what we already heard from our ninth interview, Ibn Omar, who at age thirteen, (Chapter Three) was among the *Cubs of the Caliphate* and described how they are heavily pressured into carrying out suicide attacks in bomb-rigged automobiles that they drive into enemy lines where they explode themselves.

"Yes," Ibn Mesud answers, his voice deadened from any emotion. He was only sixteen at the time.

"What did they tell you about it?"

"This will make you closer to Paradise. This is a real opportunity. That is how they approached that," Ibn Mesud answers, his voice flat. It is clear to me that he has dissociated from the terror of it—deadened his emotions—and doesn't want to feel anything as he talks. "I thought that those who were immigrants [foreign fighters], those who came from Egypt for instance should be the 'martyrs', not us, the natives. I told them, 'I don't want to go. My father is handicapped.'"

"So you joined to make a living for your family, to provide for them?"

"Yes," Ibn Mesud answers his voice brightening. "He [our *sheikh*] tried to convince me saying, 'We will take care of your family if you go. You won't feel anything.' He even showed me an envelope and said, 'You drink this stuff and then you won't feel anything.'" I feel angry listening to how they preyed upon this youth and tried to manipulate him by promising him Paradise and to care for his family after his death.

"I tried to leave them, but the one [boy] I told that I want to leave, he went to tell one of the brethren that I didn't want to stay."

"So when you finished the training and told them you didn't want to be a 'martyr', what was their reaction to you then?" Ahmet asks.

"Before that they were really nice, but after I told them that I didn't want to go on a 'martyrdom' mission, I felt that things really changed, that they were not treating me the same as when I first arrived," Ibn Mesud's voice sounds hurt, betrayed.

"So from your camp how many went as bombers?"

"There were ones from the fifteen hundred in our camp that went as bombers. The ones who agreed to be 'martyrs' they took to the battles inside Iraq," Ibn Mesud answers, failing to specify an exact number. Likely, given the numbers Ibn Omar was naming and the huge pressure to become a bomber, Ibn Mesud does not know or prefers not to remember.

"Did you have any interactions with foreign fighters, with Westerners?"

"We saw foreigners but we didn't understand them. We saw Chechens, Libyans, Iraqis, Saudis, Americans and Europeans also. But we couldn't understand what they said."

"Do you know anything about how they bring the European youth over?"

"When we saw them at the Internet center, they had long hair and looked normal, he tells us. "They would talk to friends and relatives over the Internet."

"Did they show you around the Islamic State?" Ahmet asks. He is referring back to what Ibn Omar told us about how ISIS tried to impress its grandeur and power upon the youth.

"First they showed us Deir ez-Zor [a city in eastern Syria], then they took us to Raqqa. We didn't stay long in those places, only a week or two. They showed us how big the Islamic State had become and we met some of the men and youth from *ad-Dawlah*. There were some deserters, youth that were scared. Many of those were fleeing. They stopped those who deserted and those who did get caught…" Ibn Mesud's voice fades away as he shuts down—probably trying not to remember the horror.

"Please tell us about when you started thinking about escaping," Ahmet prompts.

"I told the *sheikh* that my father was ill and needed me and that I needed some vacation time. Then I left the headquarters for home. I told my father what was going on and he convinced me to leave. I changed my clothing [out of his ISIS issued uniform] went to Raqqa and then went to Tell Abyad [the Syrian town bordering Turkey]. And from there I entered Turkey. I left first on vacation and then I deserted. I left from Gol."

"At Tell Abyad I met with a smuggler through someone who had run away before me. [Before he escaped] I told him that I also wanted to go to Turkey and he said, 'When I get there, I'll let you know how.' He later passed me his smuggler's phone number. I went to a barbershop and got my hair cut and shaved. Then, when I talked to the smuggler, he asked me, 'Are you running away from *ad-Dawlah*?' I told him, 'No, I just want to go to Turkey.' I was afraid he had allegiance to *ad-Dawlah*, so I didn't want to tell him anything." I marvel at this adolescent's grit as he disguises himself and hopes to escape from ISIS—knowing he will be beheaded if caught.

"So after you agreed with the smuggler, how did it go?" Ahmet voice is filled with curiosity.

"He demanded fifteen thousand Syrian pounds. I gave him the money. We stayed at his place for a while and he asked me about *ad-Dawlah*. I told him that *ad-Dawlah* was good. I didn't want to tell him anything negative because he might be with them. I just told him that I want to go to the hospital in Turkey. We prayed the sundown and evening prayer and then he helped me cross. He told me to go to Tell Abyad, and he told me how to get there without getting lost."

"Did anything happen on your way?" Ahmet asks gently.

As he answers, my stomach flips as my mind speeds ahead. Is he about to tell us about a betrayal? ISIS punishes deserters and has a long arm inside Turkey. Did he naively trust the wrong person? But it turns out that all went well.

"No. When I first entered Turkey, I spent two days in hiding until someone I had worked with came over. He told me to meet him."

"So how long since you deserted?"

"About four-a-half months."

"In the camp did you miss your family?" Ahmet asks, returning to Ibn Mesud's experience inside ISIS.

"Yes of course I missed my mom, my father and my siblings at the camp. I really wanted to go back home but we were forced to stay in the camp for a month and a half."

"At the camp did you ever cry?" Ahmet asks, his voice soft as he tries to get to the boy inside this young man who keeps his emotions at bay.

"Yes, I cried," Abu Mesud admits, warming to Ahmet's paternal side. "I cried because people were dying, my friends, my family… Now I think may Allah punish the person who was the reason behind this."

"Were there things you liked?"

"What I liked about *ad-Dawlah*, is that they taught us how to pray and about Islam. But they were also very hypocritical in how they treated people. Like smoking tobacco—they would smoke when they were with other ISIS members. But if they saw someone else outside smoking, they wouldn't warn him, they would hold him accountable and punish him. It was the same with shaving. In *ad-Dawlah* people were not supposed to shave or trim their beards, yet they would constantly clean their beards and groom themselves when others were not looking. There are several examples like that. Everything is *halal* [permissible to them according to *shariah*] but *haram* [forbidden according to *shariah*] to the rest of the people."

"In your view what is the difference between *Jaysh al-Hur* and Islamic State?"

"*Jaysh al-Hur* would take the Muslims money and they would sell oil and Muslims never got anything out of it. *Jaysh al-Hur* taught people how to sell oil and how to work on some things, but they would also come to a storeowner and tell him you have to pay half your earnings as a tax. As a result of this, there was a lot less business, but after ISIS came even less so," Ibn Mesud explains as his voice helplessly trails off, seeming to reflect the disastrous changes that prevented him from finding work to help support his family.

"Did they offer you marriage, slaves, money?" Ahmet asks, trying to understand how ISIS motivates young men into action.

"When I said that my father was handicapped, they offered, 'We will get you married, give you a captive girl, that you can marry as a legitimate wife.'"

"How did you feel about that?"

"They said to me, 'This is a pretty girl, why don't you marry her, in *shariah* law it's okay,' things like that. I would answer, 'Yes,' but then I thought 'No.' First of all I was convinced to marry that girl, but then I was afraid of my father—that he would be angry with me." *I'm glad to hear a young man inside ISIS maintained his conscience,* I find myself thinking.

"So during the four or five months you were with them, how did they behave with you, and with women?" Ahmet asks, trying again to open up this highly traumatized youth.

"People were afraid of them and people would not talk. They would force the women to cover. My feeling was the woman herself must be convinced and feel it, versus being mandatory and compulsory. If a woman was wearing blue or red, they would hit her just because they wanted her to wear only black. If they took a woman, they wouldn't tell her husband. They would just take her and flog her. So it [being with a woman who was not a family member] was *halal* [allowed] for these people and *haram* [forbidden] for the others," Ibn Mesud says again.

"I discussed with one guy, my friend—that this kind of thing is *haram*. At first he was afraid of me and I was afraid of him, but he initiated the discussion. He said these things are *haram*, insisting that a woman must have the *hijab*. That it's *haram* to flog a woman in front of her husband, that other women or their husbands have to correct them, not men outside their families." To address concerns like Ibn Mesud's is likely why, after some time, ISIS created the all-female *al-Khansaa* unit of the *hisbah* in Mosul and Raqqa. Although it turns out the *hisbah* women were just as ruthless as the male members, if not more.

"They also wanted us to spy and tell on other people, to route out *Jaysh al-Hur* cells, if there were any. When someone did something wrong in the camp, people would come and take him and hold him accountable. We knew there were snitches, but we didn't know who they were."

"Have you ever seen a punishment take place?"

"Yes, they brought someone to the plaza and they forced us to witness. They said, 'This guy has raped a girl and committed a felony, a crime.' He swore on the Qur'an and said he was innocent and that those people were not fair to him. So it seemed to me that he did not really deserve to be punished, but they fired on him anyway. But, with the first shot, praise be to Allah, he didn't die. Then, this other guy came with a knife to behead him. I was afraid, how his family was crying, how this guy looked, that really upset me a lot."

"There was a lot of oppression. One time there was a guy who went to get his car fixed. After, the repairman asked the owner of the car, who was from the United States, for seventy-five thousand but he protested, 'That is too expensive, the spare parts cost only this much.' Then the American called one of their [ISIS] cadres and asked him to look at the bill. After that, they brought an *emir*, an Iraqi. They started discussing and then they took the repairman and hit him in front of everyone. This poor repairman was whipped one hundred times, even though he did nothing wrong."

"So, tell us how you decided to work with them?"

"First of all, they said they would give me fifty thousand a month. I wanted to do it, at the same time it was jihad and I was serving God and the Islamic community so I wanted to join them. They gave me a salary at a time when there was no work to do."

"Did your mother and father agree with that?"

"I didn't talk to them about fighting. I told them I would become a guard at a warehouse or a checkpoint and then I would get that salary. But I didn't tell them I would become a fighter."

"Do you regret joining?"

"Yes, because that was not the right thing to do."

"It was this Saudi *sheikh* [at the mosque] who talked you into it?" Ahmet asks, referring to the ISIS *shariah* teachers who were roping in the youth.

"Yes, he recruited several young people, but each separately. He would talk to us about religion and jihad—talk like that.

"How do you feel now about being with them?"

"It was *haram*. One has to know that we shouldn't join these people.

"What food do you like?" Ahmet suddenly asks, trying to reach the heart of this young boy, separated from his parents by a vile organization.

"I like potatoes."

"So did they make potatoes for you?" Ahmet challenges, reminding him of loving hands that used to make his meals.

"They used to boil them, but it wasn't with meat or anything, not baked," Ibn Mesud answers his voice filled with sadness and longing. He is referring to the ISIS practice of serving only simple food and severely limited portions to the *Cubs*, ostensibly to toughen them up,

"Where do you live now?" Ahmet asks.

"My mom's brother has rented a place and I'm staying with him. We sell produce."

"Are you afraid here, in Turkey?"

"I am sure they have intel inside Turkey. They used to tell us that people who run away to Turkey, even to Iraq—we will catch you. They told us that in Tell Abyad we have someone there watching, and they will catch you."

"How do you protect yourself here in Turkey?" Ahmet sounds genuinely concerned.

"I don't go out. I go from work to home. I don't go to the market," Ibn Mesud answers.

This may be a prudent measure—to stay safe and undetected by ISIS spies. Yet it is also likely a posttraumatic response to all the brutality and trauma he has taken on board. People with PTSD often shut down whole areas of their lives in an effort to avoid triggers that remind them of their past traumas, to keep themselves calm and avoid the high arousal states that come with flashbacks. But they pay a high price for this in terms of a life of avoidance. Ibn Mesud, we find as we go along in this interview has literally hundreds of traumatic stories stored in his soul—stories from which he will likely never be able to completely escape.

"Once they brought someone who escaped to Turkey. They didn't let him talk and they beheaded him."

"What was he accused of?"

"He had taken the money and run away to Turkey. This guy who had run away from the fort, they hung him up for three days and then beheaded him. Before this they gave him only one meal a day and they flogged him."

"How did you feel?" Ahmet asks, now taking on the familiar role of psychologist.

"Honestly, I started crying for that guy. I tried to help him but I didn't succeed. Allah knows what is in our heart," he says, his voice becoming small and helpless again.

"What upsets you about ISIS?"

"The beheadings bother me the most. These criminal things they do."

"Do you suffer nightmares now?" Ahmet asks a question I've typed into chat.

"I see [in a nightmare] that these people are holding me and about to behead me, I've seen this twice now. I wake up crying, screaming! I pray and invoke Allah to protect me from the devil," his voice fills with alarm.

"Do these things continue to bother you or can you forget what you've been through?"

"I still feel influenced by the things I have seen and I am hoping Allah in his glory will make me forget and that I can start a new life."

"Tell us about the ordinary, Syrian people—the civilians—what do they say and think?"

"People wish that ISIS will go away and people who are wanted by them can go back to their families and things can go back to normal."

"If things go back to normal, do you want to return to Syria?"

"Oh yes, I really wish I could go back to Syria. I miss my family very much!" Ibn Mesud answers with deep longing filling his voice.

While Ibn Mesud may regain normalcy, he probably needs to feel some sense of safety before he can recover and it would be good if he had access to some mental health support—but like all of our Syrian ISIS defectors, he is too poor and too terrified to seek out help.

"Tell us a story about what you have witnessed, what you have seen that really upset you," Ahmet continues to prompt.

"One time someone was suspected of being *murtadeen* [those who abandon true Islam as defined by ISIS] from *Jaysh al-Hur*. They [ISIS] started threatening people. They made women and children leave the village and stay in the middle of the desert without anything so that they could search the village thoroughly for any hidden *Jaysh al-Hur* members. There, the children and women cried furiously. They threatened them and made them cry for three days—that is something that I have witnessed."

"Also, they would come and they would boast that they have liberated that area, or another, and make people believe that they were the strongest. One time they brought a lot of soldiers from the 17th squad. They beheaded them and put them on the trucks while they were on their cars, patrolling the area, shooting and intimidating people and showing the beheaded bodies saying, 'We are on the right path.' It was a really sorry sight."

"They are also very forceful in forcing women to cover. One time I had a flat tire in al-Shadadi and had to stop and ask a repairman to fix our tire. His shop was at the ground floor of the house. While he was fixing our tire, I saw his wife came to bring water to him; although she had her outer clothes, her face was uncovered. Just at that moment, a *hisbah* car passed and they called her. They questioned both of them, asking him, 'Why is your wife uncovered?' She had a *hijab*, and he said so, but they answered, 'No you have to wear black and completely cover her face also.' 'I just came down to bring water to my husband,' she explained but they didn't accept her excuse."

"They started insulting her and calling her *saafer* [uncovered/barefaced]. Then they flogged him fifty times, and they told her to sit so that they could whip her as well. She desperately begged them not to whip her as she was pregnant and didn't want them to harm her baby. She promised that it would not happen again, crying aloud. But, they were like stones and didn't accept her excuse. They kicked her husband out and had her sit while they flogged her twenty-five times. All the people gathered around were begging them to stop. When they were finally done with her, they ordered her to get up. She had to obey but she only weakly managed to stand up. Then I saw the blood underneath. People were saying, 'We swear, this woman just miscarried.' Later, I learned that she lost her child," Ibn Mesud concludes, his voice now shaking in horror. I feel sick listening to their barbarity and sadistic evil.

"How do they carry out these floggings?"

"They flog them on their backs. They flog the person very strongly."

"Can they get up and walk after?"

"When they tell him to get up, he has to get up, but only Allah knows how they feel. They call this whip *al-Lakhdar Brahimi*," Ibn Mesud explains. He is referring to the UN peace envoy and negotiator for Syria from 2012 to 2014 who is deeply hated by ISIS. The whip is made of a green rubber tubing and *akhdhar* means green in Arabic so it's a play on words.

"Another time there was a sister and brother walking. The *hisbah* stopped them and asked, 'Where are your IDs?' as they could not walk together if they were not related. They didn't have them on their persons. They accused the girl of being a whore and an infidel and took her with them to the *hisbah*, but let him go. He ran home to get their IDs and returned to the *hisbah*. There they told him that they didn't have her, but he insisted that they had been together when the *hisbah* stopped them. The *hisbah* accused him of lying and whipped him ten times as a punishment. Later, she was found dead near a river, close to the marketplace where she was taken."

We suspect she was raped or sexually molested but Ibn Mesud is too conservative to admit it. Ahmet presses. "So this girl, do you think they had raped her?"

"Only Allah knows," he answers, his voice going numb again. "Her family was screaming and crying. But if that happened they wouldn't say it because it could be a scandal for them," referring to the Arabic honor tradition in which the shame from the rape of their relative could also fall upon them.

The call to prayer is sounding so Ahmet excuses the group to go and pray together while I wait for them to return. When they do, Ibn Mesud shares a few more stories of his time in ISIS. Once the barrier of speaking of rape is broken, and perhaps also having had his trust bolstered by just having prayed with Ahmet, Ibn Mesud opens up and tells more stories of women in ISIS territory mistreated by the ISIS cadres.

"So one time this *hisbah* car is driven by a Tunisian *mujahid*. He saw a woman in the market who was covered properly and was shopping, doing her own business. He was following her in his car and stopped the car when she stopped to purchase things, but she wouldn't pay him any attention. He kept stalking her like this three or four times until she got home. After a while, he went to her home and knocked at the door. Someone opened the door and he said, '*Salaam Alekium* [Peace be Upon You]. The man who opened the door, as it is a local custom, invited him in to talk and offered him tea. While the tea was served they talked and this Tunisian guy started to question the man, thinking he is the father, and said, 'I saw your daughter and I want to marry her.'"

"'I don't have any daughter at marriage age,' the man answered, confused. But, the Tunisian did not believe him and insisted that he has a daughter whom he had seen several times. The man took an oath to Allah saying to this *ad-Dawlah* fighter that he doesn't have a daughter and the woman he saw was his wife. Then he called his wife, telling her to cover her face, as she was uncovered at home in another room. He asked her to tell this Tunisian who she was so that he would believe him; then asked him to leave their home."

"Still, the Tunisian remained obsessed with her. So he made a plan and made a fake report to *ad-Dawlah* about the husband, incriminating him for being a spy for *Jaysh al-Hur*. So *ad-Dawlah* arrested the guy and put him in jail and eventually the guy gets killed. The Tunisian kept going to their house harassing the woman. So, the woman in order to save herself from this man, fled to her father's home with her two little girls and three-year-old son. But, this guy didn't stop. He found her in her father's home and forced her family to marry their daughter to him."

Ibn Mesud's foot taps nervously as he continues his litany of horror, "Once our neighbor in al-Shadadi, her husband was killed as a 'martyr', she was *multazama*—[conforming to Islam and wearing the *niqab* and *hijab*]. She had four children, ages ten, seven, six and five-years-old. People were helping her out and she was trying to hold on. One ISIS guy offered to marry her. She said, 'I have to provide for my children so I cannot get married.' However, he insisted that he would take care of the children and would be a very nice person to them. He started delivering food to her from the restaurants and from the market to convince her to marry him. Then, one time he dropped off some food, but put drugs in it and the woman fell unconscious. After the woman fell down, the *ad-Dawlah* member entered the house and raped her while video recording it all. A day after he went to the woman again and threatened her with the video and that he will show it to everybody in order to force her to marry him. Eventually, she had to accept to marry him because of the video he had."

"Then, after some time, the guy invited three of his friends to their home. They forcefully gang raped the woman and videotaped everything. The next day the woman went to the court and seeing the *sheikh* protested about what happened, and said, 'My husband has the videos in his cell phone.' The judge summoned the husband, took the cell phone and saw the nasty recordings that confirmed the woman's story. However, the man accused her as having connections with *Jaysh al-Hur* adding that her brother had been in *Jaysh al-Hur* and saying she was messaging her brother over *WhatsApp* and passing him information on *ad-Dawlah*. He also brought witnesses against her. The judge, even though he saw the horrible video of the gang rape, decided against the woman and ordered her to be stoned because of adultery, and did not touch the men who had raped her. Nobody could say anything because it was her word against theirs."

After they stoned her, they left her body hanging for a couple of days. She had already died, but no one would approach her. Finally they removed her. One of her children, her ten-year-old son was sent to *shariah* camp. The other children, who were really little, were given to the woman's family."

Clearly we have opened a floodgate of traumatic recall as Ibn Mesud records horror story upon horror story.

Ibn Mesud continues, "Once I went to see a friend in Deir ez-Zor. He said that *hisbah* members raped a girl here. One man from the *hisbah* liked this girl and saying that he would marry her, he raped her inside the *hisbah* building. He kept saying that he would get married to her but it was not the case. Eventually, she went to the *shariah* court and told her story accusing the *hisbah* member, but they accused her of being crazy. They would never harm their own people," says Ibn Mesud, adding, "Whatever they do, they wouldn't punish them, but instead make them vanish and send them to other places."

I know that most trauma survivors keep their horror bottled inside and only allow brief flashes of these kinds of experiences to re-surface, as it's too painful to recall—and often floods out like it is right now with this teenager. It's likely this is healing for Ibn Mesud to have a chance to wrestle with this evil in a safe environment. But sadly, we are unable to indulge his need to recount these stories and have his traumatic recall witnessed by caring others who won't flinch in the face of its horror. We must now interrupt his flow as it's soon going to get dark and we don't want to call attention to him on the drive home.

As our time is getting short, Ahmet asks this child who has seen more than any grown man should ever see, if he has any statement for others. "We want you to send a message to the people in your region, what would you want to say to them about ISIS?"

"I wish that anyone who has followed ISIS to abandon and to flee to Turkey or go back to his family, or stay in his family. I wish every person my age and younger would not join ISIS, and listen to their parents advice, and the parents should keep them away from *ad-Dawlah* because this 'State' is lying to the poor people."

"Can you tell the others from Turkey, Europe, and youths from around the world who might think of joining ISIS about how you suffered at their hands—to warn them?" Ahmet prompts.

"In the name of God most merciful and compassionate, I recommend to my generation and the children younger than me; dear brothers not to feel tricked by this 'State'. Money is not everything. I was not aware and joined them. It is better to eat dirt than to join them. I advise you one more time this 'State' is not the right way to do things, not to be tricked by *ad-Dawlah*. I would tell them not to even think about joining *ad-Dawlah*. To stay with their families is better for them. *Ad-Dawlah* is not applying the rule of law that Allah has imposed, but they are doing whatever they want. Allah be with you. In the name of Allah, most merciful, most compassionate, I address this message to the American and Turkish young people so they don't feel tricked by *ad-Dawlah* because anyone who has gone through it and seen with their own eyes knows better. They are unlawful and making the people live in fear."

Chapter Ten - ISIS on our Trail

"They are unlawful and making the people live in fear." Those were the final words eighteen-year-old Ibn Mesud left us with yesterday. Today, Ahmet and I are about to understand his parting warning in a new light.

I'm up again early in Washington, D.C. to greet Ahmet on Skype. "Merhaba!" I call out. Ahmet tells me that they are almost ready—he just needs to start the camera while Murat, a student of Ahmet who has been helping out, mics our next defector. Today we will talk to Abu Musab, nineteen-years-old and the eldest of five, from Deir ez-Zor, Syria. He was left to fend for his family when his father was killed in the Syrian conflict. As I wait for them to start, I hear Ahmet pick up his phone. Although it's in Turkish, Ahmet, usually cheery and soft-spoken, sounds dead serious. When he hangs up and gets back on Skype with me, his voice is strained as he hurriedly explains, "Anne, I have just received a call from one of my friends and we have a report that we were followed today. I'm asking for an armored car and I'm going to find out what's happening. Our guys are already here so they will give you the interview, but I am going to see what's happening."

Before I even have a chance to ask any details, Ahmet disappears and turns the interview over to Murat who, while he has been present at all of the prior interviews, is someone I've never really conversed with directly.

"I have the questions and we can begin," Murat says in a kindly voice as he introduces me to Abu Musab. "Tell us about yourself and life under ISIS," Murat begins.

But I'm completely speechless. *Where is Ahmet? Is he safe? If ISIS followed him, do they know where we are meeting today? Should we be continuing this interview right now? Could ISIS cadres storm the studio at any moment?* My heart beats hard in my chest, as my mind races. *Are Ahmet and his family safe? What about Murat? Could they be killed at a moment's notice as I sit here helplessly, waiting to witness carnage via Skype?*

The interview is on and I need to attend to my duties—detailed note taking during the interview and typing questions into Skype chat as we go along. My Arabic-to-English translator is standing by and begins telling me what Abu Musab is saying. I start typing my notes. *Everyone else is okay with proceeding—calm down...*

As I dutifully type, Ahmet is in an armored car on his way back to Şanlıurfa, where he lives. He is weighing his options—helplessly realizing he has none, but to flee—and wonders how he will protect his wife and children. Tears fill his eyes. *If they know what we are up to, I have to get out of town—I need to vanish completely. They'll kill me! I have to talk to my* wife. *Maybe I should leave for the United States early—look for a job there?* Ahmet is fully aware that ISIS will stop at nothing. He cannot stay in town and probably can't even stay in Turkey if ISIS has learned that he's been exposing them.

"I am the eldest, I have four sisters that are younger," Abu Musab is telling us. I push my mind to concentrate on him. "We have land that we farm, but before ISIS, and the revolution, I was at school. Then the revolution took place. For some time, my father was outside [our home] fighting. Then the regime bombed the area and my father died as a 'martyr' in that bombing. I became the provider for my family. I started freelancing in agriculture, working as an itinerant farmer until the Islamic State was established. They came to Raqqa first and then to Deir ez-Zor where we lived."

"ISIS came to fight *Jaysh al-Hur* [the Free Syrian Army] and *Jaysh al-Sham*. They came in and beheaded people. It was not in the name of Allah. They labeled people in the name of Islam as infidels and *murtads* [apostates]. They forced the people to learn to pray, and go to the mosque, and pray the way they did."

Focus, Anne, focus, I think, forcing my mind onto this young man's words. *Listen—there's nothing you can do for Ahmet right now anyway...*

"We were young at the time. There were six of us, me and my friends. Al-Zarqawi was our teacher there. I joined *ad-Dawlah* under him. After *maghrib* [sunset prayer] they would give us a lesson that lasted until the *isha'a* [night] prayer. He taught us about everything—prayer and about how *ad-Dawlah* is good, about doctrine, Islamic belief, and the unity of Allah. He taught us everything about our religion. He was the person in the area of Deir ez-Zor who knew about *shariah*."

"We young people liked him a lot and went to the mosque daily to attend his lectures. We all committed to going to the mosque for his teachings. Then he asked us about declaring our loyalty to the 'State'— giving our *bayat*. He said to us, 'You, young people will be the *Cubs of the Caliphate*.'"

"I started thinking about it. My father had been killed as a martyr under the regime. I started thinking, *should I, or should I not?* The offers were very appealing. I was the only provider and life had become very difficult. I spent some time thinking about it. We also asked each other among the youth—'Should we go to the camp?' Finally, I packed up and didn't tell anyone in my family—not my mother, sisters, or my uncle. My friend Hassan and I went with two others and with our *shariah* teacher to the camp." Abu Musab was still only a teenager.

"We went to camp near Deir ez-Zor in the cotton fields. For two days we rested a little bit. We got lectures on *shariah* law. We were divided into two sections. The first section was already deployed for battles. There were consecutive training sessions, about fifty people in each session."

"Even children with their families were taken to the camp," Abu

Musab tells us. "*Mubayah* [giving our *bayat* pledge] happened after the training in the camp. At that point, we were called *mubayaeen* [followers] in the camp. They taught us to pray, about our religion, all little by little. They praised Paradise, the fight, the Prophet and his companions. They told us we need to fight because the Alliance [the Western powers/the Coalition] was striking *ad-Dawlah*. Even our area had been struck. The *shariah* teachers tried to convince us that when you die you wouldn't feel it." Again—the cynical manipulation of youth.

"In the early morning we woke for morning prayer. They had already installed toilets in this camp so we did our ablutions and came back to pray. They took us to al-Hurafi to train. There we were given about three-and-half kilo packs to carry. We came back smelling really bad. We went to the showers but there was no hot water. They told us we have to shower in cold water. Then we got a quick *shariah* lesson and then they sent us off to breakfast. Meals were not very heavy—light meals of dates or something."

"We started like that, prayer, going jogging, coming back to train for the use of weapons and so on. They taught us how to shoot and kept us constantly active so we were all in good shape. After fifteen to twenty days of training, they deployed us. They deployed us quickly because they were afraid the Alliance would strike. We were the 51's deployed to Iraq," he says referencing his unit. "Some others went to Aleppo, Damascus and the Homs area. I was sent to al-Hasakah."

"When everyone was being deployed, I asked the *emir* to stay behind because I'm the sole provider for my family."

"'If you want to be part of the Islamic state, you have to obey blindly,' he instructed me. So I shut up."

"My friend, Hassan, went with me to al-Hasakah. They told us we had to raid [against the regime]. They said, 'Get ready,' so we did. Then they took us by cars. In the first two cars were Kazaks and Chechens. They put the Kazaks and Chechens up front and told us, 'You are the defense;

the others are the attack.'"

"It took us three hours to breach [with the Chechens and Kazaks leading the battles]. There was some shooting. When we breached, there was no one left, but we found that nothing had been taken away. Everything [all the weaponry] was in its place. Everything was locked. The rockets had not been launched so *Allahu Akbar* [God is greater] we got there before *Jaysh al-Hur*."

Abu Musab is recounting the story other informants have told us of how ISIS captured the entire weaponry arsenal of the regime's 93rd Brigade's with very little fighting.[61] Some question whether there was a devil's bargain struck between Assad and ISIS. The area was well-fortified and difficult to assault, yet ISIS not only captured it easily, all the weaponry was abandoned by the regime's forces, leaving ISIS well supplied.

"We took all the abandoned ammunition that we found and put it in our vehicle. We captured a large volume of weapons, seventeen cannons at least—they were large. It was the largest weapons arsenal brought into al-Hasakah. Then the Alliance started striking. We took it all and pulled out. In this battle, there were twenty-five Chechens and Kazaks. The regime did not strike us, but the Alliance did. The *emir* said we have to transport this ammo from al-Shadadi to Deir ez-Zor."

"We went to Deir ez-Zor," Abu Musab explains, noting that the local ISIS cadres go home to their families between battles. "I got some rest. I was able to see my family, my mother and sisters. I was looking also for al-Zarqawi [his *shariah* teacher]. I asked about him and tried to find him in the area. I wanted to ask him, '*Sheikh* you told us all about the Islamic State. I wanted to stay with my family but [the *emir*] told me to obey blindly.' But I couldn't find him to ask. I really respected him and his opinion. I really liked him. He's the one who convinced me of the whole thing to begin with, so I wanted to talk with him."

"We stayed about a month in Deir ez-Zor. Then we went to the eastern part of Deir ez-Zor to battle. I had at that point been with them about four-and-a-half to five months."

"Then there was a battle with *Al-Sheitaat*.[62] *Al-Sheitaat* is a large [Sunni] tribe," Abu Musab explains. Indeed, it numbered nearly one thousand armed members at the time that ISIS decided to attack, in what many local Syrian ISIS members found to be a very disturbing chain of events [See Chapters Five and Seven].[63] *Al-Sheitaat* tribal members are Sunni, yet ISIS foreign fighters indiscriminately beheaded and dismembered men, women, and children alike, killing seven hundred and completely decimating the tribe.[64]

"We were taught if they are from the regime forces or *al-Sheitaat tribe*, then they are *murtad* [apostates]. In *al-Sheitaat* area, *ad-Dawlah* started advancing. First, we were getting ready in the morning prayer, and then we stormed. They told us, 'You, young people,' we were thirty-five in number, 'You are going to control things after us.'"

"The early storming was done by fifty Kazaks and Chechens. They stormed in and conquered the area." As we have heard from other defectors, the Chechens and Kazaks did the killing, while the Syrians job was the cleaning up and collecting of weapons etc. "The killing was done by ID cards. If you are this or that, you are killed. Even children were being killed. The Kazak and Chechens didn't usually stay long. It normally took them two hours. They were famous for their fighting skills. But with *al-Sheitaat* it took two days and we didn't win. But they were able to displace them all—kick them out. All [the men] from the *al-Sheitaat* tribe under age thirty-five got detained."

"During this battle, the young *ansar* [the Syrian local ISIS soldiers] were conscious of many things," Abu Musab explains, voicing the deep distaste the local fighters had for beheading their fellow Sunni countrymen. "For instance, that the people from *al-Sheitaat* were being killed—we thought they had *Jaysh al-Hur* [Free Syrian Army] cadres among them, but later we learned that they were just natives from the area trying to defend themselves. But there were oil fields involved. And *ad Dawlah* had killed a woman in that place. They told us about that. When a woman gets killed in that area, it's a big issue. It's an honor crime and a line you don't cross. That's how the battle got started."

While there may have been the murder of a woman involved, we will later learn from the defectors much more about the political reasons behind the *al-Sheitaat* battle that motivated ISIS, and the *fatwa* coming out of Iraq that guided the merciless beheadings. Basically this was an ISIS sanctioned genocide of other Sunni Muslims, in part because many in their tribe had resisted ISIS dominion and had also fought for the Free Syrian Army, and also because ISIS wanted to control the oil in their area.

"We came for the [oil] wells and we were told that *al-Sheitaat* were robbers and had taken the Muslims' money. But when they surrendered, the fight took a different turn." To justify the ethnic cleansing, ISIS leaders "told us, 'They [*al-Sheitaat*] stole the fortune of the Muslims, these *murtad* and thieves—*al-Sheitaat* —taking all this money. Therefore, *ad-Dawlah* has to fight them. That's why we stormed them.'"

"When I came back from this fight, we were told that they were with the regime and that *ad Dawlah* started fighting *al-Sheitaat* tribe because of this. But I went looking for my *shariah* teacher to ask him. When I was looking for him, I was told he was killed as a 'martyr' with others, by the Alliance air bombardments."

At just sixteen-years-old, Abu Musab had now lost under enemy aerial bombardments, two important male role models—his father and now his ISIS *shariah* teacher—and he has witnessed violence well beyond the pale.

"At that point I didn't know what to do. My hands were tied. That man was the one I sought advice from, but he was killed. They told us to go back home. So, I went home." Abu Musab's mother had by that time learned the news of the *al-Sheitaat* massacre and was beside herself. "My mother met me and told me, 'Don't ever leave home again. Don't go with *ad-Dawlah.*' But once I had pledged my allegiance, I couldn't leave them. All of the Deir ez-Zor [youth] had given their *bayats*. But now the local people hated us because we had killed the entire *al-Sheitaat* tribe. We had become pariahs."

"'Stay at home. You are our provider,' my mother told me. But the car came to take me when my vacation ended. She started crying hysterically, so I told the men who came to pick me up, 'I cannot leave, my mother is sick; and my sisters, they are alone'.'"

"'Jihad is more important than your mother,' they answered. I then begged the *emir* to let me remain with my mother. The *emir* said 'Jihad takes precedence over your parents. You can stay the night, but tomorrow come to the *hisbah* and don't be late because al-Zarqawi [your teacher] has died as a martyr."

"I left in the morning. My mother was really sick. Then we were driven back to the checkpoint barrier at al-Sheitaat. Those who had attended the storming of al-Sheitaat were called to a ceremony. We were considered skilled and they gave us awards because of what had happened. The leaders said, '*Al-Sheitaat* were a plague upon the Muslims and robbing them of their money.' They gave each of us one thousand U.S. dollars and said, 'Go rest at home for a week. Here are your awards.'" So with money thrust into his bloodied hands, Abu Musab, still only a teen, went back home—confused and sickened by what he had taken part in.

"When I returned home, I found my mother still sick. I went to my father's brother, my uncle, and I told him to get me out to Turkey and I gave him the thousand dollars."

"'Where did you get this money?' he asked. When I told him, he took it and shoved it in my face yelling, 'Get out of here!' and kicked me out."

"Of course my uncle wouldn't accept this money. He didn't want me to join *ad-Dawlah*. I went back home regretting what I'd done. My mother was sick because of me; my uncle had kicked me out of his home.

At first they gave us one hundred U.S. dollars, but now I got one thousand. It's really a lot of money. They were giving us a lot of things every time we stormed somewhere." Abu Musab knew he could not easily defect—to do so risked not just his own life, but everyone in his family. But, now in the face of ISIS brutalities, even his family had turned against him.

After some time, however, "the uncle who had kicked me out came and said, 'I don't want to leave you alone.' And my mother said 'These are not Muslims. *Al-Sheitaat* were completely decimated. I will not let you stay with these people!'"

"'I cannot leave you behind,' I answered. 'But if you and the girls go, I can follow.'" Abu Musab tells us his family's escape was a prerequisite for his defection.

"'Swear,' she said."

"'Okay, I won't be long,' I answered her. 'But the most important thing is that you must leave.' I knew if I left they will be attacked and I was really, really afraid."

"Only my uncle and mother knew about my plans to defect, although I wasn't sure I would defect. I gave her about twenty or fifty thousand Syrian dinars. The rest I gave to my uncle and told him to provide for them until they reached Turkey. My mother got to Turkey and to relatives. My uncle went onward to Germany. When I knew they were safe I started thinking over my plans."

My mind snaps back to Ahmet and his family. *Will they have to make a similar escape?*

"After the *al-Sheitaat* incident, when people started seeing us [ISIS cadres], they would shut the door in our faces. The same if they saw any of our family. We then had to return to al-Sheitaat for about fifteen days. They were preparing *another* raid." This time against the Kurds.

"The Kurdish fight was really dirty. [ISIS] would behead even the Arabs. We took *al-Jazal* oil field, which was the last oil field in the hands of Bashar's regime and we captured women and children. Then we went back to Deir ez-Zor, and after that had the battle of Tell Abyad. We breached several fronts again with the Kazaks and the Chechens."

"After the fight in Tell Abyad we started advancing and the Kurds retreated. It seemed almost premeditated." Again we hear that insinuation of some bargain being struck between ISIS and Kurdish forces in the battle at Tell Abyad on the Turkish border.

"Then we went to Aleppo. They would take us as allies," Abu Musab is referring to another strange situation where militias that had once fought against each other would then fight side-by-side against a common enemy."

"Hassan, who I started out with, stayed with me. There had been three of us originally, but one died as a martyr. After the fight with *al-Sheitaat* he wanted to pull out. It was a seed in our minds. We wanted to defect. There were many youths who wanted to leave but there were guards at the barricades." Abu Musab was well aware that, "anyone who tried to leave, especially to go to Turkey which was seen as a country of *murtads*, would be killed."

"Free Army soldiers were seen as *murtad* and were beheaded. We saw this. The Chechens and Kazaks would just behead them without even investigating. They would say, 'We are taking this guy straight to punishment.' They didn't even take them to the *shariah* court. Most would scream, 'I am innocent! The Free Army is on the right path. *Allahu Akbar!*' Then they would kill them."

"'We need to go to Turkey," Hassan insisted, despite the danger. "You should follow your family. It's better because they will kill us in the end also. Just like they killed the women and children of *al-Sheitaat* — they will kill us as well.'"

"But I remembered [my teacher] al-Zarqawi's words. He would tell me, 'No you cannot [desert]; and we are the Islamic State.'"

"'What are you going to do in Turkey?' I asked him."

"'I don't know, but every day we see someone beheaded,' he

answered. I started pondering what my friend said, and I realized some of it was realistic. I started crying. Then at the end of the day someone got beheaded."

"Hassan kept telling me that we should desert. I continued thinking about what he said. But at the same time, I remembered how our teacher would tell us about the Prophet's story and the *Hadith*, his Companions, and that once you commit to die as a martyr you have to forget your mother and father."

Again, this is Islam according to ISIS and has no basis in the actual scriptures. To clarify this point, I consulted with Muslim scholar, *Sheikh* Ali. During the 2003 U.S. led invasion of Iraq, *Sheikh* Ali, an Iraqi, briefly joined *al-Qaeda in Iraq* (as a propagandist) and later defected and at my request, helped me design the *Detainee Rehabilitation Program* for the U.S. Department of Defense, to de-radicalize and disengage over twenty thousand extremists and eight hundred youth then held by U.S. forces.

I shared portions of Abu Musab's interview transcript via email with *Sheikh* Ali. "I felt sick after I read the two messages," he wrote back. "But you have to notice the evidence they are using all the time, which is to apply the *right* scripture to the *wrong* incidents!"

"So first of all, definitely, there is no permission in Islam to commit suicide," *Sheikh* Ali stated bluntly, even though he had once been of *al-Qaeda in Iraq,* a group that argued not only was there permission, but also glory in committing suicide as a 'martyr'.

Sheikh Ali then explained the Prophet's story referred to by Abu Musab: "Once there was a big fight and the enemy was inside a stronghold, and they were winning as long as they could continue to hide inside it. One of the [Prophet's] Companions told his friends to throw him by catapult inside the stronghold! They did, and he went there alone and fought valiantly until he was able to open the door from the inside, and then the Muslims won the battle. Extremists regard him asking to be thrown as an act of suicide, because the possibility of his success was so

weak, and they apply this case in behalf of arguing for suicide bombers—
even alleging that there are some incidents where the bomber stays alive.
Imagine how they use such a comparison and succeed to convince young
people to make suicide attacks? The difference, as so many notice, is that
the Companion was fighting all the time, knowing that his chances to
survive were small. The suicide bomber is not fighting at all."

"Another issue," *Sheikh* Ali continued, "is that the intention
is different. The fighter's intention is to fight and die, the bomber's
intention is to die and kill, and this point is extremely important because
the Prophet, peace be upon him, basically said that deeds are related to
intentions and every person shall be judged according to his intention. And
Allah states it clearly: anybody that kills himself (i.e. intends suicide) is
going to hell."

"As for what you shared from your defector interview, this is a
weak way to handle the true texts, but it is the traditional way to brainwash
followers. The first text about forgetting parents when going to die as a
'martyr' is true only in the case with the following conditions:

1) When there is an imminent extinction danger for the town.
2) The enemy is known for his atrocities everywhere he goes
(extinction mainly).
3) If the enemy wins, he will kill everybody in town."

"So as you may notice, Anne, it is to be killed anyway. If he did
not fight, he and his parents, will be killed. And if he fights—as will
everybody in town—it is a possibility that the enemy will retreat. But it is
not a justification to commit suicide. This exceptional case is discussing
mainly to fight [to the death] without the permission of the parents. All
other cases depend on the parents' permission as prophet Mohammed,
peace be upon him, stated. So this is only an ISIS version of Islam, as well
as every other [terrorist] organization that hijacks the religious texts and
deceives the public."

"By the way," *Sheikh* Ali added, "*Al-Qaeda in Iraq* once had a brigade under the name *Al Baraa Bin Malik Brigade*, which was the name of the Companion who was thrown by the catapult. You may guess what kind of people that brigade included—only suicide bombers, and nothing else. Arab fighters were waiting to be enlisted in this honorable brigade!"

Knowing now that ISIS, and the ways in which they manipulate scriptures deceived him, Abu Musab continues to tell us his story.

"But my friend would say, 'Look what they did to the *al-Sheitaat*, and to the Kurds, the blood!'"

"I started fearing blood. They brought a *murtad* and they beheaded him. I had to turn away. I couldn't see it. But then, a Chechen started yelling at me, 'You have disappointed me! You, people of Islamic State, you have to learn to slaughter and behead!' But it made me sick how they would yell '*Allahu Akbar!*' and I thought about what Hassan said, that we should probably leave."

"Hassan and I were from the same area. We went into it together and were together throughout. But they separated us finally. Then it would go long times before I'd see him again. We'd cross on a barricade or at the headquarters. Then there was the fight in Tell Abyad against the Kurds."

"In Tell Abyad the local people were very afraid of us, because we were Arabs. They were under the Kurds and then *ad-Dawlah*. They were so terrified. They had been moved and displaced. We heard that most of them went to Turkey. The area was declared as a military zone."

"After a while I met this young man, Jamal, whose home was close to the barricades. We had opened up a barricade near Tell Abyad. In front of us were these houses. Our commander would order me go to that house and ask them for water. The first time I went, I was dressed normal, not like *ad-Dawlah*, so he invited me in and I said, 'May Allah bless you, I need water for the guys on the barricade.'"

"This guy was older than me and shaved. He gave me water and I went back. 'Do you need tea or anything else?' he asked. We didn't trust the Kurds not to drug the water, so we had them drink it first in front of us.

Ad-Dawlah taught us to fear the Kurds. Only the Kurds stayed there in the civilian areas, and no one trusted them."

"So I met this man, and fetched water from him [repeatedly]. We spent quite a while with them in that region, so we of course started talking. He asked why I followed *ad-Dawlah* and I asked him why he does not. He answered that some people are not right. I told him that I had seen honor betrayed also, because I wanted him to trust me."

"He said, 'they are not even fighting the regime; they are fighting *Jaysh al-Hur* while we wanted to get rid of Assad. These people are not Muslims.' So I started talking to this man. He told me, 'Beware, don't kill anyone.'"

"'Thank God I have not,' I answered." As a cleanup soldier, Abu Musab told Jamal he had followed the Chechen advance to collect weapons and that he was not an ISIS cadre who goes around accusing and executing others. "'When a Muslim kills a Muslim and when they kill someone from *Jaysh al-Hur,* that's someone like me,' Jamal said."

"He started inviting me to his home and I started trusting him. 'I want to cross over to Turkey,' I finally told him."

"'Why?' Jamal asked."

"'I just want to go there,' I answered, because we both [still] feared each other. There was no electricity, so it was dark at night. In the darkness, I told Jamal, 'I really want to go to Turkey.'"

"'Impossible,' Jamal said, 'What are you going to do there?'"

"'My family is there and I want to see them,' I answered, telling him the truth. Jamal had some acquaintances who used to go there."

"'How are you going to go to Turkey?'"

"'Brother I don't know; I just need to go.'"

"'*Ad-Dawlah* is killing people,' Jamal warned."

"There was an Internet post office so I could communicate with my family. When I was at the post office another guy was talking [over the Internet] to someone from Tunisia. He was calling to him in Arabic,

'Come to the fight. There are beautiful women here and there is a lot of money and cowardly men.' That really bothered me. I pretended I didn't hear and that I was just talking to my family. Later I told Jamal."

"Then I learned that Hassan got killed."

Murat suddenly interrupts, breaking the mood of Abu Musab's story as he abruptly asks, "Did you see foreign fighters in your time with ISIS?" I'm shocked at his inopportune timing. I think he is probably worried about Ahmet, too, and wants to end the interview as soon as possible. He also likely feels a responsibility to move through our list of questions and it's getting late for them to transport Abu Musab safely back to his area without attracting notice. I decide not to say anything—given the circumstances—although I really regret not hearing the conclusion of Abu Musab's defection story or his feelings at the loss of his friend, Hassan.

"Yes, there were guys from China, Kazaks and Chechens, Algerians, Tunisians, guys from the Netherlands, Germans and Turks."

"Do you know how they entered?" Murat asks.

"I don't know how they get in. They connect through the Internet, and then come in through Tell Abyad, I think." He's correct. I know this to be true from other reports and from talking to a Belgian who returned from ISIS (see Chapter 14).

"There were foreign fighters in al-Hasakah. We didn't sit with them because they were entire families, and we couldn't communicate with them. Also the *shariah* teachers wanted them separated, and for us not to talk with them. If their children are over eight they are put in *ad-Dawlah*." Again, that chill goes down my spine. *Eight-year-old fighters!* "Of most of the immigrants, we would talk only to the Tunisians," referring to the language barriers with the other foreigners.

"How did ISIS treat the Europeans?"

"They were treated much better than us, although I don't know what privileges our *emirs* and leaders have. They would send them to the best quarters. They were given everything."

"Have you heard any story of a foreigner who tried to defect?"

"Yes, of course, a large number tried to defect and they were killed—at least fifteen or sixteen people. I don't know their nationalities exactly but they were [non-Arab] immigrants. They tried to defect and *ad-Dawlah* realized and killed them right then and there."

"Were they young?"

"Yes. The Europeans who wanted to defect, they were new. *Ad-Dawlah* wanted them to go to Aleppo. They were told to go fight *Jaysh al-Hur* but they tried to escape." It is ISIS' practice to send new members without referrals straight to the front to test them and learn if they are serious about jihad. These new recruits apparently had second thoughts.

"Tell us about the prisons, who did they imprison and detain?"

"I have not seen any prisons except in al-Jafra field in Deir ez-Zor. There were some cages. Each large cage was divided into four, so you could put several people in each section. We saw the cages, but not the people in them. When we went out for a walk, we realized these were the prisons." Indeed, these prisons often feature in ISIS videos of its executions and also have been shown to us in pictures our informants have taken and share from their phones.

"In the battles how do they select the fighters? You told about the *ansar* being put in the back and others in the front—how do they do it?"

"The Kazaks and Chechens do not interact well with the *ansar*. They always act alone and lead the battles. The *ansar* are not allowed to fight alongside them. *Ansar* could not ever infiltrate them. The Chechens don't go to the camps. They are not trained." The Chechens arrive from their own battlefield against the Russians and are well-trained fighters. "In the battles, one Chechen was wearing a [suicide] belt, but you would never find a Syrian fighter wearing a bomb belt." The explosive device on his body during battle allows the fighter to blow himself up and kill his captors, and plays out the ISIS dictum (taken from the Chechens), of

Victory or Paradise!

"Tell us about the suicide bombers—how do they convince people to do it?"

"Anyone can become a button—a 'martyr'—because whoever wants to carry out this kind of attack, they chose themselves. They [ISIS leaders] don't select them. It's self-selection. They [ISIS leaders] go to the different camps and those who wish to become 'martyrs' just decide. Then they take one of them and send him for an operation," Abu Musab explains.

Fifteen-year-old Ibn Omar's (Chapter Three) assessment was quite different. He spoke of heavy coercion of children and we will hear from others that selection of 'martyrs' is not as pure as Abu Musab claims. Those who ISIS has tired of, or are problematic cadres, are simply ordered by their superiors to go on suicide missions and have no choice but to obey (Chapter Twelve).

"The ISIS intelligence it seems are everywhere, even in Turkey," Murat queries, making my mind again wonder, *Where is Ahmet?*

"You have defected. Are you still scared here in Turkey?" *Who wouldn't be terrified?* I think as I listen. *They just murdered two people in Şanlıurfa!*

"Yes of course, I'm scared. I'm one of their cadres. Look at the salaries they give us, the regular soldiers—imagine how much the leaders get," he says, inferring a well-paid member might have ample motivation to hunt him down—even inside Turkey.

"So what do you regret most?"

"I regret the *al-Sheitaat* operation the most, because they killed children, women, and old people who had nothing to do with all of this fight—and not only one or two. More than five hundred people got killed. This is a very large tribe, and it was probably more. But at least five hundred people got killed because of this fight." In truth it's likely that over nine hundred members of the *al-Sheitaat* tribe were murdered in that battle.[66]

"If you could send a message to others about your time in Islamic State and tell them whether to join or not, what would you say?"

"I want to send a message to anyone who is thinking of joining *ad-Dawlah* to say that a real Islamic State would not kill innocent people and behead them. I would tell them not to join this group. If they want to fight the regime there are other factions that are fighting the regime. I would like to send a message to every young person to stay away from *ad-Dawlah* and the war. If they have a school nearby, better to go back to school. It's much better than to involve in these things."

"What would you say to foreign fighters?"

"I address my message to foreigners who are thinking of coming. They have tortured many people and even killed women and children."

We thank Abu Musab for sharing with us and our interview ends. "Any word from Ahmet?" I ask Murat as I worriedly check my own e-mail and text messages.

"No, I'm trying to contact him but nothing yet," Murat answers anxiously. We exchange concerned condolences that don't manage to calm either of us while I remember to thank Murat for risking his life for this interview.

When we close Skype I feel sick to the pit of my stomach.

Where is Ahmet?

Chapter Eleven - ISIS Unbound: Muslim Beheadings and Female 'Martyrs'

His e-mail reads, "Anne, first of all, please keep this between us and do not share it with anyone." *Thank God, finally word from Ahmet!* It's not until the next morning that I hear from him. "I saw that we were followed at the place where we met with our subjects. I've talked to my friends in the security services and we decided that I am under a serious threat and that my family and me should leave ASAP. I have departed Şanlıurfa with my friends' help, and my family will leave by other means. Meanwhile, I am thinking what I can do and assessing the situation. I will let you know as soon as I decide. Also with my student [Murat] who helped me before, we had a great interview, so don't worry, we will complete the interviews. I am sorry for the complications but I cannot risk my family. I will figure out something. Best"

Distracted by fleeing ISIS, Ahmet had forgotten to sign his name, yet typical for him to reassure me about our research while trying to save his life!

Reading his e-mail through again, I feel a swirl of emotions. Terror grips as I wonder how difficult it must have been for Ahmet to flee Şanlıurfa and leave his family behind. I remind myself, *he probably knows best and had to run without them. But are they safe now, without him there?* I begin to feel nauseated. *And where is he?* I realize, of course, that he's not going to give me his location by e-mail. This is ISIS we are dealing with. *What can I do to help? What should we do?* I feel totally helpless. Yet a little smile crosses my face as I see his commitment to make this research succeed. *He's indomitable!* That gives me confidence that he is going to be okay.

As I think over what has happened, I realize that despite Ahmet's assurance, our research is shut down. Of course, that's really the least of our worries now and I had never expected to get even this many ISIS interviews—or any—for that matter. I mean, how could anyone have expected to get this far inside ISIS through defectors? Now, I just want to know that Ahmet and his family are safe.

He's probably with his parents, I think, recalling that they live far from the Syrian border. *He should be safe with them,* but I also know that the reach of ISIS is long and ruthless.

I don't hear from Ahmet again for an entire day.

But the next morning I open my computer and there it is, another message from him. I freeze as I read it. "I made it safely to D.C. I will e-mail again as soon as possible." He's here?! I know he won't pick up his Turkish phone so I sit on pins and needles waiting to hear more. He's here a week early for his criminology conference! When I finally get another e-mail from him, he tells me that he has a friend's car and wants to come and see me.

"Welcome!" I answer. I couldn't mean it more.

When Ahmet arrives at my front door in the suburbs of Washington, D.C., he assures me that he's already eaten. Still, I put out some snacks, light a few candles as it's evening, and put on soothing music—the psychologist in me trying to make our living room as calming as possible given his last seventy-two hours. Ahmet is wearing his usual warm smile, though his face is drawn with tension and he takes on a frown as he begins recounting his story. "I was followed after picking up our last subject and my police friends have confirmed the threat. I'm on their radar and they advised me to leave the area as quickly as possible."

"What about your family?"

"ISIS doesn't usually go after the family members," he answers, although my mind quickly flashes to the family members of *Raqqa is Being Silently Slaughtered (RBSS)* who were executed inside Raqqa—to punish *RBSS* activists. It's true though, to my knowledge, ISIS has not gone after family members *outside* of Syria; but I can't help but think, *at least not yet.*

"My police colleagues and I felt that they were getting ready to hurt me. My wife was hysterical when she found out. She insisted I take my ticket and change it to fly to the U.S. immediately—to get out of the country. I gave her my debit card and she packed me a bag and a friend took me to the airport in a car that was not as recognizable as mine. She and our children are now with her parents in the west of Turkey. Her father has a house with a big fruit and olive garden surrounded by high cement walls, but she will have to go back and pack up our belongings."

I swallow, imagining how easy it is to scale a cement wall in a rural area. And her return to their Şanlıurfa home seems foolhardy. "There's no one else to pack?" I ask.

"It's our whole life's belongings. My wife wants to go back and pack up. I don't think they will hurt her if she is just there a short time," Ahmet says, but his face betrays his worry.

"But I knew I had to run. Even though I retired as the police chief in my region, I'm not in a good position with the police these days." His situation is complicated by his refusal, at the end of 2013, to support the Turkish government's top-down shake-up of the police force. Many of his colleagues were dismissed—or worse—arrested and imprisoned on false charges. During that time, hundreds of Turkish journalists were also arrested and imprisoned.[67] "The new police force will do nothing to protect me and some may even want me dead," Ahmet informs me, his face again tightening under the strain.

"What are you going to do?"

"I have a renewable six-month visa and all my family members do as well," he explains. "I'm going to stay and find a job. Or I'll apply for asylum. I can't go back—"

"Okay…" I say, my mind racing. *I'm not sure if he can get hired in a university so quickly. Ahmet is super smart and he's written a few books and some very good published reports, but university jobs in the U.S. are highly competitive.*

We continue to discuss his situation, while Ahmet makes it clear that he doesn't want to become a burden to me. Meanwhile I keep thinking, *We've got to get him to an immigration lawyer and get the rest of his family to safety!*

Ahmet has another surprise to tell me. He's scheduled our next defector interview and his student, Murat, is going to meet this defector in yet another makeshift studio in another town in southern Turkey. Amazingly, we are going to continue on with our project. Ahmet is indeed, indomitable.

Thus we greet our next defector a few days later, both of us on the same side of the Skype screen and Murat handling the mechanics of posing our questions and videotaping the interview.

Thirty-year-old Abu Abdullah is the first of our respondents to be married to two wives, which is allowed in Islam. A Muslim can marry up to four wives and some Syrians do, although most Muslim men do not have multiple wives. It's a financially demanding undertaking that makes keeping a peaceful home (or homes) understandably difficult to manage. Interestingly, when I worked in Iraq on our *Detainee Rehabilitation Program* in Camp Bucca with *Sheikh* Ali, who is from Iraq, he told me that he planned to take a second wife. When the Westerners among us guffawed, he patiently explained that it was a charitable provision in Islam and designed not for men to be selfish, but to protect women in wartime whose husbands had been killed. "They have sexual needs, too, and that will lead to sin if they can't find husbands at times when many of the men have been killed," *Sheikh* Ali pointed out. He added that he and his wife had agreed that they should take a widow into their home as an act of charity.

On this issue, Ahmet points out that having multiple wives is usually an Arab cultural practice, although any Muslim is allowed four wives. He also concurs that it is an Islamic requirement to look after widows and children and that remarrying them as second or third wives is one way of doing this. He also points out that in rural areas in Turkey, first wives may actually request their husband to marry again so that the second or third wife can become a partner in the hard work of farming and looking after the animals. Looking back on his own family history, he comments, "My grandfather had three at the same time, but this was due to the work load and the necessity of the hard conditions of their high altitude mountain village, which was more acceptable during those times. But now even in that village I don't hear about plural wives." Ahmet goes on to tell me that his wife had been forewarned by friends in their village before marrying him—as he might want to take multiple wives like his grandfather!

Abu Abdullah has two girls and two boys. Looking back on the beginnings of the Syrian uprising, he reflects on his extended family, "We are a family of fifteen. We were farmers and picked olives. We were so poor. We were living in Syria when *Jaysh al-Hur* came and cleaned out the Syrian army. We had to join *Jaysh al-Hur,* because if you don't, you cannot get your bread [i.e. feed your family]."

"Then *ad-Dawlah* arrived in the region. *Jaysh al-Hur* fought them but was defeated. The non-fighting members who surrendered were invited for repentance and they were given amnesty after carrying out the *ad-Dawlah* repentance ceremony. They were forgiven and invited to *shariah* camp after that."

"I really loved the *sheikh* in the camp. His name was al-Jazrawi. He started to teach us our religion."

"Our *sheikh* was from Saudi Arabia. He told us the Syrian regime was violating Muslims rights and the people could not say *Allahu Akbar.* He would tell us our situation [under Assad] was really very bad. He told us, 'As soon as I came to your region I started crying for you all. You have all this oil and agriculture, but the regime violated your rights. We hope we restore those rights for you and that Muslims will get their rights.' So he made us want to join the Islamic State."

I'm reminded of how victimized the average Sunni Syrian must feel under Assad's repressive and corrupt regime, and how easy it would be to swallow the ISIS message of redemption, especially when they refer to sharing Syria's oil wealth with the common people.

"Meanwhile *ad-Dawlah* investigated us. They offered to us, to the new members, one-hundred-fifty dollars per month, that's fifty thousand Syrian, which is huge money. That also motivated me, along with my love for the *sheikh*. We were so hungry; we didn't have any money. So I also wanted to join."

But he wasn't accepted at first. "They said I needed to find an *ad-Dawlah* member who would vouch for me. I advanced to the *sheikh* and he accepted me, so they gave me an exception. Then I went to their training for two months. There, I learned for the first time, my religion and also got military training. Because they taught us our religion, I really came to love them."

"After we were done with the training, I was taken to Raqqa, the capital of *ad-Dawlah*. There I saw super nice things—for instance I saw all the women were covered. Everybody was praying regularly and going to the mosques." As a Syrian villager, Abu Abdullah was conservative in his beliefs, so the ISIS demand that everyone adhere to their version of Islamic culture was welcome to him—at least at first. "They only let us stay in Raqqa for one month. After, I was sent to Deir ez-Zor."

"Things started to change in Deir ez-Zor. I was very upset there because they were killing real Muslims who were saying the *shahada* [the Islamic creed]. After saying the *shahada*, they were killing them— which is forbidden in Islam. Once I saw a thirteen-year-old boy, a *Jaysh al-Hur* soldier, who said he was sorry and said the *shahada*, which is the guarantee for any Muslim that he cannot be killed, but they cut his throat anyway."

I'm especially sickened, yet again, to hear about the incomprehensible abuse and murders of children—though ISIS would consider a thirteen-year-old boy a young man. I wonder what Ahmet is thinking about his three boys at this moment as they face possible threat from ISIS.

"When we fought, *ad-Dawlah* would tell us, 'When you raid an area where *Jaysh al-Hur* is reigning, even if you see them praying you have to kill them because that is a trick. They are tricking you [i.e. by pretending to pray].'"

"From there I went to al-Mayadeen in Deir ez-Zor. There was a traffic circle and a checkpoint there. I was working in that checkpoint. Every day between four and ten people were brought to the circle and they were beheaded there, in front of the people. They would hang them up with a big piece of paper on their chest, where was written their crimes. *Ad-Dawlah* would force people to stop, drivers and passersby, to look at their bodies and read the writing on their chests so they were aware of the crimes these people had committed. I was so scared with the volume of bodies, and forcing people to look—the kids and everyone—stopping the cars. I was disgusted, and at the same time very scared of *ad-Dawlah*"

It seems ISIS has learned well from Saddam's former regime—how terror can be used to exert control over an entire population. It's the tyrant's solution—extreme fear silences dissent.

"I asked the *emir* to send me to al-Shadadi town. It was accepted and it was a relief for me."

"I started to work there for *ad-Dawlah*. We were collecting *zakat* [mandatory Islamic alms/taxes]. I realized they were getting *zakat* from anyone they wanted and there was no justice. They were also fining people for wearing tight pants, no beard, or the women for not wearing the approved clothing. It was expensive for ordinary people to change their clothing and people were going to a tailor for a quarter price, but *ad-Dawlah* didn't accept it, and forced people to buy from their tailor, which was four times more expensive. At the end I was so scared because everyone was afraid of everyone else and it was not Islam. I was convinced that what I was doing with them was not right and I didn't know what to do." This, I realize, is the dilemma for those inside ISIS. They bought into a utopian idea whose reality of brutality and corruption is far different, but once in, it's dangerous—if not impossible—to get out.

"I saw the oppression and I couldn't stand it anymore. My conscience started torturing me. They oppressed everybody. They took money from the civilians. This was supposed to be Islam and an Islamic state, but between me and myself, I felt Islam has nothing to do with this. I needed any means, anyway to get out. But I am a fighter of the State, if they suspect you even in the least— As soon as you left Syria they knew you would expose them, expose their scandals."

Ahmet and I exchange knowing glances when he says this— indeed, it's dangerous to be suspected by ISIS—even after leaving Syria and hiding in Turkey. We now know for sure, Turkey is not safe. Is anywhere safe?

"There was a battle. I was supposed to go participate in the raid during that engagement. I spent about three days. We would go in different groups. I had never seen before all these beheadings and all this oppression. I felt very exhausted and at that moment I wanted to go in the direction of *Jaysh al-Hur* and I wanted to get out of Syria. I couldn't take it. Psychologically I was doing very badly, so I was wondering how to take my family out."

"Thank God, I was too exhausted, so the commander let me go back home. Then I took my family out with the excuse that I was sick. I took my mother and everyone else and we went from Aleppo. I decided to get out but I didn't know how to. My situation was very difficult because they were watching me now that I had isolated myself and was not hanging out with the brethren. I would only go to the prayer. I would tell them I was afraid. Sometimes they told us, 'Fear Allah, go pray.'"

"At that point, I had decided—once I had taken my family out—there was an engagement in Umm al-Mara between the Islamic State and *Jaysh al-Hur. Jaysh al-Hur* advanced and then *ad-Dawlah* pulled out. I decided to surrender to *Jaysh al-Hur*."

"How did you do that?"

"Well, first of all I dropped my weapon and I shouted to them, 'I'm dropping *ad-Dawlah* and coming to you.' Then I took off more arms and advanced and told them, 'I am so and so and I'm from this area.' They didn't know who I was and some of them said I was just infiltrating them as a dormant cell."

"I imagined that they were going to immediately kill me so I screamed, 'There is no God but Allah!' [the *shahada*] and thought they will now kill me [as they do in ISIS, despite a Muslim declaring himself a believer]. But these people of *Jaysh al-Hur, mashallah,* [thank God] treated me so well. They, of course, investigated me. I told them of all the oppression I had seen. Of course I was used to saying *ad-Dawlah*, but I started saying *Daesh* as they repeatedly corrected me. But the word *ad-Dawlah* was engraved in my mind. I spent exactly seven months with *ad-Dawlah*."

"Have you seen foreign immigrants, like Europeans, who tried to flee ISIS?" Murat asks.

"Yes I have. There were about thirty of them. They were Kazaks and Europeans, two from Sweden, but most were Kazaks. They wanted to escape and *ad-Dawlah* caught them. They were charged with perjury and treason. They caught and beheaded them and hung their heads up. The charge was that they are agents of the regime. One of them had said they wanted to flee to another faction like *Jaysh al-Hur,* or go back to their own country."

He continues with his own journey. "I stayed for a while with *Jaysh al-Hur* with my family. They treated us so well. There was a big difference for the better and a lot of generosity in how they treated civilians. In our area, *ad-Dawlah* treated civilians with the attitude, 'You are either with us or against us.' They had just made a new decree that the boys from ten-years-old had to go to the *Cubs of the Caliphate* camps, and from fifteen to forty all the men had to go to jihad. You cannot stay home."

"Can you tell us about the camps for the *Cubs*?"

"These are camps where the highest number of participants were children. They go for a short session. Then they would take them in a car and make them swear that they would be 'martyrs'. They were brainwashing the kids from the ages of ten to fifteen in the camps about Paradise —telling them that, 'the *houris* [black-eyed beautiful virgins] will be waiting for you—to talk them into becoming 'martyrs'."

"How do they train those children? What do they tell them?"

"So for one day they tell them, 'These other people out there are infidels. They rape women. They do bad things, they drink and hurt others…' And then they send the kids to blow themselves up."

"But it's not possible for me in just one day to tell someone and then they go to blow themselves up?" Murat challenges.

"No, *ad-Dawlah* takes their time to convince them that these people are infidels. They tell them about jihad for the sake of Allah. For a while they start convincing them that jihad is good for our honor. Overtime, they become motivated to go and blow themselves up. They feel this is a good thing to do. They tell you all about your religion, about jihad, and about your brethren and the way the Prophet did things. So they create a motivation. They [the kids] don't know that these others in *Jaysh al-Hur* are also Muslims. So they go to their barricades and checkpoints to explode themselves. These people [ISIS] say that they are enforcing Allah's law."

"So how long did you stay with the Free Syrian Army?" Murat asks.

"I stayed for a while. I worked for a short period. Then I got a ticket to get out because it was better for me to leave, so I went to Turkey."

"Is it possible to leave *Jaysh al-Hur*? They don't make you stay with them?"

"No, they don't force you to stay with them. On the contrary they took me all the way in [to the border]. They helped me." This account echoes another story of a Belgian [Chapter Fourteen] who told me of being taken by *Jabhat al-Nusra* cadres to the Turkish border when he wanted to leave them.

"Brother, during that period with ISIS, certainly you have seen immigrants—foreign fighters?"

"Yes, of course," Abu Abdullah answers.

"Are they same as the *ansar* or different?"

"No, they are different. Some of them had been tricked by the word jihad, to fight for the sake of Allah. They also didn't know the differences [between the locals]. They came to the area thinking those people out there were infidels, but when they came and talked to people [they learned]. Among them were citizens from the UK, Chechens, Kazaks, Egyptians, Algerians, Tunisians and others."

"What about the Europeans?"

"They had their own translators. They were good with us. They treated us well. Of course, not everybody. For example, if someone hated someone else, he could lie and say, 'This person is an infidel,' and then…" Abu Abdullah's voice trails off and leaves the rest of his thoughts unnamed.

"Tell us about women—do they go and fight? Also tell us about captives—the *sabaya*. Do the women in the Islamic State become fighters?" Murat asks.

"No, they are sent to suicide bombing," Abu Abdullah reports, giving me a start. This is the first I've heard anything other than unspecific news reports about preparations in ISIS for deploying female suicide bombers; although Ahmet later informs me that ISIS may have already deployed one inside Turkey. As a terrorist group, ISIS is similar to al-

Qaeda in this regard. Following conservative Islamic practices, they haven't pushed women to become fighters, instead encouraging them to be wives and bear children, though the foreign women in ISIS almost all serve in the *hisbah.* My experience studying modern day terrorist groups is that those who do use women as suicide bombers, as the Chechens did right from the start, find them highly effective.[68] Female cadres can pass checkpoints much more easily; don't raise as much suspicion; can hide their bombs inside conservative clothing; and male guards are loathe to search them. Female cadres can also hide their identity if they wear a *niqab,* and they garner much more media attention when they explode themselves. Conservative groups that don't use females in the beginning often transition to using them when the going gets rough—such as Palestinians in the Second Intifada and al-Qaeda in Iraq.

Now it seems, ISIS may be getting to that point.[69] There have been many indications that ISIS may, indeed, be gearing up to more routinely engage female bombers. A new ISIS marriage certificate discovered in May of 2015 declares that women do not have to have their husband's permission to go as 'martyrs'. Instead ISIS' caliph, al-Baghdadi, is able to give them permission, totally bypassing their husbands—an ominous signal.[70] There have also been reports that ISIS cadres were approaching local Arab women, not the Europeans, to become suicide bombers.[71] And now, Abu Abdullah is telling us that he suspects women are being readied and even deployed as suicide bombers.

"They give their families money and then they send them to go and blow themselves up."

"What are their nationalities?" we ask, as we try to see if his report matches this allegation that ISIS leaders are approaching local Arab women for such missions.[72]

"There are some Syrians, some Saudis and Qataris. The majority are Saudis. They are very committed. They don't bring just one woman— they have a group and give them a lesson. They tell them, 'No one is going to suspect you. You can enter a barricade and blow it up.'" Indeed, this is exactly what happened with *al-Qaeda in Iraq*, the precursor organization to ISIS. When they got cornered, they began turning to women and sent them with bombs hidden under their *burqas* to explode themselves at checkpoints.[73]

"They execute the operations outside the province," he continues. "When I was with them I never saw any woman blow herself up, but I know they were ready to. One woman from Saudi was wearing a [suicide] belt. I know this from the others. But I didn't see it with my own eyes. The bomb master who is preparing the vests is a Saudi."

Later when Ahmet and I discuss this interview, he tells me of a case in Istanbul where ISIS may have deployed an eighteen-year-old Russian woman, Diana Ramazova, to explode herself outside a police station in Istanbul's historic Sultan Ahmet quarter. One police officer was killed and another wounded in the January 2015 attack. Ramazova, had converted after meeting Abu Aluevitsj Edelbijev, a Norwegian citizen of Chechen origin, in an online forum. The couple married and honeymooned for three months in Istanbul and then traveled in Turkey and entered Syria in July of 2014. Edelbijev is believed to have joined ISIS in Syria, and to have been killed fighting for them in December of 2014.

At that point a widow, Ramazova—illegally crossed back into Turkey—possibly sent by, or fleeing ISIS. Once inside Turkey, she made her way north to Istanbul by taxi where she stayed in a hotel until January 6, 2015, when she used two hand grenades to attack the Istanbul tourism police station. Of interest, Ramazova was two months pregnant when she carried out her attack in which she died.[74] Whether or not ISIS deployed her has still not been established and ISIS has never publically claimed the attack. However, she had enough money to take a taxi all the way from the Syrian border to Istanbul and to stay in a hotel once there. It's possible that in her grief over her husband's death, she volunteered for such a mission rather than marry another fighter. If she was operating under ISIS, she is one of the first ISIS-related female suicide bombers.

Later, in March of 2016, Mohamad Jamal Khweis, a twenty-six-year-old American-born son of Palestinian immigrants living in Alexandria, Virginia shocked the United States with his defection from ISIS when he turned himself into Kurdish Peshmerga forces after having escaped from ISIS-controlled territory near Sinjar, Iraq. The story of Khweis's journey into ISIS echoes that of Ramazova, in that he traveled from the U.S. to Istanbul (covering his tracks by going first to London and Amsterdam) where he claims he randomly met a woman connected to ISIS who talked him into traveling into Iraq. Despite his claim, our guess is the whole things was arranged—as was Ramazova's meeting and wedding in Istanbul —as it's highly unlikely conservative-minded ISIS would send a female cadre to Istanbul to randomly troll for male recruits. It's much more likely that she was promised to Khweis in marriage as the lure to draw him in, and once Khweis consummated the relationship, and had his brief honeymoon with her in Istanbul (like Ramazova), the two traveled together into Iraq, as he admits. There he claims they were separated, which would be consistent with our defectors' explanation of what happens with foreign fighter couples. She likely went to the sisters' house and he into ISIS training. For Khweis, once in ISIS, he immediately had regrets, thus his quick defection.[75]

"Do you know anything about the girls who work over the Internet recruiting others?" Murat asks, repeating another question we've typed into chat. Abu Abdullah doesn't understand and instead describes how the Internet is used to lure male fighters who are told about the women they can marry when they join ISIS.

"With regard to the Internet, they talk about how pretty the girls are and how *ad-Dawlah* is right. That is in order to trick people into joining to try to make people believe *ad-Dawlah* is carrying out Allah's law, when in fact it's the contrary. They create a pretty image that *ad-Dawlah* wants Allah's law and there is nothing bad here—that only the right prevails."

"The European girls who come, some of them are very young—sixteen and seventeen—do they get married?" we continue, trying to find out what he might know about the Western 'brides of ISIS'.

"Actually they come with their husbands or they are married to fighters once they arrive."

"Can you tell us any stories of the things that bothered you from your time in ISIS?" Murat asks, trying to coax Abu Abdullah to described what he's witnessed and endured under ISIS. Like most trauma victims, the ISIS defectors don't relish recalling the horrors they saw and rarely, if ever, exaggerate. They instead keep their horror sealed inside and only share it in an environment that really encourages them to do so.

"The things I saw…" he begins, his voice filling with a new sense of horror. I'm suddenly reminded of the *Heart of Darkness*. "It was written I should be loyal to the nightmare of my choice," Joseph Conrad had penned. Abu Abdullah continues. "They would say, 'Today we are going to behead, you have to stop what you are doing and watch.' Once there was this thirteen-year-old boy, a *Jaysh al-Hur* member, and that incident really taught me a lot. I was ordered to bring him down from the pick-up. I did not want to, but I couldn't do anything. If I didn't do what they were ordering, they would come after me. This young boy started screaming, he was just a child—thirteen. They brought him in front of the people to be beheaded. When they put his shoulders back and he fell, he started screaming. Inside of me I felt I wanted to go and free him—but they cut his head off. That really hurt me. That child was screaming, and I could do nothing to save him. I swear to Allah, that moment impressed me so much. I felt so much that child was innocent."

He continues. "If you [as an ISIS cadre] hate a civilian, you can accuse anyone as a *murtad* and whatever [ISIS] security says is considered the truth. You can accuse someone of being in *Jaysh al-Hur*—true or not. I felt the boy was not in *Jaysh al-Hur* and he was killed for nothing."

"So when you saw the reality of their oppression—the killing of the thirteen-year-old—when you and your friends disagreed, could you object?" Murat asks gently.

"No, we were supposed to just obey. If they tell you to help to slay others, you have to do it. Even if they tell you to behead your own father you have to do it. Whatever the *sheikh* tells you to do, you have to do. When we hear the order we have to execute it."

"What was the thing that bothered you the most in how they treated women?" Murat continues.

"The thing that affected me the most was that they would take a Muslim woman, for instance a [Syrian] Muslim woman whose husband was with *Jaysh al-Hur* and they take her children away from her. If they are young, an immigrant [foreign fighter] family would take them and if old enough, they send them to the camps, and they sell her. Either they sell her—it depends—or if she is pretty and good-looking, then they will take her for themselves. This is mostly practiced by the Tunisian *mujahideen*. People hate them and call them perverts," Abu Abdullah adds, reflecting a common view of the Tunisian foreign fighters as being the worst of the sexual predators in ISIS. "Otherwise they will sell her alongside the captives. That affected me a lot—a Muslim woman sold as a captive."

As a wife and mother, I find these stories—separating family members, children taken from mothers, murdering husbands in front of their children and wives, women doomed to repeated, institutionalized rape—to reflect the lowest point man can reach. How such practices are justified in the name of any god is beyond me.

That ISIS would sell Sunni believers as sex slaves we believe discredits ISIS to many who might consider joining the group and to those who defected from it. For Abu Abdullah it's likely there can be no justification for selling a Syrian Muslim woman into sexual slavery who just as likely could have been his neighbor and friend before the uprising, or the wife of a friend fighting against the regime. There is an historic basis in Islam for taking unbelievers as slaves, which could apply to the

Yazidis and Christians, although the latter are considered "People of the Book."[76] But it does not apply to Sunni Muslims.

Even a December 2014 ISIS *fatwa* on the topic of captives and female slaves claims that the Islamic basis for taking female slaves is only because they are *unbelievers*. This *fatwa* justified taking unbelieving women captive, with the following quote: "There is no dispute among the scholars that it is permissible to capture unbelieving women [of] *kufr asli* [original unbelief] such as the *kitabiyat* [women from among the People of the Book, i.e. Jews and Christians] and polytheists. However, [scholars] are disputed over capturing apostate women. The consensus leans towards forbidding it, though some people of knowledge think it permissible. We lean towards accepting the consensus…"[77] Yet, Abu Abdullah is alleging that ISIS leaders violate their own *fatwa* by capturing and pressing Sunni women into sexual slavery. This inconsistency disturbed many of the ISIS defectors who were aware of it, and Ahmet and I are eager to use it in one of our video clips to publicize this disturbing violation of Islam.

When we ask about the sale of women, Abu Abdullah answers, "With regard to that market, there was one time when I saw them selling. They were women from Iraq that had been captured. One of the colleagues told me to go take one. 'No, you cannot do that,' I answered. 'It is not something that Allah will accept, it's *haram* [forbidden].'"

"'They are Yazidi,' they said. But I saw that they are Iraqis, some Kurds. That's who was being sold. There was an area from which they took some, that they called the devil's region [Yazidis]. They would take them and sell them. The fighters of *ad-Dawlah* would take them for free, but the public had to pay—the prices they paid I don't know."

"In reality they know nothing about Allah and Islam and are just making money. Most [local] people who join stay for a while and then run away. Those who stay are greedy and just want money. But they know that *ad-Dawlah* is not correct. They stay for the money. They have cars. They think this way."

"Beside this young man, was there any other story that impacted you?" Murat presses, again coaxing him into opening up about what he saw.

"There is this story that happened in front of me. There was a young man, a poor guy who had four persons in his family. He was really poor, economically disadvantaged. They were just sitting there drinking tea. Someone from the *hisbah* passed in front of their house. The *hisbah* had ordered that we had to escalate because we needed money from those houses. They told the people, 'We don't want to come back and behead you—we need money.'" Taxation is the primary means, after their oil sales were disrupted by airstrikes, by which ISIS finances itself.[78]

"'I am really poor, *sheikh*,' this poor man answered. 'I will kiss your foot. Take whatever you want, I have nothing.' But our commander didn't accept that. He couldn't pay anything, and they executed him and his family. That situation really affected my life."

"Have you seen their prison? Do they torture?" Murat digs further for the stories that Abu Abdullah seems to prefer to keep locked in the deep recesses of his mind.

"Yes, torture was mostly hanging by the feet and flogging. I saw a guy that they hung from his arms to torture him. They spent a whole week doing it. They would sometimes give the prisoners only a half a piece of bread to eat [per day]."

"One time they brought a man. This is a real story I saw it happen. It was an older guy in his sixties. They asked, 'Where did your son go?' They hit him and beat him [to try to get him to tell if his son had gone to join a rival group]."

Trying to understand his current mental state, we ask, "Since you stayed and suffered under them, do you have any nightmares?"

"Most of the nights I have nightmares. Sometimes I get out of bed and I'm screaming '*Allahu Akbar* these people are oppressed!' Someone told me [while still in ISIS] that I am talking in my sleep. I was scared of what I might be saying. And I could see at times when I woke up that I'd been sleep walking."

Abu Abdullah is clearly suffering deep psychological trauma. Traumatic memories and normal memories operate very differently. Normally our minds work by pattern matches—we integrate our daily experiences into already known and categorized experiences. Our normal experiences are broken down into little bits of information and added to these categorized experiences as memory patterns. Our brain can only pull whole memories together again by retrieving these various bits from all the places they've been broken down into and categorized. It takes effort to pull up and reform these bits of information again into a whole and integrated picture—a mental film of sorts—which is why we only recall parts of most things we've experienced, and rarely as vividly as was first experienced.

Traumatic memories, however, are very different. Because the mind was presented with terrifying and overwhelming experiences that had no categories in which to place them—no pattern match— the mind often rejects processing the immediate experience. The traumatic memory gets stored in a part of the brain called the amygdala, as a full sensory memory and is not broken down into small bits of separated information. When the traumatic memory, now stored as a complete sensory memory in the amygdala, gets triggered, it replays itself in its full sensory glory—the film now becomes a terrible horror movie with all the sensory information intact. The sounds, smells, sights, sensations—all of it replay—flooding the mind with posttraumatic recall. Most trauma survivors find that reminders of a traumatic event can act as a tripwire, engaging these full sensory memories in a way that is so terrifying, and so real, that the person can become confused about time, and feel they are literally transported back into the horrific event.

If the trauma survivor does not work through their memories during the day, and engages in heavy avoidance and shutting down while awake, often the brain tries to make the mind process the traumatic memories at night. Dreams are one of the healing forces of the mind, a way in which the brain keeps presenting to the mind the pictures of terrifying and overwhelming traumatic realities that were too difficult at the time the trauma occurred, to integrate into pattern matches in the mind. Nightmares, sleep disturbances, sleepwalking and talking—and even screaming and reenacting the trauma in a dream state—are all common posttraumatic results.

Victims of trauma will do just about anything to avoid posttraumatic recall. The mind might provide posttraumatic amnesia for parts, or the entirety of a particular traumatic memory. Or people may try to avoid posttraumatic triggers by turning to drugs and alcohol to keep the memories at bay. When we ask about it, most of our ISIS defectors admit to having traumatic nightmares and some will also admit to flashbacks, yet none of them are receiving any psychological help, and resort instead to prayer and reading scripture to comfort themselves. I often wonder about how these defectors are living with their traumatic memories—and how they manage them—and I wish I could do something more to help them. I know sensitively listening and providing some semblance of safety for them to share their stories offers some help. But many rarely get a chance to tell their stories, they're too dangerous to tell, and listeners can't stand to bear witness to what trauma they might need to share. My heart goes out to Abu Abdullah who must be very frightened by his brain's attempts to heal him. Working through psychological trauma is very difficult, even when you have a psychologist to help you manage your terror and feelings of inescapability. He has no one helping him.

"How do you see your future?" Murat asks him gently.

"I am thinking about *ad-Dawlah*, when they leave Syria…" Abu Abdullah's voice trails off, sounding powerless, like he can see no end of ISIS in sight.

"So if ISIS leaves, would you go home?"

"Yes I would."

"Does ISIS have strong intel in Turkey?"

"No, they make believe that it is, but in fact it is very weak. They terrorize people by beheading, like beheading ten people at once. They make believe that their intelligence is strong."

"So are you aware if there are any infiltrations by international intel inside ISIS?"

"We heard about it, but I haven't seen it. But I heard they beheaded someone who was supposedly from external intel. But they don't share security matters. When I was there, there was an air raid. It was said that the raid was so exact at bombing because of a spy who gave the coordinates to the Coalition forces." We've heard alleged during interviews that spies operating inside ISIS manage to place GPS locators at positions that their forces then bomb.

"In your opinion, what country is supporting ISIS?" Murat asks, trying to explore how Abu Abdullah views international backing of ISIS, and what he may have observed firsthand.

"There is a powerful country that is backing them. There are countries—not one. I don't know which, but it's clear there is something really huge. One of them told me one day, 'Do you know who is behind *ad-Dawlah*?' I said, 'No.' He told me, 'The leaders know who is supporting them, the *emirs* know.' I told him, 'Just forget about it and move on otherwise it will endanger you and me.'" Like many of our ISIS defectors, Abu Abdullah realized that too much knowledge is dangerous.

Murat moves to wrap up our interview. "Would you please address a message to Muslim youth who have a desire to join, since you have lived inside it, what would you say to them?"

"I want to address this message to the young people all around the world, I swear to Allah that a Muslim is slaying his fellow Muslim. The talk is different than the reality. I have lived the reality. They oppress Muslims—Muslims killing Muslims. They behead a Muslim and then say we do it in the name of Allah, which is completely against Allah's rules. It's all oppression. It's for money. It's all talk. They teach you to kill your Muslim brother. There is the idea that *ad-Dawlah* is trying to disfigure or give a bad image to Islam and I swear my advice—they know nothing of Islam. Islam is innocent of what they are saying and doing. They say jihad and Islam but when you see the reality—taking Muslim women captive—don't even think of joining! They talk about the Caliphate but it's not Islamic. I spent six or seven months with them. They already were beheading Muslims. It is all to make people hate Islam," Abu Abdullah spews out, echoing what Abu Zafir (the ISIS commander in Chapter Eight) also told us—that ISIS has an aim to discredit Islamic beliefs, and portray followers of Islam as bloodthirsty killers instead.

Chapter Twelve - The Sex Slaves of ISIS

"Everything is fine, Anne. My friend, Ali, has offered me a place to stay," Ahmet tells me when I ask if he'd like to stay with us. He seems to have a whole Turkish "mafia" he can rely on and is determined not to burden me, so I imagine he's living in style. Only later do I learn that he is lodging in a small apartment with four other young guys—two of them pizza delivery guys. Ahmet's friendship with Ali was forged twenty years ago in Turkey and now Ali is helping Ahmet to settle in—albeit with students.

Meanwhile, Ahmet's busy scrambling for a job—reconnecting with the myriad of American counter-terrorism officials in the military, police, State Department, FBI, and Department of Homeland Security whose paths he crossed when he was Chief of the Counter-terrorism Unit in the Turkish National Police. Many offer to help and connect him with job leads, while I go over his resume, making sure it's polished. Even though he's got impressive credentials, I wonder, *How realistic is it to come from overseas and expect to quickly land a job that can support an entire family? How is he going to manage?*

"You've got to see an immigration attorney and discuss applying for asylum and you need to get your family all on the same continent," I keep telling him. I'm worried that once he applies for asylum, given he's running for his life, that he could be separated from his wife and children, literally for years. I know things like that can happen in asylum cases. Ahmet's face becomes drawn with distress, and the anxiety is clear in his nervous body movements each time I ask how his family members' travel plans are coming along.

"Ertugrul, the middle one was born here, but he doesn't yet have his American passport—we just applied for it," Ahmet tells me. "And my wife Hasibe, Orhan, the oldest, and Osman, the little one, are waiting for their American visas and have to get physicals." Yet he seems so sure that it will all work out.

I continue to worry. Given that activists were murdered in their town, it seems plausible that ISIS could try to harm Ahmet's family before they can flee Şanlıurfa. Although they initially escaped to her parent's home in another region of Turkey, now they are back home while Hasibe packs up their belongings. Ahmet, as usual, carries on steadily in the face of grave danger, and he's once again managed to arrange our next interview despite the chaos.

Ibn Ahmed is a young, married, twenty-six-year-old, from the Deir ez-Zor area, very close to Iraq. Ibn Ahmed is from a family of seven and studied only to the fourth grade, ending his studies when his parents unexpectedly died in an accident. "I'm the only son, I have four sisters," Ibn Ahmed begins. "Before the revolution, my parents passed away. It was an accident. Afterward, I took over the responsibilities for my family."

To support his family, Ibn Ahmed began driving his father's tanker to deliver water from the Tigris River. Then the revolution began, disrupting his life. "After a couple of months, I came across the Free Syrian Army. They said that they were the Free Syrian Army, but they were criminals. They stole my truck! I tried to find them but no one could help me. I was unemployed, under financial stress, and I went through a tough time for about six/seven months. I started selling wares on the street—each piece for ten [Syrian] lira. I did that for a while. Then ISIS came, they entered Deir ez-Zor." It took only a few days of fighting before ISIS gained control of Deir ez-Zor.

"They began ordering women to cover their faces. Smoking was forbidden for men and women. They encouraged people to attend the mosque. We started going to the mosque. A *sheikh* would come and give lessons on *Qur'an*. I don't think there was much crime at the time. When they first came, things were good—very good. It really felt like Islam."

"I started to attend the mosque for a while. I met the *sheikh*, Mohammed al Jazrawi [his name indicates he was from Saudi Arabia]. He was a scholar and would give lessons and advice on Islam and joining ISIS. I liked to sit with him. I told him I was in a difficult situation—had no income—and asked him to find me a job. He asked to visit me at home. He came and had tea. After our meeting, he advised me to join ISIS. He said, 'They were in the right. There would be no injustice. You can gain a salary and live your life.'"

"So, I went to him to go through the training. They took us to al-Jafra [an area in Deir ez-Zor]. That's where they trained us. We arrived at Jafra. They would wake us at four a.m. for the Morning Prayer. After prayers we would attend physical training. After that, we would have breakfast…Falafel sandwiches, sometimes bread and tomatoes, stuff like that." The training regime was all day long. "From nine a.m. to eleven a.m. we had weapons training on the PKM [heavy machine gun], rifles, bombs and things like that. In the afternoon, we had religious teachings until the evening."

Just as cults do, ISIS keeps their recruits constantly engaged, a bit on the hungry side, and physically exhausted. It is much easier to bypass critical thinking and install a new ideology into tired minds.[79] According to Ibn Ahmed it was in these evening lessons that, "They taught us to fight the Free Syrian Army. They referred to them as apostates and stuff like that."

The training was dangerous as well. "After fifteen days on this routine—the Coalition fighter jets hit the training camp." Twenty-two of the fighters were killed—eight foreigners and fourteen Syrians. The trainees were moved to a different location, and as new ISIS fighters, were immediately deployed.

"When they deployed us, they realized I was illiterate," Ibn Ahmed explains. "[I] could barely read and write, and couldn't memorize the Qur'an. So they made me a guard for the *hisbah*."

"Every day [in the *hisbah*] they would bring in about one hundred men for crimes—smoking, not going to prayers, etc. They would have us administer a flogging at the station, or they were given monetary fines, and then sent back." We ask if they also killed prisoners and he tells us, no. "At the *hisbah*, there were nine foreign fighters in charge of us— two French and one American, two Tunisians, one Egyptian, two from Kazakhstan and one Iraqi. It was the Egyptian, American and Tunisian who were in charge of the area," Ibn Ahmed explains. I feel intrigued to find an American there in charge of the *hisbah*.

We ask if he had any communication with the foreigners, but Ibn Ahmet replies with what we've heard from the others, "They speak a foreign language. You can't understand them. They just say *As-Salaam Alaikum* [Islamic greeting meaning peace be unto you]. That's all they know."

"How do they communicate with each other?" we ask.

"That's something we couldn't figure out. We didn't get it. The Kazakhs spoke a foreign language. We couldn't understand them. We wondered if perhaps they had common languages among them. As a local fighter, you can't ask a lot of questions, but we can tell from their accents," Ibn Ahmed tells us.

Around the time of his deployment (August 2014), ISIS conquered Sinjar Mountain, the area in northern Iraq where many Yazidis, the ancient sect that ISIS considers to be devil worshippers, had fled. ISIS began slaughtering the men on Sinjar mountain and taking the women captive.

"They brought the Yazidi women in covered cars. You couldn't see them, so the locals wouldn't see such a sight." It sounds like even ISIS who flaunts its brutality, in this case was hiding its genocidal misdeeds. "Nine [Yazidi women] were left with us. They took the rest of them to Conoco [the oil pumping factory]."

My heart is racing with the realization that *we are talking to a man who has had inside experience with the Yazidi women who were trafficked as sex slaves.* I am horrified and brace myself for what is likely to come.

"Each foreign fighter got a Yazidi captive," Ibn Ahmed continues. "This was considered a gift from Abu Bakr al-Baghdadi. I swear this happened. I'm telling the truth," Ibn Ahmed wants to be sure that we believe him. "This was a gift from Abu Bakr al-Baghdadi for our brothers, the *mujahideen* fighting in Syria."

"They told us they were Yazidi infidels," Ibn Ahmed explains, repeating what the Tunisian leader had told the local Syrian fighters. "He said they were our captives—they will repent at our hands." I feel myself getting nauseated.

We hear again the Islamic State's rules of the spoils of war: "The captive [girls] were for the foreign fighters, not the locals. We were just guards."

"We asked why the local fighters couldn't [have sex slaves]. They said if you were to go to Iraq or Libya then you would get a captive woman." Ibn Ahmed admits that at first he, too, wished to have one. Although that desire didn't last long. "Each of them took a captive. I saw them crying and one [Yazidi woman] cried out, 'This is not Islam!'"

"How old were they?" we were genuinely shocked by this first person recounting of systematic rape.

"Most of them were married. Most were fourteen-years-old and older." We ask about the usual age for marriage and Ibn Ahmed admits that he was married when he was nineteen and divulges that these Yazidis were just girls.

"After a week of seeing the Yazidi girls, I couldn't take it anymore," Ibn Ahmed confesses.

Distraught as he recalls, Ibn Ahmed continues, "I went to the *sheikh* that I met earlier, Abu Mohammed Al-Jazrawi, and told him I wanted to transfer from there." When the *sheikh* asked why, he told him he'd like to go to Conoco, the large oil station but did not admit his reason.

"'No problem. There is jihad in both places,' the *sheik* answered."

So Ibn Ahmed managed to get himself transferred to Conoco, hoping to see less horror, but in fact that was where he would see far more.

Ibn Ahmed explains the Conoco structure to us. "It has approximately seven hundred rooms. Each was about the size of this room," he gestures to the office where we are videotaping him [it is around eighteen square feet]. *Sheikh* al-Jazrawi gave Ibn Ahmed paperwork that he was unable to read, to give to the *sheikh* in charge at Conoco named Abu Baraa al-Maghribi [meaning he was from the Maghrib or the West]. "I came the next morning. He gave me a set of clothes: pants, boots, ammo vest, a jacket and a rifle. He said a soldier will come and you will be a guard with them inside the jail. The soldier who later came strongly warned me, 'You cannot leak anything.' It was absolute secrecy or they threatened to behead me. 'In case the [Assad] regime or the Free Syrian Army tries to get information from us, you have to keep what's happening here a secret,'" they threatened.

"The next day when I went to the warden [at Conoco], the soldier repeated that I could not say anything about what is happening there. He called another warden and told me I'd be working with him. So that was my job, a warden."

We ask why they chose that job for him.

"They asked me if I was studious. I told them I could barely write—I don't know how to write. That's when they told me I'd be a warden. They said this was all for Allah. They said if I want to go to Paradise, I should obey them." Thus we again see how ISIS manipulates believers to follow orders. "Then I started as a guard at the gate. I didn't even walk down the corridor the first day. After, I became friendly with the other guys and started going down the corridor."

That's when he saw what was hidden inside the Conoco oil station. "There were four hundred seventy-five women captives, Yazidis and Iraqis. Some were wives of Iraqi army soldiers. Some were Syrian." Which means, according to Ibn Ahmed, it was not exclusively Yazidis who were being enslaved. The female slaves were the wives and daughters of *all* their enemies, regardless of religious or ethnic background, including those who could have been his former neighbors, relatives and friends. "They were mixed. Anyone whose husband worked with the Syrian regime—some from Raqqa, Shaddadi—any province under ISIS control."

Ibn Ahmed was in complete and total disbelief that ISIS would enslave even Sunni women and horrified at the system of sexual slavery that ISIS was setting up. "When I walked down the corridor, I was shocked looking at all these women. Some of the Yazidi girls would cry. I would ask them, 'Why are you crying?' They would answer that ISIS took their children. Some were one and two-years-old. They would ask, 'Is this your Islam?'"

Ibn Ahmed didn't have an answer to that. "I just walked away and left, to stand at the door," he says, his voice sounding numb.

I try to imagine the horror of having a nursing infant pried out of one's arms, and the threat of being killed after your male relatives were executed. But these women were not doomed for simple death. Their souls were going to be killed as well, as their bodies were assaulted time and again.

"The next day, after being there a week, I started going inside the rooms with the foreign fighters. Conoco has five hundred fifty rooms, like small offices," Ibn Ahmed explains, referring to the building where the foreign fighters are housed. "Each foreign fighter had a room and a TV. Some even smoked *hookah* [Arabic water pipe]. I saw them. Of course, no one can say that, or you'll get beheaded."

"After a week or two, we got news that each foreign fighter could pick a captive woman for himself in his room." I feel my stomach retch.

"How many foreign fighters are there in Conoco?" we ask, trying to gauge this mass rape event.

"Between four hundred and four hundred fifty are in Conoco. That's not mentioning al-Jafra oil refinery, al-Omar refinery and the others that were full. When the foreign fighters got the news that they would get captives, I could hear them cheering in the corridor."

The system of rape was methodical. "The prison warden would bring ten foreign fighters at a time because they could not be brought in at once. We would guard the doors and they would go in and choose a captive woman. Then he'd take her by the hand and leave. This went on for three days, each taking one by the hand. We'd stand at the door and watch these women crying."

We ask about the actual logistics of taking these women to their rooms.

"She'd stay in his room until they brought more captives," Ibn Ahmed explains.

"They take them and stay in their rooms?" we ask again— dumbfounded and disgusted by mass institutionalized rape somehow legitimized by perverted ISIS beliefs.

"There would always be more captives," Ibn Ahmed answers patiently. "They'd bring four hundred and distribute them. Then they'd bring more or transfer them. When foreign fighters would leave, they would take their captives with them. We'd get more foreign fighters who would each get a captive, and so on."

All three of us—Murat, Ahmet, and I—are stunned, and speechless, that we have hit upon an ISIS defector with so much inside knowledge about the sex slaves. We are all so horrified that it takes a moment before Murat manages to formulate our next question.

"So these women stay in their rooms with them, or go back into the prison after?" he asks, as we wait—wanting, but not wanting—to hear more details.

"She'd stay with him until he leaves. Then they'll bring her back to the prison. Most of them would be forced to start praying. Then they'd marry them and she'd stay with him. But some [foreign fighters] would return them [to the prison] when they transferred," Ibn Ahmed explains.

I feel a part of my mind beginning to block out what he's telling us, trying to deny the appalling reality of what he's saying. But I force myself to pay attention and record it as he speaks.

When it was still only an idea, Ibn Ahmed had asked his superiors why the local Syrians wouldn't also be granted a sex slave. But when it came down to the reality of mass, institutionalized taking of females for rape, he was totally horrified. "The next week, I requested a three-day break to go home and rest. I felt tired and uncomfortable. I lost my appetite. I thought of them as my sisters."

"So you went home?" we ask, relieved for his brief respite at home—as it gave us respite as well, from listening to such horrors.

"When I went home, Abu Mohammed al-Jazrawi started to come and check up on me."

"'You're not yourself. Are you okay?' he asked me."

"I told him I'm okay and remembered the words of the soldier who warned me I'd be beheaded if I said anything. So I told him, 'Everything is okay and hopefully we'll get our Caliphate and there are no problems.'" Too afraid to even admit the horrible reality to his ISIS teacher or his family members, Ibn Ahmed received no comfort at home, save for a brief break from the horrors.

"So I went back to work [at Conoco]. Then they brought a Sudanese foreign fighter. This Sudanese guy picked a captive woman for one night and then left her to go back to prison. That's when I started thinking I should leave. I advised my friend, 'We should leave ISIS. This isn't Islam. This is not okay. See these women how they cry and are away from their children? One of them was nursing her child when they took him from her! She didn't know what happened to him.' That's when I decided to leave."

The breaking point for Ibn Ahmed was an incident that happened with the Sudanese fighter. "The Sudanese foreign fighter picked a fifteen-year-old girl. I swear he raped her. She started bleeding badly. An ambulance came to take her. They said, 'Don't speak of this. Captives are captives. Do as you please with them.' [But] the girl had internal bleeding and died from her injuries."

"After she died, one of the *sheikhs* [at Conoco] put the Sudanese fighter in prison. Even though I was thinking about leaving, I wanted to see how they would punish him—then I would leave. So, I worked for another week. They let him go after seven days and he went back to his post." Ibn Ahmed was devastated by the hypocrisy and lack of justice.

"The next day I went home. My sisters and wife asked me, 'What's wrong? Why are you upset?' I told them what happened." Ibn Ahmed's all-female family was shocked and horrified as well and now fearful for their own fates.

"'We have to escape to Turkey as soon as possible!' they cried. 'If something were to happen to you, then the same thing would happen to us!' So, I went to Tell Abyad and got out."

It wasn't as simple as that, of course. Ibn Ahmed explains how he risked death as he bluffed his way across the border, with his whole family in tow. "First, I took time off for three days. In the morning, I planned a trip to my aunt's house in Tell Abyad. That is what I was going to say at the checkpoint—I'd say it was a one-day trip and I'd be back tomorrow. And they did stop me and asked me." It was a brave move, as being questioned at an ISIS checkpoint when attempting an escape is like having the knife blade almost at one's throat.

"I had my whole family with me—my sisters and family. And I told them at the checkpoint that if they wanted to speak with the *sheikh* that I would give them the name of my *emir*." This, too, was a bold move, as he should have had paperwork to be able to travel, but luckily Ibn Ahmed's bluff worked and the ISIS guards let him pass without phoning his *emir* to check. When he got to Tell Abyad, he gave a smuggler money for passage into Turkey. "He got us tickets [from ISIS] to cross the border safely." Apparently ISIS issues tickets for its members to show at the border crossings, to prove to whoever is checking for ISIS, that they have permission to cross into Turkey.

Life as a refugee is tough. He works as an itinerant farm laborer, moving from crop to crop with the growing seasons. "When work comes, then I'd pick potatoes, tomatoes, vegetables and cotton."

Murat, I've noticed, is a lot like Ahmet—kind-hearted, often taking a hospitable attitude toward our defectors now living in Turkey—showing a sense of responsibility toward their safety and wellbeing.

"How much do you make every month?" Murat asks.

"It's barely enough to feed us. We'd work for three days a week. Every fifteen days we'd work eight or nine days. It's been a month since we have had any work." It's growing cold now and the growing seasons are finished until spring planting.

But Ibn Ahmed says he is glad to be out. "The farther from ISIS, the better," he reflects. "We can sleep comfortably after the horrors that they committed." Although in truth, Ibn Ahmed does not sleep well.

"So you stayed with them for five or six months and then you fled. What have you seen? Do you remember anything else? Do you have bad dreams?" Murat asks, trying to keep up with the flood of questions we are typing into Skype chat.

"Every so often I dream that they are pulling my hair by the scalp and about to slit my throat, and I startle awake. I dream they catch me, and because I'm wanted, they try to behead me."

When we ask him how he is doing psychologically, he tells us, "The nightmares will not go away. It will stay in my mind. It'll drive me crazy. I try to forget even though a nightmare is so difficult to forget. I still remember the woman huddling in the corner crying, and you can't do anything for her. You can't forget..." His voice fades off. I imagine how the horrors of the Conoco station still haunts him. Genocide doesn't come free and lives on in the hearts of those who kill and torment innocents.

We ask him what else he recalls from his life under ISIS. Once again we hear of ISIS' gruesome, and public punishments.

"One day, I was about to leave on my motorcycle. There were three older men in their fifties brought in. They didn't even look like they could carry a rifle. They were being punished. I asked the other [ISIS] guys why they were there. They trusted me so they told me that these men's sons were fighting with the Free Syrian Army. I said to myself that it wasn't their fault and walked away. Later on, they beheaded and hung them in the town square. They took photos and spread them around—just because their sons were serving in the Free Syrian Army."

We encourage Ibn Ahmed to tell us more about what he witnessed and he obliges.

"Another older man had ten members in his family. He went to the *emir* of finance/treasury in another village and said, 'We're starving and have nothing.' The *emir* answered him, 'The Prophet [Muhammad] used to tightly tie a stone to his stomach and the hunger pains would go away. Why don't you try that? Allah be with you.' The old man headed home with tears in his eyes."

This treasury chief in Ibn Ahmed's story was quoting from the *Hadith* of al-Bukhari, but we see another twisted ISIS interpretation. According to *Sheikh* Ali [the Iraqi former al-Qaeda member and Islamic scholar who helped me in Iraq], the Bukhari *Hadith* does tell this story. However, as *Sheikh* Ali explains, the Prophet Mohammad would never have responded to the poverty of a supplicant in such a cold-hearted manner and would have condemned the Chief of Finance for his greed and lack of care. *Sheikh* Ali wrote to me, "If the Prophet and his Companions tied a stone on their stomachs this means that the treasury was empty, which according to the incidents of the life of the Prophet you will definitely find happened many times. But that treasury was mainly founded to satisfy the needs of the poor. Moreover, when the treasury was empty, the Companions and the Prophet gave alms to the poor from their own money."

"I remember one day there was a truck that was going to Iraq through Tartoos," Ibn Ahmed tells us. "It had six passengers. ISIS stopped them at a checkpoint and asked them where they were from and they said, 'Latakia [a port city in Syria] and we're going to Iraq carrying cargo.' They were asked to leave the vehicle and asked if they pray. They said they did. ISIS asked how many times a day they prayed. There was a conflict. They put all six of them on the highway median, then shot and killed them. A car came to take their bodies and they [the ISIS fighters] stole their truck."

"Another thing that happened—the wheat, the wheat silos ended up going to the regime—to Latakia," Ibn Ahmed tells us. So, while the ISIS treasurer did not provide food for the hungry in their areas, ISIS leadership sold the wheat stores under their control to the Assad regime. The hypocrisy is unbelievable.

We force ourselves back to Conoco. "You said almost all the prisoners were women?"

"Yes, and there's a section that is a regular prison for thieves. I was assigned to the women's section."

"Can you tell us about how life is there? What did you feed the prisoners? Were they tortured? How did the captives feel?" we ask, trying to encourage Ibn Ahmed to return to the horrors of the prison—although a part of me doesn't want to hear any more of it.

"The [female] prisoners were sure that they would be killed. This made convincing them to go with the foreign fighters much easier when compared to the prospect of death," Ibn Ahmed explains. But he says at some point the women put up some resistance. "There was a time when they were on hunger strike. ISIS fighters then told them, 'You're Muslims like us and we'll take you back home.' So they started eating again. Then after a while they were given as captives again," continuing their sexual enslavement.

Ibn Ahmed turns to our question about food and other issues of daily life in the prison, "They would make them rice, and pasta, and they were given water. For a while they were in their own clothes that they arrived in. They brought them clothes every now and then. Black clothes and an *abaya*." So, even the sex slaves had to wear the regulation ISIS clothing.

"What about the bathrooms?" Murat asks, to get to the details of the prison.

"The bathrooms were off to the side. She'd shower in private," Ibn Ahmed tells us.

"The women captives, you said there were four hundred. Can you give us more details about them?"

"From Iraq, about fifty—they were soldiers' wives."

"They were Yazidis?" we ask.

"No, soldiers' wives and wives of militiamen."

"Sunnis?" we make sure again.

"Yes. From Raqqa, there were wives of [Assad's] soldiers. Yazidis, they brought about three hundred. There were another fifty from other areas in Syria."

Ibn Ahmed is re-confirming that the sex slaves are not all Yazidis—which is horrible enough—but many of them were also Sunni women enslaved and offered for rape, a practice that violates the very writings of ISIS on the subject of female enslavement.

"Among the women captives, where there also Christians?" I ask.

"Not as far as I know in Conoco. But they bring them from everywhere. But in Conoco, I already told you what I know."

"These women—some were widowed, some had their children taken away from them as you mentioned—they are raped; what is their mental state?" we ask.

"Of course, you see her sitting in the corner with her head down, tears in her eyes. She doesn't really sleep properly. She just huddles in the corner," Ibn Ahmed answers. Murat watches him closely and types into chat that he looks deeply ashamed. His voice sounds wracked by guilt.

"Tell us the story about the Yazidi woman and the foreign fighter with a gun," Abu Said, our fixer prompts. He knows this story from having talked to the defector beforehand, and now prompts him to tell it to us.

"This person was a foreign fighter. He was Tunisian. He went into the room to rape her."

"Was she his captive?" Murat asks.

"No, he just liked her. So he went in and put his handgun to one side and left the room to wash up. She was in the corner, terrified. When he came back she took the gun and shot him in the head." I admit that I smile in satisfaction hearing that—cheering her on, in fact.

"So when she killed him, what did ISIS do to her?"

"She killed him and they said she ran away. There was a story I heard, which I believe is true, that there were Free Syrian Army cells that helped her get away to safety," Ibn Ahmed explains. He sounds pleased with this story.

"I'm sure you heard the women talking. What did they say among themselves? What conversations were held?" Murat asks.

"I heard some of them tell each other to be patient. That maybe they would be released because they are Muslims. Others said, 'No, they will behead us.' Another asked, 'Is it possible they will let us go back to our children, because they are an Islamic State after all?' They were shocked at the rape and ill-treatment."

"Have you witnessed torture and interrogation of these women?" we ask—as though institutionalized, systemic, and repeated raping isn't torture enough.

"I remember an incident when foreign fighters went to pick. One of the women spit on them. They took her outside in the hallway and kicked her and stepped on her stomach until she started bleeding and then they threw her back in the prison." Again I admit finding myself pleased that the woman had the courage to spit on her captors, although the punishment sounds like it wasn't worth the satisfaction it temporarily brought.

"When you went home on your break and spoke to your family, your wife helped you decide to leave? Or was it you alone?" Murat asks.

"I decided to leave because I saw how the women were tortured and I considered them my sisters. Then my sisters and wife encouraged me and said to me, 'Imagine if we were in there? What would you do?' So I decided to leave and Allah helped us."

"Do you remember other stories from that prison?"

"I remember they brought one woman from Raqqa because her husband was with the Syrian regime. ISIS went to her house and took her away from her children and brought her to Conoco. Her father-in-law came to try and get her out. Of course he was elderly. He said he wanted to free this woman and they asked how he was related to her. [When] he answered that her husband was his son, they beheaded him. They asked a fighter to bury the body far away." It appears that in ISIS, family members often pay the price of their family member's supposed transgression— which makes me worry again for Ahmet's family. *They need to get out of Turkey and soon!*

"When you were working with the *hisbah* – how did they treat women?" we ask.

"As infidels," Ibn Ahmed answers.

"If they saw someone not dressed appropriately?"

"First of all they take her and flog her."

"So you'd take her with you?" Murat asks.

"Yes."

"But how can you take her—as [male] strangers?" Murat challenges.

"She has to be punished," Ibn Ahmed answers, defiant, even now after being out of ISIS.

"But religiously you don't have the right to take her since you're strangers," Murat pushes back.

"No, it's allowed because she's not with a man to begin with. I'll have to punish her. So I'll have to take her to be punished." Ibn Ahmed may be a defector, but he hasn't totally shaken the "listen and obey" mentality he had under ISIS as he repeats it now for us.

"So you're arresting her because she's alone or with a strange man. But you are a strange man. As far as I know that's not allowed [under *shariah* law]. How is that allowed?" Murat challenges again and I wonder to myself how this will play out.

"You're obliged to carry out orders without arguing," Ibn Ahmed's answer cuts to the heart of the matter. Inside ISIS, no one but the leaders are allowed to think things through.

"When ISIS first came in and started teaching you about your religion, how did you feel?"

"To be honest we were happy. We thought we were in a different world. They make poor and rich equal. No one will want for anything. They taught us prayer—religion. We felt very comfortable. [Then] we noticed they were all talk and no action."

"What's your biggest regret about being in ISIS?" we ask.

"The thing I think about most is that I shouldn't have left," Ibn Ahmed says, totally shocking us. Then he adds, "I should have gone to each room and sprayed [them with bullets] and died. That's it." *So he believes in 'martyrdom'?* I think to myself. *Maybe some things are worth 'martyring' yourself for? While I generally don't support violence, some agents of violence and genocide maybe need to be killed—even if it means losing your own life to fight them.*

"How do you see your future?"

"I felt happy when I got to Turkey," Ibn Ahmet's voice brightens. "I see my future *after* ISIS leaves and I can go home." I agree with him— ISIS cannot be chased out of Syria and Iraq fast enough. Although we both know, given the proxy war that ISIS plays out between the Gulf States and Iran, and the corruption in Turkey and Syria that provides support to ISIS, their presence may be long, and their defeat difficult.

"So who do you think is behind ISIS?" Murat asks.

"Iran, Russia and the [Syrian] regime," Ibn Ahmed answers, adding, "I won't change my statement because I'm one hundred percent sure."

"How so?" we challenge, because Iran, Russia and the Syrian regime are all on the Shia side of the Sunni/Shia divide and ISIS is a Sunni and Takfiri group.

"Most of the [ISIS] *sheikhs* speak in a Shia accent, which is the Iraqi accent. You hear them say one thing and do another on the ground. That's why we're sure it's Iran, Russia, and the regime behind ISIS," he answers. "I'll give you another reason why I'm sure. Both Iraq/Maliki and Iran gave ISIS weapons. The Syrian regime is still giving up ISIS areas, like Palmyra, without a fight. Russia still hits the Free Syrian Army and doesn't hit ISIS." We hear it so many times that I begin to wonder if these things are not more than just the results of bad intel or what happens in the heat of battle. It's hard to avoid considering the conspiracy theories when data keeps being spewed out in support.

"How did ISIS get their weapons? Who did you think was supporting you?"

"I noticed every time ISIS took ground from the Free Syrian Army, then the [Assad] regime would give up an area where weapons were kept," Ibn Ahmed echoes the common view among many of our ISIS defectors that the Assad regime and ISIS are working together to fight the uprising. (Indeed, it later comes out in captured documents that the two trade in oil.[80)]

"For example," Ibn Ahmed continues, "when ISIS took Deir ez-Zor, the [Assad] regime gave up the al-Maylabiya checkpoint in al-Hasakah. There were enough weapons to arm five thousand fighters. The regime also pulled out their Air Force and personnel and ISIS took over."

"Do you think there are ISIS recruits in the refugee camp inside

Turkey?" we move to another topic of great importance. "Do they have any influence there?"

"In the camp, not at all. Some give different opinions, but those refugees haven't returned to Syria after ISIS. They might think ISIS is right. But I don't think there are [active ISIS] supporters in the camp."

"Do you fear speaking about ISIS inside the camp?"

"Most of the refugee camp hates them. They speak openly about how much they hate them. They say it isn't Islam. The moment ISIS leaves, they hope to go home. They hate ISIS more than the Syrian regime." Tragically, this is very telling—that the Syrian uprising has now resulted in an even more hated enemy.

"Did ISIS ever recruit someone from the camp?" we ask, pressing the point.

"No, because they [ISIS] are surrounded [in Syria]," Ibn Ahmed believes that ISIS cadres inside Syria cannot get into Turkey now. We know from other stories that he is wrong—but it's his belief and we don't challenge it. "There are some ISIS who want to escape. If they get to Idlib [a northwestern Syrian city], they run into the Free Syrian Army. If they are caught they'll be killed. If they try to leave through Tell Abyad, then the Kurds will catch them and kill them. That's why they are stuck now. It's hard for them to get out." He does have a point on that—it's become much more difficult in recent times for ISIS to reach all the areas that they used to control along the Turkish border.

"Have you been in touch with anyone from ISIS that's trying to escape but can't?" We've learned that there's actually a lot of communication between the defectors and those still inside and living under ISIS—when they can get Internet. When there is communication the refugees and defectors learn what continues to unfold inside ISIS from those left behind.

"No, there's no phone signal there," Ibn Ahmed answers. "We ask civilian refugees what's happening there. They told us ISIS recruits are trying to leave, but can't."

"What I meant was, do you think ISIS can recruit inside the refugee camp?" Murat asks, wanting to revisit our earlier question that we feel remains particularly important. Ibn Ahmed's answer remains the same, "No, not at all. No one likes them in the refugee camp."

"What do you know about Abu Bakr al-Baghdadi?" we hope he might have seen the elusive leader of ISIS.

"I only know that he is the Caliph. We only hear that he's going to establish the Islamic State and that kind of thing. In the beginning we were convinced and tricked; but later we realized this was not true. For example, if you go to my neighborhood [in Syria] it's very, very poor. So where is the Islamic State? Where is all the *zakat* [charity] and oil money? Billions of dollars and people are starving. If someone says they are hungry, they say, 'Tie a rock to your stomach!' Take the refugee camp [in Turkey] for example, if ISIS left [Syria] then it would be empty. Most of the refugees fled [Syria] because of ISIS."

Even though Ibn Ahmed personally witnessed all of these horrors and turned his back on ISIS, he still respects the *sheikh* that recruited him into ISIS. That makes us curious. "Tell us more about your *Sheikh* Jazrawi...why do you [still] like him?" we prompt.

"He is a man who opens up the Qur'an and teaches about prayer and *wudu* [Islamic cleansing]. He starts with you from scratch. He gives advice and will help people in need." Yet this man who did help Ibn Ahmed, is part of a group that denies food to the poor while selling it to their enemies. In defense of his ISIS teacher, Ibn Ahmed adds, "He's also been tricked [by ISIS]. I felt like he didn't know what was really going on out there. I didn't dare tell him what was really happening in Conoco."

We realize we are deep into this interview and have yet to touch on the other deeply disturbing subject—suicide bombers. "Do you know anything about the suicide bombers?" and wonder if he had direct experience with them.

"Suicide bombers are kept in a station where the high-ranking *emirs* are. Local fighters are not allowed near that station. They have a list of these bombers. It's very organized. Their names are put on a list with the date of their bombing. No one can see them. Wherever ISIS tells them to go, they will. For example, if they are told to go bomb the Free Syrian Army, they will."

I try to imagine being put on a list for 'martyrdom'. I know from interviewing suicide bombers who wore their vests but were arrested before they could detonate, that the terror of contemplating taking one's own life in an explosion seems to kick off a powerful sense of euphoria.[81] I also saw these same phenomena induced in a "thought experiment" I conducted in Belgium with university students who were asked to role play that they had been suicide bombers caught and imprisoned at the last minute, before being able to carry out an attack. When asked to imagine how they felt putting on their suicide vest—half of them said things like they were suddenly overwhelmed with a feeling of bliss, that they became dissociative and began floating above their bodies, or felt greatly empowered.[82] Perhaps if one is indoctrinated enough into the 'martyrdom' ideology, the hope of Paradise coupled with what appears to be an endorphin-induced effect, keeps them in a blissful, calm, and determined state through the moment they are ordered to go and detonate themselves.

"How old are these bombers?" we ask.

"They are young. Twenty-seven, seventeen, nineteen."

"Their nationalities?"

"Mostly Chechens, Tunisians and Kazakhs. There are some from the Arabian Peninsula, from Saudi Arabia."

"Do you really think foreign fighters are there to be 'martyrs' or for something else?" we ask.

"Foreign fighters really came because they thought it was a true Islamic state and jihad. When they sat with the *sheikhs* they were brainwashed with a few passages from the Qur'an. Passages that focused on women captives and fighting the apostates. The moment they sit together, the foreign fighters are told to 'listen and obey.' 'You will kill when we tell you to kill.'"

"How did the foreign fighters—the Europeans for example—treat you?" we ask.

"The Europeans, they think they are coming to protect the Syrian people," Ibn Ahmed echoes other ISIS defectors' views. "The foreign fighter would go to the frontlines and fight the Free Syrian Army. They think the Free Syrian Army is the same as the Syrian regime because they fight back."

"So the foreign fighters don't really know who they are fighting against?"

"They don't. When they first came to Deir ez-Zor, they said they freed it from the regime. They thought they were fighting the regime, but it was the Free Syrian Army."

Our interview time is almost over—Ibn Ahmed needs to leave while there is still a lot of activity and before dark to go unnoticed from our meeting place and back to his home. Ahmet and I would like to talk to him much longer, but it isn't possible. That we have been able to interview an ISIS cadre who personally witnessed the enslavement and organized rape of hundreds of women is totally amazing to us. Ibn Ahmed also is knowledgeable about the suicide bombers. While each interview contains nuggets of fascinating information and another piece in a puzzle we are trying to piece together, Ibn Ahmed, we feel, has given us an entire section.

"So if I come to you now and say I want to join ISIS what would you tell me?" Murat asks.

"I'd tell you not to believe them and the moment you're there, they will put you through the training and you'll see rape and murder. You'll see torture and flogging. You'll see poverty and you can't do anything about it. And if you want to leave you'll be killed—or you do what they say, 'Listen and obey.' I'd advise you not to."

"What message do you have for anyone in the Arab world thinking of joining ISIS?"

"In the name of Allah, the Most Gracious, the Most Merciful. I advise all Arab men not to come to Syria. Those who wish to come to ISIS should think about the rape and killing of the poor and the oppression. If you think about leaving, they will kill you. Once you get into the sand, it'll turn into quicksand—as soon as you're in it, you'll drown. That's why I wouldn't advise anyone to come. No one should come because once you join, you'll have to kill and rape. It's not an Islamic state."

Chapter Thirteen - A Father's Daring Rescue

T he horror of the November 2015 Paris attacks still hangs in the air as we gather in Tariq's apartment in a European city—a location I have agreed not to disclose—in order to not place his daughter in greater danger than she already is. She is a rare, European ISIS defector and a bride of ISIS. "I am ready to do anything for my children," Tariq tells me as we begin our interview. It's just days after the deadly Paris attacks in which ISIS dispatched cadres—most of them originating from Belgium—to open fire on innocent civilians and carry out suicide attacks on multiple targets that included a rock concert and a soccer stadium. One hundred thirty people died and hundreds more were injured.[83]

Tariq and his family are Palestinian refugees who fled from Lebanon to Europe in the eighties during the Lebanese civil war. He and his wife, Sana, greet me warmly at the door of their fourth floor apartment. Sana is dressed in a rose colored *abaya* and is wearing a headscarf tied under her chin. Her smile is friendly, but she looks frightened about our meeting. Tariq is dressed in khaki pants and a button-down shirt. They invite me in and tell me that their daughter, Laila, will arrive soon.

Janni, the police chief in their city, introduced me to them over the phone. I know Janni from giving a counter-radicalization talk to their police force and I've asked him for European leads on our *ISIS Defectors Interviews Project* as I do in every country I visit. Janni is also a trusted confidant of the family who tried, unsuccessfully, to prevent Laila's husband from going to Syria, and helped them while Laila was living under ISIS control. I'm now capitalizing on all that trust he has built with Laila's family.

"We are a good family. We don't have any problems," Tariq

quickly informs me after we are seated on low divans around a blonde wood coffee table. I've taken my laptop out and after getting their permission, I take notes as I listen with great interest, having been given this rare opportunity to talk to an actual European "bride of ISIS" who escaped. Most do not.

Sana quietly serves us tea and a few snacks as she lets her husband do all the talking. They speak multiple languages fluently and their English is good enough that we don't need an interpreter. "We have three daughters and one son. Three are married and are here in Europe. One lived in Lebanon for three years, but she returned now," Tariq tells me, as his face wrinkles into an anxious expression. "We are a very simple family with *no* problems." He seems to want to make sure I understand that it was not their family that drove his daughter into her current situation. "Then our youngest daughter, Laila, fell in love with this man," his expression darkens, recalling Mohammed, the young man who took his daughter to Syria—to join ISIS.

"We didn't know anything about him at first," Tariq explains, rubbing his hand through his black head of hair, that familiar gesture of angst we've seen so many times throughout this project. "She met him in the town, with social media." Even though he's now transplanted to Europe, daughters meeting men over the Internet isn't the way it's supposed to work in Tariq's Palestinian culture. According to tradition, the girl's parents are supposed to pick good families with sons of the right age and moral pedigree and do the introductions. No one is forced to marry, but the parents chose the pool of potential recruits from which their daughters can chose. He continues, "We didn't know anything about him. We didn't know anything about his life," Tariq says, shaking his head in disbelief; to not know the family of the man his daughter became involved with is an anathema to him. "I didn't agree in the beginning," then he reminds himself—as he continues, "In this country freedom is the first priority. I cannot say no to my daughter. We live in Europe, not an Arabic country anymore."

Tariq and his wife found themselves forced to accept the new ways in Europe. His daughter went behind his back, met and dated Mohammed, and eventually fell in love and married him. So, even though it violated their cultural traditions, Laila's father allowed her to choose her own mate when she felt ready. But departing from the old ways has dangers, and in this case the danger was in Mohammed's long-term intentions that were unknown to them.

"Slowly, step by step," Tariq tells me, "we learned that he had been thinking to go to Syria. First, after the engagement he tried to go several times. But Laila phoned to Turkey and she got him back."

I know this part of the story as Janni and his colleagues briefed me before I made this appointment. Laila is well known to them because she had called their special intervention team for help when her then fiancé told her he wanted to leave for Syria to join ISIS.

"You've got to help me," she had told the police. "I don't know what to do." Janni, the police officer who was in charge of the counter-radicalization effort, was a warm-hearted man who calmed Laila down, and instructed her to try to talk Mohammed out of it, keep a strict eye on him, and call immediately if he made a move—which Laila did the minute she learned that Mohammed had gotten on a plane.

"He's left! He's on a plane to Istanbul," Laila had reported to Janni between fearful sobs. Istanbul at the time was, and still is, the gateway for militant jihadis from all around the world to join the various rebel groups in the Sunni uprising against Syria's dictator, as well as the gateway to joining ISIS. Taking that route into Syria, one flew first to Istanbul, continued on by plane or bus to Ahmet's Turkish town, Şanlıurfa (Urfa), and then met up with the "brothers"—*Jabat al-Nusrah, Jaysh al-Hur* or ISIS—who helped their new recruits cross the porous southern Turkish border into Syria.

Mohammed would have continued on to Şanlıurfa but for Laila's phone call to the police, which resulted in his uncle intervening in Turkey and convincing him to return home. But the so-called ISIS "Caliphate had captured Mohammed's imagination" and his wish to join ISIS continued even after they were married.

"He gave her two choices," Tariq tells me—divorce or go with him. "If she didn't want to join ISIS, she would have the right to leave. Mohammed gave her this choice and she believed it," Tariq grimaces. It's something he's obviously gone over and over in his mind—how any daughter of his could have gone to join a terrorist group. "What I believe is," he explains, "she was twenty-one and this is the first love in her life. It's living tragedy and drama—all girls of this age are in their dreams. He is the first man and the best." Tariq's voice drops off.

How naïve and trusting his daughter was to believe that she should follow her husband into terrorist territory. But at the same time, Tariq raised his daughter to respect her husband, and she agreed to follow him, even if it meant into danger.

"She didn't tell me because she knows that if she tells me I will kill him! She knows before they married I was not comfortable." At this point I assume, but am not totally sure, that Tariq is speaking only figuratively— he has such fire in his voice as he says it. He's clearly still very angry over what this young man did to his daughter, and now the state is preparing charges against her.

Tariq explains the logistics of their leaving. "I was in Lebanon when they flew to Turkey. I was visiting my mother, she was sick!" The anger and the anguish in his voice is clear over being betrayed by his son-in-law, and lied to by his daughter, at a time when his aging mother needed him. As a son, he was dutifully tending to his elderly mother, only to return home and learn he lost his daughter. Tariq can't accept that he was absent at a time when his daughter needed him to step in and stop her. "My wife called me in Lebanon to say, 'Laila has gone with Mohammed.'"

"How did you figure it out? Laila didn't come home at night?" I ask, turning to Sana. I've learned from countless interviews with shocked and grieving parents of terrorists around the world that this is a typical way parents will learn that their son or daughter has gone on a suicide mission, or these days in Europe, that their child left for Syria and Iraq. The normal routines are disrupted. Their son or daughter doesn't arrive home on time and the worrying vigil begins—until they learn the shocking news.

"His sister knew, his sister told my wife," Tariq's voice is flat. Remembering his pain and panic, he sounds dull and powerless; though at the time he sprang into action as soon as he learned the news. "I took a plane from Beirut to Istanbul, and on to Gaziantep [a neighboring city to Şanlıurfa] to catch them near the border. I talked to her from Lebanon first."

"'I have to go with my husband,' she told me when I got her on the phone. 'I have to live with him. He explained that life will be good there. I can live as a normal person. It won't be dangerous,'" Tariq is incredulous, recalling her words. "She doesn't know about war," he shakes his head because he knows—having lived through the Lebanese wars in the eighties. "She only knows war on TV! Him too, he's in Rambo thinking!"

"'We are waiting for someone, to go in,' she told me by phone while I was in Gaziantep." By "someone" Laila was referring to the smugglers and guides ISIS uses to bring foreign fighters across the Turkish border into Syria. "'I love you Baba [Daddy]! I love my family, but I have to go with my husband,' she told me. 'Nothing is going to happen. We are going to help the children and work as civilians.' She was crying. I knew it was not going to be that way. I couldn't talk her out of it. I didn't have a chance to stop her." Sadness fills his eyes and voice. "I arrived two hours too late."

"Were you able to stay in touch?" I softly ask.

"She had Turkish Internet," because they settled in Syria close to the border, Tariq explains. "I tried. I stayed one week. I tried to talk her into coming out. No chance. She was still crying very much, but she was determined. She didn't know that once in, she couldn't come back again. She told me how Mohammed said to invite me. I said, 'No thank you, I know the situation very well in Syria, I have been many times,'" bitterness again fills his voice.

"At that time, Laila didn't feel any danger. They were living in al-Bab, in the city. There were restaurants and it was normal life at first. She sent pictures of herself in a restaurant. After two months they got an apartment. They rented it from a civilian man, [even though] the city was under *Daesh* control. He was a Syrian man who lived in Turkey." Tariq uses the derogatory name for ISIS. The Syrian, it turns out, didn't want to be part of ISIS, so he had fled to Istanbul but he kept relations good enough with the ISIS fighters, so through relatives he managed to rent out his apartment to ISIS fighters and the like.

"She has Internet there. At that time, she called every day saying, 'I'm sorry Mama, I have to be with my husband,' and she's crying but she stayed."

"After two months she got pregnant," Tariq says, his voice sounding devastated.

Yet I ask, "Were you happy about this?" I can't help wondering if becoming grandparents would outweigh the horror of their daughter living under ISIS.

"At that time no, we were not happy," Tariq answers, his voice flat. It's clear he is very much a family man but these were not the circumstances for celebrating new life. "They were happy. But I was not happy. They said they have what they need, but we were afraid for her." Tariq throws his hands in the air as he asks, "This baby, if born in Syria, which kinds of papers will he carry? She can't carry the child out to see us! It's useless! I am losing her because she will not get out without her baby. I can't get a baby out of Syria without the father agreeing," reflecting his immediate recognition of Arab customs and laws. "While Europeans believe it's her son, it's not like that in Syria. But what has happened has happened. She tells us she is very happy," Tariq smiles wanly.

Indeed, later in March of 2016, I will hear a story from European police who tell me of a woman they tried to guide, by phone, out of Syria to escape with her child born inside ISIS territory. When she got to a checkpoint near the border the police received news from their embassy in Turkey, with whom the police had been coordinating closely, only to learn that it would be impossible for their European embassy in Turkey to issue the child's passport without both parents being present and proof that the child is actually hers. "But the father is a fighter in ISIS and the mother and child are escaping! The child was born under ISIS!" the policeman argued to no avail with his embassy consular officer. Rules were rules.

Many modern, Western countries have created laws that bar a mother or father from obtaining a new passport for their child without both parents being present. Such laws were made so that neither parent can abduct their child out of the country during divorces and custody disputes. But in the case of a child born in ISIS-held territory, this policy is counter-productive and traps the child in Syria and Iraq unless both parents are present and willing to risk escape—which traps women who want to escape with their children born inside ISIS—unless they are willing to abandon their children. In this tragic case, the police informed the mother of the dilemma in obtaining a passport for her child born in Syria and that there were no exceptions. So she turned back to stay with ISIS rather than escape with a child who she couldn't legally return to Europe.

"So I made another plan in my mind," Tariq continues as he tells me about Laila's pregnancy under ISIS. "I know her husband has brainwashed her a bit, so I will clean it, and give her the correct information. Let me explain—she is not endorsing much of [extremist] Islam except for the relationship between husband and wife, that a wife should follow her husband even if he goes to hell. So, I try to explain to her, 'Yes, you should follow your husband—but not to death, not to a war zone, not to stupidity.' And she started to believe me."

"Do you know what Mohammed's role in ISIS was?" I ask.

"I don't know exactly," Tariq answers. "She said he was going out. She told me at that time Mohammed was helping with the food, that he brings food to the fighters. He was like a cook, a delivery guy. Mohammed went out of the town from time to time, to carry guns to the fighters."

At this point the interview becomes sensitive. Laila's trial will be held soon and she and her parents need to be careful about how much they admit. As a bride of a fighter, ISIS would automatically consider Laila part of their group; but in the European country she has returned to, all that matters now—in terms of her prosecution—is if there is evidence that she actually committed crimes. This European country won't prosecute her for simply having gone to Syria; but having joined and supported ISIS is a crime, and if she signed on to be part of the *hisbah,* as many foreign women do, or took on another role in ISIS, she and her family should not admit to that. It could lead, not only to a conviction, but also a more serious sentence. As usual I don't want anyone to incriminate themselves for our research.

At this point in the interview, Laila arrives home. She had agreed to this interview with me, and her father called her home to meet me. Like her mother, Laila is dressed in a full-length *abaya,* sky blue in her case, and a matching headscarf tied neatly under her chin. If she was formerly wearing the drab, black burka and *niqab* of ISIS women, she's now abandoned it. She's also very heavily pregnant—due in only ten days time, which makes her appear vulnerable, though she looks healthy and strong.

Laila's face is open and she has a kind smile as she peers at me from her wide, almond-shaped eyes. I can see that she's trying to take my measure as well. Janni, the policeman who sent me, has her full trust. So she, like her parents, immediately trusts that I don't have any intentions to twist her words or sensationalize her story.

"I'm so sorry about your husband," I tell her while I stretch out my hand in greeting. I already knew that her husband had been killed while they were in Syria. She shakes hands with me and takes a chair across the coffee table near her mother, ready to join in the interview.

Our conversation continues with Tariq explaining how Laila's husband was killed, "They told her he was in a building with some of their group. American planes flew overhead and bombed them. He was killed. Three of the guys were wounded and they took them to the hospital. The rest were buried alive. No one saw anything."

Although I've totally fallen for Tariq, I'd like Laila to take over now and tell her story in her own words. He's clearly a father who is protective of his family and I know that he's the one who got Laila out, so in my eyes he's already a hero. I don't want to offend him, so I turn gently to her and ask in a very soft voice, "You were pregnant at the time, how far along?" hoping she will pick up the conversation.

"I was five months pregnant," she answers and begins to explain. "I knew it was a dangerous area. I didn't hope so, but I knew he may be killed," she says, referring to the common practice among ISIS brides to want their husbands—and even themselves—to be 'martyred' in order to earn Paradise, and for those left behind to earn a place of honor in the group. Laila is signaling she wasn't of their beliefs.

"So you didn't want him to become a 'martyr'?" I ask to be certain.

"He believed he was a 'martyr'," she answers, making it clear that her husband shared those beliefs. She also appears uncomfortable discussing what his eternal status might actually be—given he may have mistakenly given up his life for nothing. "I was against everything," she explains, "But it was hard to let him go [to Syria] alone. We were a new couple. It was very difficult to leave him. I was trying to stop him. I called the police. He was determined. He was upset," her staccato statements trail off as her voice becomes small and powerless.

"Living in two cultures is hard," Tariq interjects. He's reluctant to give up the floor, having told their story so far. "Some families don't take care of their children. The freedom of which they sing in Europe—they let their children grow up free—but then try to say no later." Tariq clicks his tongue in the Arabic style of saying "no." In his mind, this Western way of raising children doesn't work. "Mohammed's father is like that. He had good parents. They work and try to make money, but he did what he wanted."

"When he was with his friends he lived a moral life," Tariq continues. "Then he started to go away from them. He went back and forth between the two." This is often the rub with Muslim, immigrant families. For Muslims growing up in Western culture a strong tension exists between conservative Islam and Western freedoms. If their friends drink and smoke pot, wear revealing clothing, have sex—all things forbidden in conservative Muslim culture—then the youth have to somehow find a way to walk a tightrope between the two. It's difficult not to disappoint their parents and seemingly fail their Islamic heritage, and still fit in and succeed among their Western peers.

For some it only works to create a double identity—and this hidden "sinful" self is something terrorist recruiters in Europe know how to manipulate. On the one hand they push their recruits into deeper devotion to Islam, while peddling an extremist version of it, and also encourage them to live a secret life in which they begin to plot against the West while allowing them to keep up their Western "vices" of criminality, drinking, using drugs, having sex, etc. The terrorist recruiters tell them that its fine to cheat and rob from the *kafirs* [unbelievers] among whom they live and deceive them by living their Western lifestyle, but that when the time comes they should cleanse themselves and wash away their "sins" through 'martyrdom' and terrorist attacks against the West.

When I was in London, I learned of an al-Qaeda recruiter who was taking gang kids on weeklong camping trips teaching them that they could continue their lives of criminality but that they should convert to Islam, give a portion of their "war booty" to the extremist cause, and be on call for 'martyrdom' because if they died in the gang lifestyle without Islam, they were going to hell. But if they converted and joined the terrorist group while contributing a portion of their "spoils" of criminality to the "brothers" [i.e. al-Qaeda], they wouldn't simply die a gang-related death, but die a 'martyr' and win all the rewards of 'martyrdom'.[84] It seems Mohammed might also have suffered confusion between his two worlds and gravitated into extremism in one of them.

"He read on the Internet how to be a good Muslim," Laila jumps to defend Mohammed and try to explain where he picked up on the pro-ISIS ideas. "He also went to a *Salafi* mosque," a fundamentalist strain of Islam. "Although, I think most of it came from the Internet, because when he went to the mosque, he made his *salah* [prayers] and went home. He didn't spend a lot of hours there. But he was on *YouTube*, etc." Likely, Mohammed was watching ISIS recruiting videos—exactly the type of online recruiting that we hope our videos will work against.

Salah Abdesalam, one of the Paris attackers living in Belgium, also lived a double life. He was known to watch jihadi videos while smoking joints. He and his brother both had suicide vests for their 'martyrdom' attacks in Paris, but while Salah's brother, Ibrahim, carried out his suicide attack, Salah—a not-so-true believer—apparently chickened out, ditched his vest in a trash can, and returned to Belgium. He was apprehended in a Brussels neighborhood where I had been conducting an interview only minutes before. But that's a story for a later chapter.[85]

"He was not stable," Tariq adds. "Sometimes you'd find him in the disco and other times in the mosque." Mohammed, it sounds, had the typical double identity of a Muslim growing up in a conservative family and relaxed Western society.

The police have already shared with me that those who went to Syria from Laila's neighborhood, nearly all attended an extremist mosque in the community. It doesn't mean the mosque is sending them, but their radical *Salafi* message may be one that is supportive of ISIS thinking, reinforcing its rhetoric rather than opposing it. This, too, is a difficult issue for *Salafi* Islamic preachers facing ISIS. They want to teach their scriptures and conservative interpretations of Islam, but when they do, they face the possibility that these will be twisted by groups like ISIS in ways that adherents find hard to question, because they originally learned them as "the truth". Terrorist groups like ISIS are adept at building upon existing dogma to make their extremist message acceptable in the minds of those they wish to poison. For instance, Islam teaches that on the day of judgment, sins will be weighed against good deeds, hell exists, and martyrdom wipes away one's sins. These widely held fears and beliefs provide the terrorist group with a religious basis to sell suicidal terrorist attacks as a form of 'martyrdom' that can cleanse a person of his sins. Likewise, pride in the former Islamic Caliphate and hope of someday restoring it, is also manipulated by groups like ISIS.

"How about you?" I turn back to Laila. "Did you also party with him?" I ask, knowing that many Muslims end up joining extremist groups as a means of trying to cleanse themselves from past "sins.""I did many sins," Laila answers, her face very serious.

"Partying?" I probe, realizing this is highly awkward to explore in front of her parents. She nods, but doesn't divulge details. Who knows? She may have slept around, had an abortion, done drugs, or been drunk a lot—but I don't want to ask her these kind of questions point blank while her mom and dad are listening in. I decide to digress.

"Was Mohammed scared about his sins?" I ask.

"Yes," she answers solemnly. We both get stuck there, as I can't ask her why exactly, without possibly putting her in a bad spot in front of her parents.

"Do you know how he became convinced to join ISIS?" I decide to avoid any more discussion of either of their "sins" in front of her parents. I may be able to meet her again, alone, and I can ask more then.

"I don't know what was the beginning," Laila says. She looks me in the eye as she talks and seems to be very willing to openly discuss their lives in ISIS. It appears that she is sincere and has truly walked away from it, and now has very little to hide about that part of her life at least. "He saw many videos of why they should come and be there. He believed it would be good for the afterlife. He didn't care for the life now. He was willing to die. On the Internet they convinced him of 'martyrdom'."

"Were you convinced?" I ask, trying to keep the horror I feel out of my voice, as I look at this lovely young and pregnant woman and imagine her young husband so willing to give up his future, this future.

"I was not thinking like that," Laila answers.

"He wanted to be a fighter when he got there?"

"Yes," she answers in a soft, calm voice. "He was obsessed to live there."

"So it was exciting for him?"

"Yes, he was excited."

"And you?"

"Everything was new for me and I was scared," she admits, as she relaxes a bit. "It was a city that they had control over, so there was not fighting going on there."

"How did you feel about going to Syria to join them?" I ask, trying to get at her side of things.

"I didn't want to go there, but I couldn't leave him," she repeats, sounding like a young girl still in love—maybe even more in love now that Mohammed has been killed. This in fact, could create a vulnerability in her as well—to taking on 'martyrdom' if she was traumatically bereaved enough to want to join him in death. "He was not like other religious guys. He was kind to me, and our relationship didn't change," she says, referring to how hard some extremists can be on their women.

"Did Mohammed make his *bayat* [pledge of allegiance] to them?"

I ask.

"Yes," she answers.

"Did you make your *bayat* also?" I ask, before realizing that this is an incriminating question.

"I didn't have to make *bayat*, but was for a month in a sisters' house," Laila says, referring to the time when Mohammed was away for his *shariah* and military training with ISIS. "Most of that time I was sitting alone. I was scared to get to know people. I didn't think I had much in common with them. They were too much like my husband. They would talk about [Islamic] clothes too much, about how the women should dress, and following all the rules." Laila smiles self-consciously, "I wasn't like them."

"Was he changed when he returned?"

"No, he was the same." We talk a bit about the Syrians I've been interviewing who have fled ISIS and are now hiding in Turkey, about their observations about the Europeans and Westerners that come to ISIS. I ask Laila what she observed of the Europeans, since she had the advantage of sharing their language. I would also love to hear more about the other brides of ISIS.

"I didn't notice so much," she claims. "I wasn't there for a long time." She returns to the subject of her husband. "His job was not to fight," she notes. Perhaps Mohammed was simply a logistics guy, but if he went to both *shariah* and military training he certainly had trained to be able to fight with the others and very likely was required to behead his prisoner upon graduation from *shariah* training, like the others have told us. "He was very slowly going in, but when he was at home, he'd go out and play football," Laila explains, as though life inside ISIS was more or less the same as living in Europe.

I smile and ask her how she handled it when he was gone, how she went out—if she had to enlist another "sister" given she had no *mahram* [chaperone].

"I went out alone," Laila says. "They didn't stop me." I express surprise and she continues. "I wore *niqab* [the head and face covering], no one goes without."

"I thought it was forbidden for a woman to go out alone?" I ask.

Laila shrugs and tells me she did all her shopping in the market without worrying about having a chaperone. "I only knew a few Syrian people," she tells me. "That was enough for me."

Then it dawns on me that she is a native-born Arabic speaker and could, as a result, get around very easily on her own—as long as she didn't draw the attention of the *hisbah*. During subsequent interviews, we also learn that foreign fighters' wives don't require a chaperone so she wouldn't have gotten into trouble going out on her own—as long as she wore her thick *niqab*. We talk a bit about how speaking Arabic made her adjustment in Syria much easier for her than for most Europeans who go there.

I ask her more about her observations of life and violence under ISIS; about the beheadings, floggings and so on. "I heard stories, but I didn't see it," Laila answers innocently. "I thought it was horrible. There were punishments in the city but I didn't see it."

I find it hard to believe that she avoided all the horror, but she has no posttraumatic response to being asked about it. Perhaps becoming pregnant two months after arriving isolated her and she simply slept through a lot of it, as feeling exhausted is quite common during the early months of pregnancy.

"What about Mohammed, did he see these things?" I ask.

"He didn't talk about it if he saw it," Laila answers. She's amazingly calm—and believable. Then after considering, she adds in her soft voice, "I don't think he saw it either, because he would tell me. One time he saw a guy bring cigarettes. They burned the cigarettes and maybe put him in prison one day. But he wasn't afraid of them."

I return to her husband's death. "How did you learn he died?"

"Strangers coming to the door," Laila answers, her face suddenly contorting into grief—another sign that she likely wasn't lying earlier as her emotions are that close to the surface for things that did traumatize her. "They told me what happened. It felt like the building was shaking [when they told me]. A Syrian woman stayed with me. She took care of me. I was screaming so much."

"What did you do then?"

"I wanted to leave. When I started to ask about leaving they told me, 'You can leave. You just have to go and talk to them and leave.' But others said no. I didn't want to take the risk."

"Did you think they would pressure you to marry another ISIS fighter?" I ask, knowing that's likely the case.

"They said, 'We don't force you to marry again,' but I was scared of it. How can I live there without family? I don't have anyone. I was afraid of that risk. I didn't want to get married again," her eyes filling with fear.

"My father sent me three thousand dollars through Turkey and someone brought it across to al-Ab."

"How could he send you money?" I am incredulous at how some normal things—like transferring funds—can continue to function even in a terrorist zone.

"He sent it to a smuggler and that person took a five or ten percent commission. Also they [ISIS] gave me fifty dollars a month."

"Is that what Mohammed was paid by ISIS?"

"He was paid one hundred dollars a month," she corrects me. So as a widow, they remained true and paid her widow benefits—although only half his salary. "It was very cheap to live there. They gave him money for the rent, too."

"Did they provide a car?" I ask.

"Everyone that works with them gets a home. I don't think a car," Laila is speaking of the foreign fighters. I ask her to tell me more about the "sisters' house.

"The girls from the sisters' house, they were all married. All their husbands were in training, too." I share with her information from the other ISIS defectors about European girls gathering in a house in Raqqa to work the Internet to bring other Western girls into the group. I ask Laila if she was invited to talk other girls into coming? I want her to tell me about these European female recruiters, if she knows about them.

Laila shakes her head in consternation. "I didn't have a relation with them," she answers. "I didn't work with them. I lived as a civilian to the last moment. I kept my passport." ISIS cadres usually turn in or destroy their passports when they give their *bayat;* she is clarifying that she never formally joined ISIS. "They took Mohammad's passport. I don't think he minded," Laila adds. "I think he had a very good heart and believed that if he asks about it, then they will give it back to him."

"I heard a story of a Russian widow, her husband died, too," Laila volunteers. "She asked if she can go to Turkey to go see her mother for three days. She wanted to leave, but they didn't let her. When I heard that story, I didn't want to take the risk of asking them if I can go out. Maybe they will start watching me."

"I told her not to ask too much," Tariq jumps in. "They can transfer you or watch you. I was telling her, 'Be quiet, learn the situation, but be slow. Don't ask anyone [to leave]. Be quiet at home.'" Tariq was clever, guiding his daughter.

"I was scared," Laila explains. "I was crying too much on the telephone."

Meanwhile Tariq was plotting how to get his daughter out of ISIS' grasp. "It was like a movie," Tariq describes. "I was gambling. I played my cards and I played my last card." Tariq's gamble is that he hired a smuggler to attempt to get her out of the ISIS-held stronghold. "He told me exactly—'It costs our heads if we get caught.'" The lives of Laila and her smuggler would be on the table—her father was gambling all that he had.

"If they catch me with him maybe they will think I have [an illicit] relationship with him," Laila explains, and she's right. Inside ISIS, if she's caught with a man she's not married to—especially in the middle of the night when they were planning to spirit her out—she can be killed or, as she already feared, forced to marry another fighter.

"I say I am going to play, because if she stays there she is already dead," Tariq continues with his gambling metaphor.

I'm drawn in, now anxious to hear about Laila's escape. "How did you get her out?"

"We decided with Laila," Tariq explains. "She agreed she has nothing to do there after her husband died. So we [all] agree she has to come out and she would like to go. I started making my contacts. I put together two plans to get Laila out. In the second plan I go in and get her," Tariq explains how he was prepared to risk his life trying to take his daughter back from ISIS.

There are some cases where parents actually have done this, mothers and fathers. In Belgium, I met the attorney of the uncle of an ISIS cadre who went to get his nephew out, but arrived too late. The nephew was killed days after his arrival, but once in, ISIS didn't want to let the uncle to leave. After some time of winning trust, the uncle found a chance to get himself to a smuggler; made his way over the border into Turkey and then back to Belgium, where he faced charges for joining a terrorist group. The risks of rescuing a family member are many.

"I traveled to Istanbul. I stayed there three days," Tariq continues. "Laila helped me in this way. That owner of her apartment was living in Istanbul and he is not with *Daesh*." Laila connected him to the Syrian owner of her apartment in Istanbul.

Laila jumps in. "He was there in al-Bab [when we arrived in Syria]. He was smoking and normal. He rented us the apartment. My husband is very open and told him, 'You can smoke with us. I am not like them.' He does not judge others."

Tariq continues, "I telephoned him in Istanbul and told him, 'I want to meet with you. I am the father of the lady who is living in your apartment. He gave me an appointment the next day at ten in the morning. I met all his family and we drank some tea together. I explained, 'I have to take my daughter out of this place. You are going to help me and I will pay however much it costs me—I don't mind.'"

"Of course the Syrian people are out of their land, poor, and need money, so he said, 'Okay I will find out.' So I went back the next day to learn what we are going to do."

"The next day I felt he was changing his mind because it's very dangerous. I talked very long with him. After, he told me that all his family like me—and his daughters told him, 'Father you have to help him.' So we traveled together from Istanbul to Gaziantep [on the border of Turkey and Syria]."

"His daughter told her father," Laila adds, 'If you don't help this man *I* will go and take his daughter out!'" I imagine these girls convincing their father to help rescue another father's daughter from danger.

"In Kilis, [a city in southern Turkey bordering Syria] we took a hotel," Tariq continues. "There we saw a big mess—thousands walking the streets. It was two days before *Eid* [a major Muslim holiday when families gather]. There were thousands trying to go *into* Syria. Most were sleeping in the streets. Our new friend tries two to three times to cross but the Turkish border was closed, and it was dangerous to go over via an illegal crossing."

"'So what should we do? I ask him."

"'I have a friend,' he answered. 'But it's very dangerous.'"

"He has a friend that loves money," Tariq knew the costs and consequences.

"So he rang to him and told him, 'I have something in al-Bab, I'd like to take it out to Azaz, how much you want?'"

"'What's the material?' the friend asked. 'Which kind?'"

"'A lady. She has to go out, from al-Bab to Azaz.'"

"'It costs my head,' he immediately responded."

"'It also costs my daughter's head. I would like to gamble,'" Tariq told them. "We agreed to a plan. At four a.m., he will take her from her home to his family. He won't use a car. He will use a motorcycle so that no one can see the number and find out it was him."

"I told Laila, 'Your father is waiting for you,' and I gave her a password to know the guy."

Now Laila looks terrified, reliving her fear during this middle-of-the-night rescue. This stranger, she interjects, a Syrian man, arrived at her door early that morning, "He said, 'Come with me.'"

"'No! What is the password?' I asked him. Then he said it, but he was very scared. He said, 'Hurry up!' then took me to his place. I stayed for one hour. Then we went to a place where we can cross the *Daesh* border."

"Why did he take you to his home?" I am surprised that he involved his family and home in this dangerous effort.

"He took her to his house with his wife and three children because they are not allowed to drive before sunrise," Tariq explains, making sure I understand that his daughter was never alone with this man in his home—her honor never compromised.

Indeed, I later learn about two French young women who also escaped ISIS. In one case, the girl's smuggler raped her when he had the chance and another girl was forced into granting her smuggler "sexual favors" to get across the border. Escaping ISIS isn't easy for anyone, but it's fraught with even more despicable dangers for women.

"Then they took the tuk-tuk [a small three-wheeled auto rickshaw] with his wife and three children to cross the *Daesh* border," Tariq continues.

Laila explains that inside Syria different areas are controlled by *Jaysh al-Hur* [the Free Syrian Army] and ISIS, delineated by checkpoints.

They were at one of these interior checkpoints, about to cross out of ISIS territory and into *Jaysh al-Hur* territory when, in this no man's land, things suddenly got even more terrifying.

"It was [Syrian] regime bombers attacking. We were dodging the bombs! I was between *Daesh* and *Jaysh al-Hur* borders. We were running back and forth [between checkpoints]. They started firing at each other and bombers came overhead. A car exploded nearby," Laila breathlessly recounts the trauma. "We had to wait from six in the morning that day until four p.m. Everyone else fled. Even his wife and children left on foot. But we stayed in the tuk-tuk. Then we walked finally at four p.m. We arrived at Azaz at nine in the morning." I can't help but remind myself that she faced this journey pregnant, with no food or water, and terrifying stress.

I ask Laila how she was able to cross the checkpoints and borders without being detected. She reminded me that she was dressed in a *niqab* and her escort presented her to the checkpoint guards as one of his wives. They left her alone as a result and she could pass without being identified. Not unlike a female suicide bomber, I thought. In this regard females have an advantage.

"When I crossed into *Jaysh al-Hur* territory, he showed his ID card. He's a normal Syrian so he can cross," Laila explains. "Then he put me in a bus. I was still in Syria. I took a bus, to Azaz, then later crossed the border [into Turkey] at Bab al-Hawa."

Still breathless, she adds, "I lost two phones in the bombing."

Tariq takes over. "She then asked someone to ring me [on their phone]. She told me where she is. She described the place where she is waiting. I told her to go to the office and buy some food."

"I was very tired." Pregnant and she probably hadn't slept the night of her four a.m. escape followed by another day dodging bombs. "I just wanted water, I hadn't eaten since four in the morning."

But it turns out her story didn't end there, even though she had made it all the way to a bus station so near the Turkish border. ISIS was about to learn of Laila's disappearance, which made it too risky for her to stay at the bus station in Azaz for long. Tariq backed up and started to fill in the details about what happened between Laila's time in Azaz and when she finally crossed the border into Turkey.

"There were too many spies in Azaz," Tariq explains. "So I called someone from inside Syria to take my daughter to Aleppo." Tariq made the difficult decision to not immediately bring Laila across the border into Turkey but move her further into Syria, knowing she might be more easily caught at the border. "He was a guy with a wife and three daughters. I told her not to go in the car before she talked to me first. She waited some hours. Also he gave me the number of his car," Tariq explains, recounting the security measures he took to help ensure Laila's safe rescue.

"He rang me when he arrived and they found each other," Tariq continues. "She could call me from the garage, so we were keeping in contact. I told him to take her inside Syria, directly to Aleppo," a Syrian city in an area that ISIS didn't control. "She sat at his home for four days, and I waited in Antakya [Turkey]," Tariq explains.

Things were heating up. The threats started. ISIS realized that Laila had gone missing and they were angry. "*Daesh* began looking for her. They began sending us SMS [text messages] to our phone saying, 'We will kill her. You are going to lose. Laila is in danger with her son.'"

I ask how they knew his phone number. "It was my wife's phone. They must have known it from Laila's time with them."

"They said, if she really wanted to go out she can, but she has to give birth and nurse the baby and give them the child first, because it's a child of *Daesh*," Tariq explains, as I feel a chill move down my spine.

"I told my wife not to answer them. "I told my friend not to sleep too much—just watch my daughter and your family."

Indeed, his friend in Aleppo had taken a grave risk. "They [ISIS cadres] can arrive in Aleppo if they know she is there," Tariq says, and

Laila adds, "They can shave [their beards] and come after me!" her eyes widen with terror.

"I warned him to take care," Tariq repeats. "It was the last day of *Eid*. We decided it's better to cross at the beach. This is the last Turkish border in Turkman. It was up in the mountains, one-and-a-half-hour from Antakya [where Tariq was waiting]."

"How can she safely pass the Syrian border without ISIS knowing?" I interject, explaining how we've been told that ISIS has a lot of informants among the border crossing guards.

"They used his wife's identity card," Tariq explains, again being concealed under a *niqab* playing in her favor. "I warned my friend that Turkish border guards should not see her European passport in case they work with *Daesh*. They crossed the border with his wife's special mission—a paper his wife has because she is a special agent in the military. They thought she [Laila] is his wife and working with the Syrian and Turkish officials."

"She crossed the border," anxiety still filling his eyes, "but I was afraid to move from Antakya. I was afraid someone might be watching me and if I went out of town they might follow me. For this reason, I didn't move to the border [to meet her] but waited in the hotel. As soon as she got here I rang to Janni [the policeman back home that helped them before]."

I marvel at this dangerous, and costly, mission of love. Tariq says he spent fourteen thousand U.S. dollars to pull off the rescue of his daughter from ISIS. And the journey is not yet over.

A tone of bitterness enters his voice. "They wrote about Laila in some of the newspapers saying *Daesh* sent Laila back to Europe [as an active ISIS cadre]."

I nod my head in understanding. His daughter didn't return home to attack, but was hunted, and still may be hunted and killed. ISIS has killed hundreds of its cadres accused of deserting. Recently, a German national was sentenced to prison, in part for his role in hunting down ISIS deserters inside Syria on behalf of ISIS[86].

"Are you afraid?" I turn to Laila. She's heavily pregnant and probably at the most vulnerable place in her life as a woman. There are many ISIS cadres that pass back and forth from Syria to Turkey, usually crossing to Greece, and from there into northern Europe. It's the path taken by the Paris bombers and later by those who staged the attacks in Belgium in March of 2016. That ISIS could and might send an assassin to kill her is not out of the question.

I feel fear for her even as I pose the question; perhaps as a mother myself, I feel a strong desire to protect her. And I feel guilty that we are recording even a word of her story. I know I must be especially careful with this information.

"I'm scared to go out alone," Laila answers. "I don't work now."

"She has to finish her schooling," Tariq interjects. He wants to assure me that Laila is not just lazing around or hovering in fear at home. "She goes to the [redacted] school," explaining what her future profession will be, which I also will not disclose here.

"We have to stop the people arming them [ISIS]," Tariq says as we begin to conclude this interview. "They can't bomb and fight without these." As a Palestinian, he's seen many conflicts and understands that the engine that fuels conflict is often the cash and weapons flowing through back channels from outside, interested countries that supply terrorist groups.

"It's politics," Laila adds, making an important point about the draw of ISIS. "But the young people, like my husband, don't think like that. They think the fight is about Islam." We discuss some of the factors that likely radicalized Mohammed. Laila explains that in her husband's case, it was the feeling of exclusion from mainstream European society, and anger over geo-political events that get mixed in with extremist ideologies purporting to be the real Islam. It's an extremely common story in Europe. Muslims of immigrant descent, darker skinned especially, face a lot of discrimination from white, native Europeans while they also watch, in dismay and anger, as Western countries violently interfere in Islamic countries.[87]

"Islam and Christianity are very close," Tariq reassures me. "We are against all this killing and also prophet Mohammed was against killing civilians."

"The Prophet says you make a sin if you destroy even a tree," Laila assures me.

"Even our greeting is '*Salaam Alaykum*' which means peace be with you," her father adds.

We wrap up our interview and I begin to pack up my things and ask for help calling a taxi. Tariq refuses. "I'll drive you." I smile as I see that I've worked my way into this family's affection. I leave thanking them and agree to write carefully to completely disguise Laila's identity.

"You know you really inspire me," I tell Tariq, as he drops me at the hotel on this rainy night. "In this whole story you are the hero. You are the hero Dad. God bless you!"

We smile and part as I wonder the rest of the evening, *What will happen with Laila? Will she be separated from her new infant and be sentenced to prison for her time in ISIS, even though she went reluctantly with her husband as his obedient wife? And if she fears prison, would she consider running away—even going back? Does ISIS have any lure for her? Has she been honest?* I feel she has—but can one ever know for sure?

Later, I learn from someone in her circles that she has stayed in contact with one of the men in Syria, someone from their circle of European friends still there. They fear she could now be in love with this male friend. It's heartbreaking to hear. As a young woman, already a widow, and about to be a new mother—she is so vulnerable, and likely confused by grief and trauma. I know the police and the court system will watch her carefully and be as compassionate to her as they can; and hopefully help her rehabilitate back into European society so that she and her baby can live full and good lives, rather than be caught in the clutches of ISIS.

Postscript: January 2016, I learn that Laila's baby boy has been born and mother and child are healthy. Two months later, the charges against her have been dropped and she is free to resume her life in Europe. I just hope and pray she never again falls prey to a man heeding the call of ISIS, or to ISIS cadres who may want to hunt her down inside Europe. I think again, *Does ISIS have any lure for her? Has she been honest? Can one ever know for sure?*

Chapter Fourteen - Not All Returnees are Defectors

One can never know for sure.

Twenty-seven years old, Younes Delefortrie is telling me about his return to Belgium after spending five weeks with ISIS in Syria in 2013. "I hid in the house. Even the children didn't know I was there. For three days the police came by asking [my wife], 'Did you see him?'"

It's February 2016, and I've come here to interview Belgians and family members of those who have traveled to Syria to join ISIS, *Jabhat al Nusra*, or other groups in the uprising. Belgium is disproportionately represented among ISIS foreign fighters coming from European countries. Five hundred Belgians have disappeared into Syria, many to ISIS, and one hundred and twenty-five have returned.[88] Half of those are imprisoned and the other half are on the streets of Belgium. Younes is one of them.

Only a few months ago, it was a handful of Belgians who had returned from ISIS training in Syria, took up arms and suicide belts, to nearly simultaneously attack the Paris concert hall, stadium, restaurants and bars. Abdelhamid Abaaoud, the alleged ringleader of the attacks, was a Belgian national from the Molenbeek area of Brussels. He was discovered hiding out in a Paris apartment and killed by the French police shortly after the attacks. Likewise, Salah and Brahim Abdeslam, brothers and French nationals had been raised in the Molenbeek neighborhood. Brahim exploded himself while Salah ran and returned to this neighborhood to hide out. Twenty-five-year-old Chakib Akrouh, also born and raised in Belgium, exploded himself after the Paris bombing, during a police raid. He is believed to have been involved in the bar and restaurant attacks. Other Belgians of North African descent were involved in preparing the attacks and aiding Abdeslam's escape. Many will be identified in the coming months and it will be discovered that they traveled through Turkey to Syria and back again through Turkey and Greece to attack. However, at the time we are interviewing Younes, only some of this is known.[89]

When I lived in Brussels from 2000 to 2007 during my husband's diplomatic career, I traveled to places like the West Bank, Gaza, Morocco, Jordan, Iraq, Uzbekistan and Russia to interview hundreds of terrorists, their family members, close associates and even hostages.[90] Eventually it dawned on me—I didn't need to leave Belgium to find militant jihadi extremists. There were plenty right in my neighborhood. In fact, numerous al-Qaeda inspired plots involving Belgian cadres had been stopped during the seven years I lived in Belgium, including a suicide operative who planned to detonate himself inside the U.S. embassy in Paris.[91]

It is against this backdrop that I find myself in Antwerp, one of Belgium's main cities, sitting in a small office just off of the Radisson hotel lobby, drinking Belgian coffee and listening to Younes tell his story. Having arrived in pants that are cut short, well above his ankles, in the regulation manner of *Salafi* traditional dress, Younes greeted me with a friendly, but nervous smile. According to his brand of Islam, it's forbidden to take a woman's hand, he explained, as he tensely said hello without a handshake and I wondered if I would be able to get much of an interview with him. But now that we are into it, I see that I've gotten him talking freely in fact. I think I may have hit the returnee mother lode.

With the Islamic State's declaration of a "Caliphate" in June 2014, what had been low-level but significant militant jihadi activity in Belgium ramped up on steroids. As the uprising against Assad began and no one came to the aid of the rebels, alienated young Belgian men and women already resonating to the call of groups like al-Qaeda, began thinking they could help the anti-Assad rebels. *Salafi* extremists had been cultivating the ground in Belgium for years, working in the streets and out of garage mosques, converting disaffected immigrant youth to their extremist brand of Islam. The young recruits already accepted al-Qaeda's premise that jihad against the West was called for because Islamic peoples and lands, and even Islam itself, were under attack, and 'martyrdom' missions against the enemy were an instant pathway to Paradise. Already primed, they easily fell for the call of ISIS.

From 2013 onward, Belgian youth became enamored of the idea of adventure, upset by the lack of global support for the uprising against Assad, and strongly resonated with the idea of an Islamic utopia and the alternative world governance of the "Caliphate" offered by ISIS. They began streaming by the hundreds through Turkey into Syria. These Belgians joined the monthly deluge of a thousand to fifteen hundred foreign fighters flowing in from around the globe who made it possible for ISIS to suffer the steady degradation of Coalition airstrikes and still renew its ranks.[92] These recruits from Belgium are part of the group of foreign fighters who our Syrian ISIS defectors consistently described as "true believers", fully indoctrinated into militant jihadi ideas upon their arrival.

Ten years ago in Antwerp, these North African second-generation youth were already disaffected, telling me how alienated they felt in Belgium and France and how angry they were over geopolitics. In fact, when the Paris attacks happened in November 2015, I would have pointed to Antwerp as more of a hotbed of militant jihadi activities than the well-known Molenbeek neighborhood of Brussels, from where the Belgian Paris attackers came.

On this trip, I wanted to learn why young men and women from Belgium would leave circumstances so different from the Syrians who often joined ISIS out of a lack of alternatives, coercion, and pressure to provide for themselves and their families. Were the "true believers" who returned to Belgium, defectors, like the Syrians we'd been talking to? Or were they simply returnees—still deeply entrenched in militant jihadi beliefs and still dangerous? Here in Belgium, and across all of Europe, government security officials were especially concerned about their citizens returning home after serving time in groups like ISIS, a concern now greatly heightened by the Paris attacks. How many of those who went to Syria might constitute a threat if they returned home? How many would remain ideologically indoctrinated and were already weapons trained?

I knew it wouldn't be easy to make contact with ISIS defectors inside Europe. We had hit a pipeline of them in Turkey thanks to Ahmet's efforts at winning trust, but those who return to Europe would be reticent to talk for a number of reasons. These defectors would fear ISIS just like the Syrians in Turkey. They might not want to admit they had joined ISIS because doing so means they could face prosecution in their European home country. They also might not appreciate an American asking them questions, given the Coalition bombings in Syria. And if they hadn't really defected, they might be seriously dangerous. I knew if it was the latter I could potentially be putting my life in danger. It was a calculated risk.

Before I left, Ahmet commented, "You always have a police guard with you on these interviews, no?" I turned to him, incredulous. Sure, I would have loved a trained police chief, like Ahmet, along on these interviews, but our budget didn't allow it. So I went alone—unprotected—as I had done for most of the hundreds of interviews I'd conducted over the years. I never had the luxury of a guard alongside me, except inside the Department of Defense prisons in Iraq.

Younes Delefortrie was seated across the room, speaking in English to me. [93] We are using his real name, with his permission. I already knew from reading local press about him that he was a convert to Islam, grew up in a Flemish family of five children and that it wasn't a happy home. His mother was an alcoholic and his father was unable to control her violence or her drinking. Younes was the oldest and may have had it the worst. I'd also read that he doesn't like talking about his childhood, so I'm treading gently as I ask him to tell me about himself—how he grew up and later became involved with ISIS. [94]

We had the camera rolling as he agreed to a video interview. Describing himself as a hyperactive child unable to pay attention, I nod, knowing that this description is often the fate of young boys who grow up in chaotic and violent conditions. If a child who is trying to organize himself doesn't have a reliable attachment figure with whom to make a strong and reliable bond, he will often fail to organize himself well, or even learn to pay attention to authority figures.

"It was a difficult situation," Younes says, describing his early family life while ruminating on whether or not he was "normal" as a young boy. "Normal needs two parents," he reflects as a sad expression crosses his face. "I ruined a lot of things in my life—school and education, and had a lot of energy," he says, easing into his childhood pain carefully.

"Everybody can be a mother. Not everyone can be a mom. My mother left when I was twelve or thirteen."

"That's a pretty tender age to lose your mother. Did it break your heart when she left?"

Younes expression becomes sardonic, as he answers, "A mother who has a drinking problem is not something you will miss very soon. I was actually relieved. It's better for children if there is an unnatural abnormal—it's best to change the situation. I was also sure that it would improve the situation."

His mother got so drunk each day that she couldn't care, cook, or clean for her children. Later, an associate of Younes tells me that his mother was violent as well, and tried to make Younes responsible for the other children, blaming and hitting him in her drunken state when he didn't manage to take up the slack. Given that, it probably was a relief when she jumped ship.

Younes's father put their mother into alcohol treatment three times. On the third time she decided to run off with another alcoholic in the program. After abandoning her five children, she went on to have five more children with the next man. "She lost my appreciation of being a mother," Younes sarcastically notes, shaking his head. "She was drunk, annoying, aggressive," whereas he tells me that his father returned home to try to pull the family together after he "worked eight hours in hard labor."

"Occasionally he'd drink on the weekends, normally after dinner, or at dinner, or before television at night, but he got up each day at seven a.m." Younes' father, a team boss in a metal construction factory, I'd also later learn from others who know Younes' story, would come home and did try to hold the family together. But he would also sometimes give in and drink right along with his wife. Younes' father was not as much of a saint as his son made him out to be.

After his mother left, his grandparents stepped in. "They came at six a.m. to make breakfast. My grandmother cleaned the house and they came back at four p.m. to take us from school," he says as though everything was fine. In fact, he was not fine. Like many young boys who haven't any coping mechanisms to deal with their emotional pain and act them out through constant motion, Younes became severely hyperactive to the point that he was put on medication. He describes how he was "bored in school, not feeling good, and eventually failed." Rather than high school he went into a "learning contract" to learn the Belgian art of making chocolate and pastry production. It seems like such a contradiction—from pastry maker to ISIS

As a teen, Younes went on a wild streak for some years— using drugs and partying with girls. "The partying and the girlfriend relationships without any value made me realize that life without borders was not the right life to live, better to have borders and standards. At that moment I was also an altar boy. I was religious. My father and mother were very religious and took us to church, but I had only Western society borders, and those of the Catholic Church—and those two borders were not very good. They didn't look like borders to me."

Like all youth, Younes began searching for meaning to his life and as an alienated teenager found his answers among other youth who would sit on the riverbank smoking hashish. "They opened me to search new knowledge—what is Islam, what are the borders." He explains: "This is clear cut, no grey. Black and white, no doubts—till today I didn't find doubts. Before, I had non-authentic beliefs," referring to his Catholic upbringing and likely the hypocrisy he witnessed in his family, torn by drunken violence, living out what they claimed as their creed. Younes was searching for limits, discipline and certainty, and Islam offered all three. And his emotional pain made him receptive to more extremist versions than what he learned from his hashish-smoking friends.

"So-called moderates," Younes calls them, "that was my [first] version of Islam. I can describe them as non-well informed. They don't do acts that put them out of religion, but they just accepted the entry card. We have the five pillars: i.e. saying the *Shahada* [the Muslim testimony of faith], keeping the five daily prayers, fasting during Ramadan, giving *zakat* [charity], and if possible taking at least one pilgrimage to Mecca; but in our [*Salafi*] opinion that is just the passport to calling yourself a Muslim. Human beings are what they are and quickly satisfied with those things. But they need to go deeper."

"Converts are more motivated—'radicalized' is the claim—but the truth is we are just more interested in what we believe. Born Muslims think they get it all. That is a big problem of what we have now. America [American policy makers and political pundits] says we cannot change Islam from inside and said we need to change and renew," Younes reflects. As a *Salafi*, he roundly rejects the idea of moderating or innovating on Islam in any manner. "Who said we wanted to renew? Our religion has been changed. Catholics made many changes over times, the Jews rejected the Torah and made their own," Younes repeats a common militant jihadi and extremist line that Jews rejected what was given to them and therefore fell into sin, but true Muslims stick to the old interpretations and ways.

"Everything created by human beings, everything created by people, fails." Younes seems very sure of himself and very dependent on beliefs that sustains his sense of certainty.

It makes sense that he wants something solid and unfailing. Younes grew up with failure—his mother's failure to nurture and stay sober; his father's failure to control her; his grandparent's impotence in the face of her negligence; and the Catholic Church's numb inability to step in and protect the children. For Younes, his strict version of Islam meets his needs. And like many European converts, he learned about Islam from friends who came from close knit, extended, immigrant families where he saw another way of living.

So while they smoked hashish, Younes began to take an interest in all things Islamic. Christened Michael by his parents, he converted and renamed himself Younes. As a Muslim he became convinced and calmed by a strict system of rules that promised to keep him "safe" from the dangers of his childhood—certainly from alcoholism—as alcohol is banned in Islam.

I ask him about marrying—knowing he's married multiple times with two children. Younes explains that he went to Morocco as a young man in search of his first wife. "I was of the opinion that Muslim women here are too westernized. People told me that from the mountains of Morocco, the women are more laid back and not feminist, and if they felt oppressed, they know it's the fault of society, not of a man." Younes was looking for someone who would not be a repeat of his mother, who had blamed and hurt him throughout his childhood, and whom his father couldn't control.

"So I went [to Morocco] in Ramadan. I met the family of the mother of my children. The guy said to me we have a sister that wants to marry. She stayed [with me] five years so I knew she wasn't just looking for citizenship. I knew it was risky. It took a year to finish the papers—sixty [government] stamps to get the marriage papers. We have two children, but the marriage didn't last," he explains getting a pained expression on his face. "I am very strict, and not easy to live with."

He was also looking for more than this Moroccan woman saw as her wifely role. "I expected love, Romeo and Juliet, and she thought she was doing enough to cook and clean and take care of our children. I expected love, but I got the boring sheep. She's a good mother and takes care of my children," he admits, "But that was not enough for me. I wanted love." Of course he did. He hadn't been loved as a boy and he grew up in the West where love and romance are normal expectations in marriage.

"So it didn't work," Younes continues. "I was alone." Still anxious for limits, certainty, and strict guidelines, Younes fell in with *Sharia4Belgium.*

In 2010 British extremist, Anjem Choudary, who headed the extremist organization *Islam4UK*, began working with Belgian extremists, including one named Fouad Belkacem, formerly arrested for possession of drugs and burglary, to set up a similar organization based in Antwerp. The Antwerp based organization was called *Sharia4Belgium.* At its inception, Belkacem stated in a video message: "We believe *sharia* will be implemented in Belgium and worldwide... Democracy is the opposite of Islam and *sharia*... Belgium is a dirty, perverted community."[95]

Sharia4Belgium, like al Qaeda and ISIS, followed an extremist version of Islam that encourages practicing *Takfir,* meaning they believed only they had the true Islam and could declare other Muslims as apostates deserving to be killed. At first Belgian authorities were lenient toward the group. Perhaps because they made laughable statements like Belkacem's call for ex-first lady of France, Carla Bruni, to convert to Islam: "I ask Allah to guide Carla Bruni, to turn her into a *niqab*-wearing Muslim, and to make her divorce that unbeliever, [French ex-president] Sarkozy, may Allah fight him."

As the uprising occurred in Syria, *Sharia4Belgium* quickly aligned itself with *Jabhat al Nusra*, and later ISIS. Over time it became a feeder organization for unemployed and disenchanted Belgians who wanted to join the uprising, sending them off to Syria to train with these groups. Now Belgian authorities took notice. In 2014, Belkacem and forty-five other members of *Sharia4Belgium* were indicted and in December 2014, found guilty of membership in a terrorist organization—half of them sentenced *in abstentia*—as they were either suspected dead, or still fighting in Syria.

As *Shariah4Belgium* was activating in Belgium, Younes remarried, "a Moroccan lady from Holland," he tells me, but was again quickly disappointed. "She was divorced and was not at the point to start over again, so that became difficult." Younes lacked the social skills to keep a relationship with a woman intact; never learning from his own parents and with a raging hurt inside, he feared that his wife might turn out like his mother. Unable to make this second troubled marriage a success, he escaped—by going to Syria.

"In December 2013, we broke up again and I left to go to Syria. The war was getting heavy" as was the political situation with *Sharia4Belgium*. "In Belgium there was no place to talk freely anymore. We got arrested every time on the street [proselytizing], put in jail for twelve hours, and we were under surveillance, with them checking us, and everyone's phones tapped. We were under the eye of the state security. It's not fun to live without privacy or freedom of speech."

Younes glances around and gestures beyond the room as he continues, "If you see this neighborhood, twenty meters further there is an African church. They try to gather people to their church, but if we tried to do it in the streets, [the state accuses us] 'he's radicalizing and calling for hate and violence.' We were confronted every day of the week with double standards, on television and in the news," Younes complains. *Although the African church was probably not offering to send anyone off to join a terrorist group in Syria, whereas Younes' group was engaging in such activities*, I reflect.

"If you don't see the possibility to make yourself in your society, you change your society to where you can be useful," Younes continues, echoing hundreds of interviews I've made in Antwerp, Brussels, and

Paris with North African, second-generation immigrants. The significant discrimination leads them to believe they can never be accepted and succeed in mainstream Belgian or French society. In France, youth in the ghettoized North African immigrant suburbs of Paris told me during the riots and fires in Paris in November of 2005, "Liberté, égalité & fraternité [Liberty, equality and fraternity]—these things don't apply to us."[96]

That was before the rise of ISIS, and it was mainly al-Qaeda that, as a result, could recruit such youth into their ranks. But to join al-Qaeda, one had to really prove himself, ideologically and as a trusted cadre, before he'd be accepted into going to an al-Qaeda training camp. Today under ISIS, there is the declared "Caliphate" to escape to, and the dream of a utopian, alternative world order where frustrated young men and women are promised significance, purpose, belonging, honor, adventure, jobs, and marriages. And for the men—even sex slaves. The rise of ISIS gives these disenfranchised youth a place to go, and it's not hard to get there—a quick flight to Istanbul, then a bus or an internal flight to a town close to the border--and then an ISIS-arranged smuggler to get them into Syria.

Younes references the militant jihadi view that *hijra* [migration] to Muslim lands and joining jihad are duties of every Muslim. It's a view that was popularized to Westerners by al-Qaeda's Anwar al–Awlaki (see Chapter Seven). Younes explains to me, "You have to prepare for your life after. It's a religious duty—*hijra* to Syria and Iraq. It is religious aspects of why they leave." Then suddenly turning defensive, he adds, "My history, my choice to go over there has nothing to do with my childhood. It's very sad that people try to search for another reason [aside from religious duty]. We are honored when we take this step. I hope it is religion that motivates everyone else."

"Also, not everyone is going to fight. I know five people who went to live there with their families. Why go to a country at war? Why, when one hundred thousand families are running from it, you go to live there?" he asks and then blames the political situation in Belgium. "That is the fault of the society we live in. They are making peoples' lives unlivable."

Then turning to the immigrants who are streaming into Europe from Syria, he states, "They can leave the women and children here. They have no protection anymore; they are more breakable. But all the guys from ages twenty to twenty-four should be sent back. Half are war criminals. They fought with the army of the regime. The rest are running away from *shariah* and Islam and don't want to live under those rules so they run. But they are going to confront their Creator sooner and later. They are blinded by democracy here. They have to sell their religion to live under the safety of democracy." Younes still believes that life is better under the "Caliphate."

I want to know about his journey to Syria, how he made it in, and why he then left and returned to Belgium.

"I went in the evening. I took a bus to Cologne [Germany]." Typical of his impulsive nature, he failed to let the "brothers" know he was coming and to make arrangements to be met by ISIS cadres at the Turkish border. "I left without asking someone," he says but defensively adds, "I didn't have to ask permission to go where I wish to go. I went to Dusseldorf, then flew to Istanbul, and took another plane to Adana [in Turkey] near the border of Syria. I stayed a week in a hotel but didn't find someone to help me cross the borders. At these times it's more difficult to join, but at that time in 2013, the Turkish [authorities] had one eye closed. For everything related to Kobanî [a Syrian city on the Turkish border overtaken at that time by ISIS], the Turkish government was helping— with weapons, shotguns and pistols—unofficially or not, I don't know. The logic was that it was official." So once again, we hear about Turkish complicity in supporting rebel groups—including ISIS.

"I was searching on Facebook. I was searching for someone already there, profile pictures, asking, 'Abu [xxx], do you have a connection [inside ISIS]?' The ball gets rolling. After six days I found someone to take me in. We went then and stayed five days right on the border in a Turkish house." Indeed, Ahmet later confirms that in some places in Turkey, the houses are very near the border, their backyards only meters away from Syria. Younes went to stay in an ISIS smuggler's home, making it easy to run through backyards late at night to cross into Syria.

"[Before crossing into Syria] I met two women from Holland. I was asked to escort them through the border. We went to the [smuggler's] house and met also a Kazak family there—a father and his son, his wife and two daughters staying in another room. They tried to cross a big field where there was big barbed wire, but they were stopped and sent back."

"So the Turks do control the border and try to prevent people from going to join the rebel groups?" I ask.

Younes smiles mockingly. "They didn't want to see it openly. It's like the child's game—one, two, three, piano—you turn around and if you are caught moving you have to go back." He returns to his story. "We crossed at five in the morning. The sisters and me were allowed to take only one bag. The rest came later."

"All of the people who were gathered in the house crossed. We went over the barbed wire. There was a place where it was pressed down." Then a small comic tragedy occurred as Younes ran, carrying that one bag for the sisters. "I was trying to get over the barbed wire and the bag I was carrying opened and *burkas* fell out. The barbed wire caught and tore these *burkas*. The women over there asked for good quality burkas, so they [the Dutch women] brought a lot for the other sisters. They ended up all hanging on the barbed wire! She was not happy," Younes looks rueful over the mishap. I laugh to myself imagining the sun rising on black burkas, caught on the barbed fence, flapping in the wind—the symbolism shining in the morning sun.

"When we'd crossed two hundred meters there was someone waiting in a big van. We stayed in the van until the morning. Then we went to the Islamic police. It was not yet the Islamic State. It was ISIS, but they hadn't declared the Caliphate yet."

Just as the Syrian ISIS defectors have been telling Ahmet and me, the European newcomers were housed near the border and checked carefully before gaining free entrance to the group. "They checked everything. There was another Younes—Younes Bunting. He left a month before I came. He was also a convert and they discovered he was working with the *Mossad* [Israeli intelligence]. So when another Belgian Younes came without announcing, they found it strange and suspected me. They searched my phone, my computer, everything. Their lives and security depend on it. If a spy is able to infiltrate and tell their location, the Coalition can send a drone to kill all the foreign fighters."

Shaking his head regretfully, Younes adds, "All those American soldiers who died after 9-11—their blood is spoiled for nothing; but in our situation our blood is not spoiled. We believe Muslim blood that is spilled for implementing the *sharia* state—you get your efforts rewarded in the afterlife." I nod, thinking this belief in the afterlife gives a lot of terrorists courage to risk their lives.

"They gave me a choice. They asked me, 'What are you going to do here?'"

"'I want to make myself useful in every way possible, as good as I can handle, according to my capacities,' I answered. "They searched for a place [for me] with some Belgian fighters, but there were some issues with the guys from Belgium who were still upset over the Younes who came before me. They didn't want another troublemaker. So [the ISIS leaders] assigned me to a group of Frenchmen and Libyans. It was not a bad idea, my French was not that bad," Younes tells me. As a Flemish Belgian living in Antwerp where Flemish is the dominant language, French would be less necessary. Being tri-lingual says something about his intellectual abilities. It's obvious to me that he's smart, despite having failed in school.

"It is something special—all these people speaking many foreign languages," Younes says, his voice filled with appreciation. "They put me in a house and I was welcomed. The first day when I came in they were doing evening dinner, eating on the ground [in the traditional Arab style] in a big house—a mansion really," Younes' face lights up describing it. Clearly it fit his fantasies of belonging to a traditional and welcoming culture and religious community where men are honored and share a strong sense of brotherhood. But all was not good—even from the start.

"I got in and then in the first week, I started noticing the situation—evening bombings. It's overwhelming at first but you get used to it very quickly."

"Was it loud and frightening?" I ask.

Younes nods looking like he was quite frightened but tries to downplay it, saying, "You just try to find your tranquility."

"Did you take *shariah* training?" I ask, knowing it's the pattern in which ISIS moves its new recruits to swearing their *bayats* before becoming trained fighters.

"There was no *shariah* training at that house," Younes responds. "They asked me to give allegiance, *bayat*, but I rejected and they found that strange. 'I don't want to be stuck to an organization,' I explained to them. 'I want to know what it's all about. I am not against you. I want to make myself useful. I will check out the houses, do guard duty, but I don't want to be forced to stay with you.'"

"They accepted this," Younes explains. "Now, with the Caliphate, it will not be accepted. If they are soldiers [of ISIS] they must give *bayat*. You cannot make *hijra* and then have them say, 'okay you can leave.' Adani's statement [the spokesman for ISIS] says, 'You will leave with a bullet in your head.' It's logical," Younes says, justifying the murderous deserter policies that ISIS now implements as normal for any state.

"So what kinds of things went on while you were there?" I ask.

"After the second week, they gave me an AK-47 and explained how to clean and reload it, and grenades—two grenades. I slept with them under my pillow. Once we were attacked by the Free Syrian Army and I carried five RPGs [rocket propelled grenades] on my back." He also posted photographs of himself posing with weapons on his Facebook page, where he named his employers as *Jabhat al-Nusra* and *Revolusi* (Revolution) *Dawlah al-Islamiah* (ISIS).[97]

"The regime attacked our village in the beginning," he explains. "It was a mixed up place—with *Jabhat al-Nusra*, ISIS, the Free Syrian Army—but everyone was cooperating at first. Since January 2014, it all changed." Younes looks perplexed and abruptly stops this line of conversation. Perhaps he doesn't want to doubt ISIS, or he doesn't want to talk about carrying arms for a terrorist group.

"Why did you leave so quickly after arriving to ISIS?" I ask him.

"The [second] wife from Holland—our relationship was tough. She was missing me and I was missing her. I didn't find it smart for her to come. Everyone was starting to fight each other. We decided that we will meet up in Turkey and decide what to do. I ended up coming instead to Holland. I thought then we can get money. The Free Syrian Army stole my laptop, money, and things, and I saw the opportunity to replace my money and materials, and perhaps get my wife back."

Younes likely knew that as a Belgian he might be lucky enough not to show up on another European country's terrorism list for having departed to Syria. "The airport of Holland was not a problem," he tells me; he passed through Dutch security unchallenged. This is a fundamental problem in Europe—the national borders are open, but the intelligence agencies and police do not always share information as openly across these same borders. Younes makes sure I understand how he departed ISIS. "I didn't run away, I asked them, 'Is it okay to go back?' They [ISIS] tried to convince me to stay, that it's not a good idea [to leave]. They were totally right. Now, I'm in the exact situation they predicted."

His broken second marriage underwent its final twisted challenge. "I had my last one hundred euros with me that I had from the brothers. She was at the airport but [not realizing she was there waiting for me] I took a taxi to Rotterdam. We missed each other! Even at home, she came to the front door, but I went to the back, to not let the neighbors see me. At the front, there were police waiting at the door so I hid in the trunk of the car. The police arrested her. They didn't know that we were texting each other."

"The Dutch police try to manipulate, use people, and not be according to the law. We cannot expect something else," Younes complains. "They released her and she returned home with her ex-husband and children. I wanted to kill him at that moment. I was so disturbed. 'You cannot stay, they will watch the house,' she said, so I decided to call the police myself."

"I called and asked, 'What do you want from me?' I met them at the gas station. They asked me to raise my shirt. They thought I had a [suicide] belt. Then they let me go." It seems incredible that a young man who could be a suicide attacker is so easily let go after being checked, but that's how he tells it.

"I went and I hid in the house. Even the children didn't know I was there. This went on for three days. The police came and asked my wife, 'Did you see him?' Then they came with papers from Interpol saying the Belgian police want to speak to me."

Realizing he needed to face the music, Younes explains, "I returned to Belgium after a week. I did five interviews with the media. I didn't want to be put silently in prison. I did my story before I reported myself to the police. That way they cannot do whatever they want. They have to apply [the law] according to the book," Younes explains, as I think, *This guy is a clever operator.*

Younes was prosecuted and received a sentence of three years with suspension and a fine of fifteen thousand euros also with an extension. "If I am brought in court again, I have to pay it," Younes explains. "I had an empty file [no criminal charges] before this situation. The judge told me, 'You have a critical profession—to be a baker, so go make some bread and be quiet.'" This makes me laugh—it's so Belgian. But on the other,

I am convinced that Younes should have been sent to some kind of de-radicalization or disengagement treatment, at a minimum.

Younes did go back to baking and even opened his own bakery, but Girt Wilders, a far right, Dutch, anti-immigration politician saw fit to shut him down by publicizing his terrorist affiliation. "'There is blood on this bread,' he said in the papers," Younes tells me. As a result, people stopped coming to the bakery. "He'll pay for it—legally," Younes threatens, making sure not to issue an actual threat to the politician, "in this life or the next." This is no light thing in the Netherlands. Another outspoken Dutch critic of Muslims, Theo van Gogh, was stabbed to death; implying violent wishes against Girt Wilders is risky. I wonder what Wilders was thinking when he shut down the business of a known extremist who was trying to make it in society and earn an honest living. Didn't he see how that could drive Younes right back into his former extremist activities, increasing the danger to himself and to society?

A month after our interview, Younes, wearing a black hoodie adorned with the drawing of a Kalashnikov and the ISIS logo on the back, tells an *al-Jazeera* journalist that since his conviction he finds it hard to find work, and when he did land a job, found that his mid-length beard doesn't sit well with his new boss who urged him to "trim it a bit". Likewise, he complains about his own father's racial slurs against "brown" Moroccans, adding that in Antwerp he faces a barrage of continuous assaults on his Muslim identity.[98] An associate of Younes also tells me that he lives a very isolated and lonely life, caught inside the certainty of his extremist beliefs that keep his childhood pain at bay, and unable to reach out for the help he so obviously needs to socialize and rehabilitate himself back into society.

When I ask Younes, who is not wearing any ISIS branded clothing in our interview, how he feels about the recent Paris attacks he tells me that they are "understandable". I ask if he thinks it's appropriate for a group to target innocent civilians to which he answers that these civilians vote for their governments who are carrying out troubling actions in Islamic lands.

"Targeting women and children?" I push.

Younes agrees that children are always innocent, but won't go further than that. "The Ottoman empire was not created by honey and bees. It started in war, crusades," he argues. "Even your American revolution was won by shedding blood." I don't think to tell him that our rebel forces never pointed their guns at civilians in their marketplaces.

"I still believe it's better to be living under Islamic law than to live under a democratic system that is not applying the laws of our Creator. I'm sure of it," Younes says with conviction. "We will never be able to practice our religion completely," and tells me that he still believes in the dream of the "Caliphate" and wants it to be extended throughout Europe. In an interview only months earlier with *Paris Match*, Younes is reported to have shown reporters the black flag of ISIS proudly hanging over his bed.[99] He still clings to the certainty of convictions, identity, and hope in a utopian Islamic future that ISIS offers troubled youth.

I ask him, if I were Belgian, would I be able to practice my religion freely if there were a "Caliphate?" He cracks a dour smile and tells me, "there will be rules to follow."

As I listen I again wonder why the Belgian judge let him go back freely into society and failed to address the fact that Younes is still heavily radicalized and in need of treatment to disengage from the extremist mindset. He's still vulnerable to becoming a dangerous element in Europe. Moreover, during his prosecution, Younes spent only a few months in prison but he says to me, "Thirty years in prison—your life is over. Better to kill me now—so I don't have to sit in jail."

That gives me a chill, remembering how Zakaria Zubedi, the head of *al-Aksa Martyrs' Brigade* in Jenin, on the West Bank, also told me that he'd rather die than be imprisoned again and was nearly killed, rather than be re-arrested. We also know that Chechen would-be suicide bombers-turned-fugitive have booby trapped their homes and bodies so they can explode themselves upon arrest rather than undergo torture and imprisonment by the Russians.[100] We even heard the same about Chechens operating inside Syria—that they constantly wore suicide vests. *Victory or Paradise!* their motto.[101]

Indeed, the threat of imprisonment can drive individuals who believe in 'martyrdom' into enacting it and that makes them especially dangerous. Little do I know, as Younes and I finish up our interview and part ways, in only a month's time we will see exactly that scenario play out in Belgium. And I will be there.

Chapter Fifteen - A Mission that Matters

I return to Belgium in February of 2016 and as I reach out to ISIS returnees, I e-mail Younes asking if he'd like to talk again or if he has friends who would agree to an interview with me. His reply is disturbing for the *Salafi* beliefs he purports to follow: "…my testosterone was going high with you…I have a weakness for mature women," he writes. He tells me that no one else in his circle will give me an interview, but if "you are alone and bored we can have a one-on-one."

Deciding to pass on that offer, I spend the week talking to the Dutch and Belgian police and some lawyers defending ISIS returnees, and I continue to interview parents of those who've gone to Syria. Among them is Fatima, the mother of a young man currently serving as an ISIS commander. She emigrated from Morocco as a girl and now has six children, all born in Brussels.

"I found out when the feds came to our house," Fatima tells me. She hadn't known her son, Mohammed, had left for Syria in 2013. He was twenty years old.[102] Fatima collapsed into hysteria when she learned of her eldest son's fate.

The reasons for Mohammed leaving to join ISIS are similar to many in Belgium: sympathy for the uprising in Syria and concern that no one was helping them; longstanding anger over Western actions in Iraq, Afghanistan and other Muslim areas of the world; many psychosocial vulnerabilities that could be exploited—discrimination and hopelessness for his future. According to Fatima, her son "was funneled into the technical track [in elementary school] and his teachers said he wasn't qualified [for the university track]. He was only twelve when they determined that," sarcasm in her tone. When he graduated high school, like many men of North African descent, he had trouble finding a job. "He got only a six-month contract and the promise of a job after, but he didn't get it. They brought someone white instead," she tells me.

Fatima, who wears a traditional Moroccan *abaya* and a large headscarf that covers her head, neck and shoulders, tells me that she finds Flemish Belgians "quite racist". When I ask if Mohammed faced discrimination, she answers that it's not just her son; she has had white Belgians say to her, "This isn't your country. What the hell are you doing here? Go home!"

Discrimination, unemployment, frustration, lack of purpose, a longing for significance, wanting to impress the girls, even wanting to be a hero in someone else's conflict, are very common psychosocial vulnerabilities among North African youth in Belgium. These kinds of vulnerabilities can make them ripe for groups like ISIS.

Yet none of these issues are enough to create a terrorist. Mohammed had the additional essential ingredient.

Mohammed was exposed to a terror network and a neighborhood recruiter who introduced him to the group's ideology, convinced him it was correct, and helped facilitate his travel to Syria along with providing him with everything materially needed to join ISIS. Thus, he was exposed to the lethal psychological cocktail that creates a terrorist: the group, ideology and social support that strongly resonated with his inner vulnerabilities.[103] Traits that often resulted in rejection in Belgium— his Muslim and North African heritage were now, positive traits. He could imagine himself enjoying the relatively high status of being a foreign fighter in ISIS, and likely under his recruiter's manipulations, he envisioned a life that took on new purpose and significance. Any ISIS recruiter would have promised him a job, a free house, and both a wife and a sex slave for joining, not to mention the eternal benefits of possibly becoming a 'martyr'. So Mohammed, like hundreds of other Belgians, suddenly disappeared to Syria without giving his parents even a chance to try and pull him away from ISIS' grasp.

Fatima recalls how her son made his goodbyes without telling her he was leaving. "The last night he came home. I was lying on the sofa and didn't feel well. He asked, 'What are you doing? We are going to dance a little bit.' He took me in his arms and we danced and laughed. Then he looked at his watch and said, 'I have to go pray.' He held me tight and then left." Her eyes overflow with tears.

When I ask how he left undetected by the authorities, Fatima admits that she and her husband think the police knew their son was preparing to go because Belgian intel was following his recruiter. Yet, she says the police did nothing to stop him.

Unlike many other cases where a brother or sister leads the way, fortunately, Mohammed has not tried to lure any of his siblings into following him. But damage is being done to the family. One sibling became extremely depressed and another tried to commit suicide because she was so upset by the social stigma of having a brother in ISIS. Fatima and her children have received no psychological assistance from the government.

"I don't know if I'll ever see him again," Fatima tells me, as she wipes the on-going flow of tears from her cheeks. Her pain is palpable. She tells me he's now a commander with a young wife he met in Syria, and a nine month-old-baby. Fatima shows me their pictures on her phone. His wife, in a picture taken at home that he surely meant only to have for himself and to share with his mother, is uncovered. She has beautiful, long, dark, curly ringlets that fall around her shoulders and Mohammed sports a big Islamic beard and traditional *Salafi* clothes as he reclines on a mat cradling his baby daughter, who is dressed daintily in pink. It's oddly normal, this happy-looking family scene.

Mohammed calls his mother over WhatsApp whenever he can get a wireless Internet connection. Fatima takes the opportunity to tell him that she loves him and that he should return home. At first Mohammed returned her kind words, but now she feels he's become hardened and ever more convinced of his violent and extremist views. Recently, however, she says something has changed and she's not sure he can speak freely. "The sense I get is someone is with him, that he is being dictated to or he is reading some kind of statement."

Her family members all firmly oppose the terrorist group and its ideology. "It's not religious. It's political," Fatima says. "Religion doesn't tell people to go kill others. And it's not our problem, or our job, to go fight in Syria, and it has nothing to do with religion."

Fatima's deep sadness over losing her son is so overwhelming that when we end the interview, I feel moved to take her hands in my own and tell her, "Don't give up on your son. Keep telling him to come home. Don't ask. Command. You're his mother and he is still in touch for a reason. Keep telling him, 'Come home.'"

Then suddenly Fatima says, "He wants to come home. He told me last time I talked to him. He's wounded, [they all are], his wife also, and the baby, too—in the back of the head. He wants to get out."

"He wants to return here?" My eyebrows arch in surprise.

"Yes, he is trying to find the way out, but he may not be able to travel. He's in Deir ez-Zor and wounded." My heart starts beating wildly at this sudden turn in the interview.

"He will cross into Turkey?" I ask. "He's willing to turn himself in to the authorities?" That will be necessary if he wants to return to Belgium—legally at least; unless, he wants to continue on his jihadi path like the Paris attackers.

"Yes, he wants to turn himself in—inside Turkey. He'll go to the consulate if he can get to Turkey," Fatima explains. She seems so diminutive, huddled in her chair with her large headscarf wrapped around her. Suddenly I want to protect her from the heartbreak.

"It's very dangerous," I inform her, recalling all the Syrian defectors who told us about Europeans caught trying to escape. The European men are beheaded on the spot and the women are taken back to

Raqqa to an unknown fate. "The ones that try to escape and don't make it are beheaded. He must choose his smuggler very carefully," I warn her. "Some of them are working for ISIS and will betray him unless he pays them very well," I instruct her, and am suddenly aware that I may be giving advice for a criminal act that breaks some unknown laws.

"He told me last time we talked that he needs twelve thousand Euros to get out. He wants to hire someone to take them out." A look of pain crosses her face. I feel terrified for her and wonder how she can appear so calm. Maybe she's just so relieved he's willing to leave.

I decide not to ask her if her son has asked her to send the money. Many ISIS cadres ask their families for money and much needed medical supplies. Some are sincere, but others are bilking their loved ones to support the terrorist group. In either case, sending money or medicine— even to their own children once they are inside ISIS—is the crime of offering material support to a terrorist group and can be punishable if discovered. Fatima has a lot of angles she must maneuver to get her son home safely. I don't know what to say to help and I desperately want to help her.

"He and you understand that he will be put in prison?" I want to make sure she knows the best of all the possible outcomes of helping him is imprisonment.

"I prefer him to return," she states calmly and clearly. "I can bring him oranges."

"Have you told the police?" I'm now wondering if they might help.

"They don't want to help us. When he left, we went to the Ministry and asked for help, knocking at all the doors. The police told us that the only person they will repatriate is the King. We know that we don't belong here."

"But they must listen when he calls?" I've listened to Fatima and others bemoan how little Belgium authorities currently offer families in terms of support—before their family members leave, and after (although some new programs are starting to emerge). Parents here, whose sons and daughters have gone to ISIS, tell me that they feel as though the Belgians, even those in their ethnic community, think they intentionally raised a monster. So in addition to their shock and grief, families often also feel rejected and judged by both the authorities and their own communities. Yet as parents, they also feel as victimized as everyone else by the terrorist recruiters who poisoned their children's minds and played upon their vulnerabilities.

"I'm sure they listen," Fatima responds, but Belgian intel has never visited or contacted her after his calls, nor have they ever coached her on how to talk her son into returning to Belgium.

"If ISIS listens [to his phone calls] it can be an issue as well," I tell Fatima. I begin to feel anxious and nauseated by all the actors who could betray his wish to defect from ISIS and cause him to be killed. "You must be very careful when you discuss this with him—Belgian police may contact the Turks and it may somehow leak to ISIS. And you can be overheard without realizing it, if he's talking to you by Skype." I recall the ISIS defector who told us about overhearing a Skype conversation in Raqqa.

She nods. "I have a burner phone [disposable and untraceable] for these conversations." I smile to myself, realizing that even the parents here have learned how to avoid Belgian intelligence and clearly don't trust their own authorities to act on their adult child's behalf.

"Do you know if I will be able to keep the baby if they come out?" Fatima suddenly asks, as though I can decide these things. I'm confused by the question and then realize she knows her son and his wife will be imprisoned, if and when they return, but she wants to have her granddaughter. Heartbreaking.

"I don't know," I tell her honestly, as my mind flashes to the image of the baby girl dressed all in pink.

When I later ask the police and others if they can help her—

without divulging her identity—an officer in one of Brussel's de-radicalization units warns me, "Anne, you must be very careful if you decide to help her. We had a similar case not long ago. I was talking to the so-called defector myself over WhatsApp, while he was still in Syria. He said that he was a defector and had escaped out of ISIS's territory and was going to come across to Turkey and turn himself in at our consulate. When he got to Turkey, our authorities searched his phone and opened all of his Internet accounts. They found out that he had a plan in place to attack in Belgium, knowing full well he would be charged, and then set free on bail. He had friends getting weapons ready for him when he returned to Brussels." It's not beyond belief that someone in ISIS would claim to be a defector as his way of quickly and legally getting back into Belgium, when he wasn't a defector at all and intended to carry out an attack once home.

"He was going to mount a suicide attack?" I ask, but my interlocutor suddenly realizes he's said too much. He clams up, telling me he can't reveal any other details. *Is Fatima's son also using her, and any money she might send him, to launch an attack in Belgium?* Having already spent two and a half years with an extremely brutal terrorist organization, he may no longer have any limits on who he will exploit to hurt others. Perhaps, seriously wounded, he may also now be ready and willing to die for his cause. Or, they're really injured, and now with a wife and young child he needs to protect, he needs to defect from ISIS. Even for a mother, it's impossible to know.

During these last two trips to Belgium, I have been able to interview five parents about their sons' sudden disappearances to Syria—four mothers and one father. Parents tell me how ISIS recruiters managed to drive a wedge between fathers and sons by telling these vulnerable, young men that their real purpose and Islamic duty is to go and help their Syrian brothers in their uprising against Bashar al-Assad, and to build the "Caliphate". The recruiters work to discredit the fathers, telling the young recruits that their fathers could not be serious Muslims because they decided to raise their families in Belgium, which is a land of *kufr* [unbelievers].

"You need to take *hijra* [travel to Muslim lands] and live with the believers to truly be following Islam," one mother recalls her son being told. When he repeated these statements to his father about being a failed Muslim living in *kufr* lands, it caused an argument and furthered the rift between them. It's a rift that the recruiter promptly filled with ideas of manliness; convincing his target that the path to manhood and true Islamic identity—not to mention purpose, significance, dignity and belonging—were in joining the militant jihad in Syria.

Another mother, Hala, tells me about her son dying with ISIS in Syria. Daoud was radicalized like the others, in his Brussels neighborhood, by a recruiter working out in the open. Like many of the other mothers, Hala had tried to stop her son. She arranged for her son to meet with their local imam. However, when the meeting took place, her son's limited Maghreb Arabic and the imam's limited French didn't permit much of a substantive discussion of the extremist views he had come to endorse. Daoud, like the others, had fallen into the belief that his future was with the true Islamic path to establish the "Caliphate" first in Syria, and then spread it to Europe and beyond. Tragically, his local imam was without the language skills to even try to talk him out of it.

This is frequently the case in Belgium and in other European countries as well—many imams in Belgium can speak fluent Arabic or Turkish but not the Belgian local languages of French, Flemish and German. This inability to speak the local languages is an issue that European countries are beginning to address. There is growing support for imams serving in Europe to be trained there, speak the local language, perhaps time for a "European" Islam. Likewise, there is also concern in Europe about mosques continuing to receive foreign funding from countries like Saudi Arabia and Turkey. Austria, for instance, recently passed a law banning foreign funding for their mosques, which resulted in many imams paid for, and sent from Turkey, to return home.

"He was smart and spoke multiple languages," Hala says of her son. Like other boys, Daoud was a second-generation immigrant from North Africa. "But his high school teacher discouraged him and made him feel like he could only be a factory worker or garbage collector, so finally he dropped out of school. Then of course he could only get exactly those types of jobs—so he felt totally humiliated. The terrorist recruiter promised him much more." It's a common story I've heard from North African and other Muslim youth in Belgium and France. Their teachers track them into laborer jobs, and if they do go to university, they won't be hired for what they really can do. The discrimination is daily and systemic.

As an experiment, while I was teaching at Vesalius College in the Free University of Brussels from 2002 to 2007, I asked my students to prepare two resumes with only the name and linguistic abilities differing. The "Moroccan" applicants who claimed fluency in a European language and Arabic were routinely told the job was filled while the "white European" who spoke two European languages was offered a job interview. Others have replicated the same results, showing discrimination. A survey that made headlines in Belgium recently found that two-thirds of temporary employment agencies agree with client's wishes to discriminate against personnel of immigrant descent in hiring cleaning personnel.[104] In Antwerp, one of the government officials fighting radicalization also confirmed to me that it's extremely difficult to find jobs for immigrant descent youth—that no one wants to hire them.

Indeed, the unemployment rates in some areas of Belgium are above forty-five percent for young men of immigrant descent, in contrast to what ISIS offers: paid employment, free housing, relative privilege vis à vis the Syrians, status, adventure, dignity, respect for being Muslim, and for the men—a wife and sex slave. It's not a stretch to see how many economically and socially disenfranchised youth find the dream of trying to build an alternative Muslim utopian universe with ISIS attractive, in comparison to their gray future ahead in Belgium. Sadly, it's a lot like Soviet citizens who believed in Stalin's "five year plans", or anarchist promises of destroying and rebuilding, that never materialize no matter how many lives are sacrificed.

Once at a meeting with the Belgian anti-discrimination minister I asked him how I could witness young men systematically being turned away from nightclubs with the comment, "go home Moroccan", when EU law so clearly made such discrimination illegal. His answer? "Well you know it's the Moroccans that cause all the problems in the nightclubs." Shocked at his response, I almost spit my coffee back into the china cup I was holding.

It has seemed to me, as I've witnessed the situation in Western Europe over fifteen years time, that the nightclubs, landlords and employers in Belgium and many other parts of Western Europe, discriminate with impunity. When I ask North African and Muslim victims in Belgium and France why they haven't fought back in court, they tell me that they would never get justice. Indeed, Belgium's pathways to obtaining justice are highly bureaucratic and the penalties are paltry.

When one of my students interviewed a young Moroccan man about the discrimination he faced and how he felt about it, he answered, "If all the white Belgians think I'm a monster, then I might as well be one."

Not all the parents whose sons join ISIS that I've talked with are of immigrant descent. Some have sons who converted to Islam and the causes of their offspring's feelings of alienation are different. Their vulnerabilities included parental divorce, feeling lost, mental instability, depression, having no clear and hopeful life path, alongside the youthful and naïve belief in utopias. They, too, can be ripe for a slick ISIS recruiter who sells them certainty, purpose, and belonging with a close-knit group, and a mission that matters. These young men seem to block out the brutality of ISIS that is all over the news—or perhaps as in the case of

Younes—it appeals to some inner rage that they cannot express, so they express it on behalf of Syrians whom they believe are the ultimate victims of injustice.

According to our interviews, vulnerable siblings receive no support despite the fact that their ISIS sibling might try to recruit them (although new programs are starting to be developed that may change that). And those who do return from ISIS, if they manage to evade being imprisoned, deal with their psychological traumas alone. I saw that with the clearly still-radicalized Younes, who was not receiving counseling. Yet we know something can be done. France has a program that helps talk young fighters into returning home and helps them reintegrate back into society, with success.[105]

For female ISIS defectors, the road back is even more harrowing. One mother told me about her daughter-in-law who had been forced to re-marry after her husband was killed. She finally fled ISIS, but her ordeal didn't end there. "The smugglers rape them or force them into having sex in trade for getting out," this mother told me. For the women, it's one trauma after another; and then their families may reject them when they return. I wonder how vulnerable the female defectors may be to becoming suicidal; and I wonder if some might return to ISIS if they find they can't adjust to being back home. The combination of wanting to return to ISIS and becoming suicidal after returning home is also a lethal mix.

Thus far, most parents in Belgium have been extremely frustrated with the police and intelligence agents. Some called the police for help before their sons left, only to be told *after* their sons left that there was nothing the police could do to stop them because they weren't minors. All of the parents tell me that their adult children in ISIS keep in frequent contact with their mothers. They know intel agents listen to the phone calls, but as in the case of Fatima and her son, the police and local authorities never contact the parents after their son or daughter calls, nor do authorities offer any assistance in trying to talk them into coming back home.

Many parents felt that the authorities were actually glad when their sons left Belgium and hoped that they never return. I wasn't surprised to hear this sentiment. I found that attitude openly stated by some in authority—they preferred those with jihadi leanings to stay or even die in Syria rather than return and cause problems in Belgium. Let their problems play out elsewhere. In some ways, you couldn't blame them for this attitude, particularly after the Paris attacks demonstrated that Belgian citizens were capable of coming home to cause carnage. Yet there have been many reports of Europeans who have gone to Syria specifically to be groomed to return and launch attacks in Belgium and France; it seems shortsighted to hope that the problem will simply remain inside Syria.

Indeed, in December of 2015, after the Paris attacks, a twenty-seven-year-old German ISIS defector from Bremen (Harry S.) told the German weekly, *der Spiegel,* that he and many other Europeans who went to join ISIS were repeatedly asked if they would return to Europe to mount terror attacks.[106] By February of 2016, attacks in Belgium and France by those who had been trained by ISIS in Syria, or inspired by their Internet campaigns, were beginning to mount up. Among them, French national, Mehdi Nemmouche returned from Syria as the alleged gunman who opened fire on bystanders outside the Jewish Museum in Brussels in May of 2014.[107] And just days before I arrived in Brussels for this trip, a shootout occurred between police and terrorists who were hiding out in a Brussels commune [municipality] called Forest. Many believed the escaped shooters were Paris attacker, Salah Abdelslam and an associate, hiding in Brussels after the Paris attacks—but they ran from the police and vanished into thin air.[108]

On this Belgium visit, I decide to go to Molenbeek to visit a de-radicalization center. It's the community where Salah Abdelslam, his brother, and many of the others had lived. The center was closed so I walked with my filmmaker, Camille, around the area, getting a current feel for it. I'd been to Molenbeek many times and know a lot about the area from when I lived in Brussels. Tensions here can run high. One year during Ramadan, a Muslim man stabbed and killed another who dared to eat in public before the fasting ended at sundown. Yet I would not, at that time, have named Molenbeek as the hotbed of terrorism that pundits are now labeling it. But extremism has definitely increased inside Brussels over the last decade, particularly since the Syrian uprising.

Fraud and crime within this North African immigrant community have always been rife. Many families take full unemployment benefits from the state while they also find ways to work in the black market. The area is well known for its youth who deal in drugs, pick pocket, and routinely troll Brussels streets, especially around the nightclubs, to harass young "white" women. Little is done to stop them. A police officer bemoaned the lenient judgments that allowed one second-generation Moroccan youth to be arrested seventy-five times before he was finally jailed. "They know we will arrest them and they'll be free the next day," he said. "The judges here do nothing."

Being a young, white female dressed in an acceptable manner for Western culture can court serious and violent aggression from within this community. All the female students I taught had their stories of being threatened and assaulted by North African immigrants (first or second generation, no one was sure) for "displaying their sexuality" in ways that apparently made the men believe they were nothing more than prostitutes.

A Danish girl I taught at Vesalius, with beautiful blonde, short ringlets who dated a second generation Moroccan Belgian who lived in Molenbeek, shared, "The Moroccans often insult me on the tram going to his house. One time one of them poured a Coca Cola over my head because I wasn't wearing a scarf." An American student studying abroad here, waiting at a central Brussels subway stop [De Brouckère], became incensed and demanded a North African young man stop groping her girlfriend's behind and putting his hands up inside her dress. In response, he boxed her violently on the side of her head with a closed fist. She is permanently deaf in that ear as a result. Another student, a Norwegian with long, wavy, blonde hair was jumped in Watermael-Boitsfort, a tony Brussels commune, while walking home in the early evening. The North African who attacked her threw her down on the pavement, kicking and beating her. Recalling the incident, she asked, "I couldn't understand—why he didn't rape me or take my purse? I had cash and my phone, but he wasn't interested. He apparently only wanted to punish me for walking with my hair down and smoking in the darkness as I walked along. He probably thought I was a prostitute."

Another of the female students came up in the subway stop in Molenbeek after nightclubbing on a weekend to find five North Africans surrounding her. They asked her which she wanted, an "angel's smile" or to be gang raped. Not knowing what an "angel's smile" was she chose that. One of them then took out a knife and carved a hideous line from the two ends of her mouth to each ear—forever disfiguring her face.

I found it absolutely terrifying to hear these young women's stories and didn't write about it at the time for fear of retribution.

A male Flemish student told me of news reports in which young men, appearing in court for rape charges, were accompanied by their parents who protested that their son couldn't be guilty because he only accosted a prostitute. Clearly the culture clashes in Molenbeek and some of the other areas where immigrants have congregated inside Brussels reflect serious issues of assimilation that fuel a hatred that seems to go in both directions.

Now walking around Molenbeek, I feel acutely aware that Camille and I are the only females without headscarves and there are very few women on the streets at all. It's mostly North African men; many dressed in Moroccan-style clothing. As I take in the charming cobblestone streets and the three and four-story stone townhomes, some of them with ornate wrought iron balconies, I wonder if we will encounter any aggression?

Hopefully we are out of the age range to be mistaken for the young women who are so often "punished".

A Belgian police officer who served his career in Molenbeek commune shared what he saw as a serious problem, already a decade ago, that has led to the current state of affairs, "There was no priority on community policing. In fact, while the *Salafi* movement was growing in Molenbeek, the intel guys told us to stay out of the garage mosques, that they had their informants inside. We saw criminality decrease as the young men grew beards and insisted on the women wearing scarves, but now I know it wasn't good. We should have been at all the meetings and talking to everyone, but community policing is still not a priority in Belgium."

I wonder as we walk around, just how radicalized this area is. An hour later, I get an answer. Safe inside my hotel, I watch television footage of Paris attacker Salah Abdelslam arrested very near to where we were just walking in Molenbeek. Bullets flew as the police entered the house where he was hiding. Parents with two small children were inside as he was dragged from the house and put in a police car.

That night, I go back to the spot and talk to some first and second-generation young men hanging out on the street. "Do you think many knew he was hiding here all this time?" I ask.

"If they knew, no one would dare say anything. He would be punished if he did," a first-generation Syrian tells us. A second-generation Moroccan tells me, "You risk having your building set on fire if you rat out community members. They can attack you or your family."[109] I recall talking to another young Belgian in Antwerp who had refused to turn in an al-Qaeda recruiter operating in his neighborhood. When asked why, he answered, "You don't understand our culture. We would never turn someone in our community into the police."[110]

Indeed, this may explain how Salah Abdelslam managed to hide out in plain sight in Brussels for four months after returning from the Paris attacks—no one wanted to risk retribution or the ire of a brutal group of killers like ISIS. Afterward, I talk with Ahmet on Skype. "You shouldn't go out interviewing anymore. Stay in the hotel," He warns me. "They may be planning a retaliation attack."

It's possible but I think, *nothing more will happen, they rounded up the last of the Paris attackers.* I continue my interviews and traveling around Brussels, though Ahmet's warning sticks in my mind. I notice many young men with that aggressive look I know well—belligerent defiance in the face of societal rejection, and there are more headscarves in Brussels than I remember from only five years ago. The belligerent look doesn't win the men many friends among "white" Belgians and the tensions make me feel more nervous than normal.

My last morning in Brussels, I sit savoring my Belgian coffee as I correspond with a Dutch colleague who offers to help me get more interviews on my next trip to Europe. No one knows how to make coffee like Europeans. My phone rings. It's Hamid, a friend who has introduced me to the lawyers of some of the ISIS returnees in hopes of gaining interviews with them. He's hysterical. "Anne where are you?!" he screams over the phone line. "Where are you?!"

"I'm about to get in the taxi to the airport," I answer, confused as to why he's screaming at me. "What's wrong?"

"Don't go to the airport," he shouts. "They blew it up!"

I'm stunned. I let him begin to explain, while he calms down realizing I'm not already there. The explosion happened less than forty-five minutes ago.

Next, my friend Anamaria, who I'd seen the night before, calls hysterically. "Anne?! Are you at the airport, are you okay?!" She's breathless. By now I've opened my computer and am seeing the first photos of the Zaventum airport bombing. The entire departure hall has been blown away and a just-posted Internet video shows panicked passengers running from the smoke-filled building. When I assure her I'm safe, "Oh thank God!" Anamaria cries out and breaks into sobs. I feel tears filling my eyes, too. It's worse imagining it the way she did—me in the midst of all that carnage.

When I think about what I should do, I momentarily consider going to the airport to photograph it. Instead I try to find out what hospital they are taking the survivors to and who to contact at the U.S. Embassy to volunteer. I had done so when 9-11 happened and NATO was mentioned as the next target. I can help again. I gather my things to go on the subway toward the embassy when I hear the next shocking news. The Maelbeek metro station has just exploded. The subway line I was about to get on. This time I opt to follow Ahmet's advice and stay in the hotel. Sirens are screaming everywhere in the center of Brussels.

It's not academic this time. It's not terrorists telling me what they think and why they do it. It's the airport I'm supposed to be at—it's the subway line I was about to board. I stare mutely at the television footage, at the hanging shards of cement and rebar, the blown away floor tiles and windows blown from their casings and the bodies lying about injured and dead, as I think, "Yes, thank God."

But they are thanking God, too. Or so they claim. The Belgian extremists who pushed luggage carts of explosives into the crowded departure hall and exploded themselves; reportedly screamed, "*Allahu Akbar*!" as their last words.

God *is* great, but what they believe is all lies. How can we make them understand that there will be no "Caliphate" to end worldly injustices and no utopian Islamic place where they will be honored? This false utopian dream comes with a terrible cost—thousands of lives and unspeakable brutality. There's also the terrible cost to our societies when fear entrenches bigotry. And there are the corrupt dealings between ISIS and its sworn enemies. Three quarters of the oil wealth that ISIS is thought to have brought in during 2015, according to captured documents, came through trades with those close to the Assad regime, just as our defectors told us. ISIS sells oil to the same regime that sends it back raining down in barrel bombs upon their heads![111] How could this corrupt, brutal and un-Islamic terror group ever deliver any true remedies to injustice?

It takes me four days to get home. Before I leave, I attend the impromptu memorials of flowers and candles in Place de la Bourse. I notice all the TV trucks that no police could ever possibly have entirely searched. *What stops someone from driving up with a van full of explosives?* I can't help but wonder. Similarly, when I go to the *Eurostar* at the Midi train station in the heart of a Moroccan Belgian community to finally exit Brussels and fly out of London and back to the U.S., I see all kinds of large trucks parked nearby. *Is one of them filled with explosives and just waiting to be detonated?* It's oh-so-easy to see how fear divides people.

Belgian police cannot possibly be on top of everything in this city, despite the now deployed Belgian military. Soldiers in camouflage wielding machine guns are everywhere. The police have already made multiple arrests in Schaerbeek and Molenbeek. When I hear that a rented home in Schaerbeek was the site of the terrorists' explosives factory and from where they launched their attack on the airport, I recall my students coming to tell me, in 2006, about a pop-up ad that appeared on a computer at an Internet café in this same neighborhood. It was sponsored by al-Qaeda and asked the user, "Do you want to join the worldwide jihad?"

A jihad is certainly raging worldwide and it seems to have come to the heart of Europe—Brussels, the capital of the European Union. In the United States, the FBI admits to having over one thousand open ISIS-related cases that cover every single state. And the June 2016 Orlando massacre was carried out by an American, second-generation Afghan. He was a lone wolf, a consumer of Anwar al-Awlaki videos and a "wannabe martyr"—a homegrown terrorist inspired by ISIS.

The Zaventem airport reopens in two weeks. Many friends tell me about injuries and deaths of mutual friends. Everyone feels touched by it. A girl who went to my son's international school in Athens was killed there. Europeans try to return to normal, but there is no normal anymore with news of ISIS trying to mount multiple attacks in multiple European countries. Turkey vows to close the borders and keep more Syrians inside their country. Greeks are overrun with refugees as European countries to the north begin closing their borders in succession. EU officials try to coordinate their intelligence better. Every Western country offers Belgian intelligence much needed assistance, as Coalition air strikes continue to degrade ISIS, killing more leaders and diminishing its taxable territory and capacity to sell oil. Yet ISIS thunders on.

Ahmet and I continue our mission as well. We continue interviewing the Syrian ISIS defectors who hide in Turkey, and those we can gain access to in Europe and other parts of the world. Those who agree to speak on video are recorded and as quickly as we are able, our volunteer video editors are producing short video clips of these ISIS insiders telling true stories of what life is like inside the "Caliphate" and denouncing the group for its brutality, corruption, lies and un-Islamic core. We have thirty such interviews to date and more from European returnees and parents of those who have gone to Syria and ISIS.

We load the first short videos of the ISIS defectors onto the web, naming them things like "Come to the Caliphate" and "Glorious Cubs of the Caliphate," hoping that those who are already consuming ISIS products might also mistakenly view ours. Likewise, we produce Internet memes – electronic posters with strong quotes from the defectors that denounce ISIS. Each is paired with compelling photos, from their phones, or from ISIS itself. We will tweet these out under ISIS hashtags with pro-ISIS names. We are forming focus groups to learn which of our video clips and memes have the strongest effects. We are sure that there are no better voices to fight ISIS than those who have been on the inside.[112] Our work gives these defectors a platform to release their words to the world— denouncing one of the most evil terrorist groups in history. We hope with these insider voices, along with international efforts to defeat the group, and political efforts to address its root causes, ISIS will one day be wiped off the face of the earth.

Ahmet and his family have found safety from ISIS. They've settled into the United States, he having earned an *Individuals with Extraordinary Ability or Achievement Visa*, and together we run the *International Center for the Study of Violent Extremism (ICSVE)* to fight ISIS and other groups like them.

We laugh at how fate plays itself out—that when we met I couldn't travel to the south of Turkey because our funder thought it was too dangerous—I'd disappear, be kidnapped or killed—and my trust in Ahmet may turn out to be a mistake. Turns out that trusting Ahmet was one of the best decisions of my life. That I was far closer to being killed by terrorists in Brussels, in neighborhoods I knew well, is an irony not lost on either of us.

Our work continues.

Epilogue - Breaking ISIS

The *emir* who told us, "They took the love inside children and put evil in its place…"

The father speaking of his pregnant daughter trying to escape ISIS, "They said, if she really wanted to go out she can, but she has to give birth and nurse the baby and give them the child first, because it's a child of *Daesh* [ISIS]…"

The young man, "If they tell you to help slay others you have to do it. Even if they tell you to behead your own father you have to do it. Whatever the sheikh tells you to do, you have to do. When we hear the order we have to execute it…"

These words and many more will forever echo in our minds. They are pieces of the ISIS utopian ideal and the glory of its "Caliphate." Building upon existing al-Qaeda ideology claiming that Muslims, Islamic lands and even Islam itself are under attack by the West, ISIS pursues an End Times quest to establish its so-called just world order through brutality, violence, bloodshed, corruption, devil's bargains, terrorist attacks and murder of the innocent.

But to understand ISIS is to understand that it is not just a terrorist group.

ISIS is a revolutionary ideal that appeals to those who have lost faith in existing models of governance and do not see justice being delivered to them in any other way. It is a "brand" that captures the hearts and minds of disenfranchised, marginalized, angry, frustrated, bored, and even mentally ill individuals all around the world. Capitalizing on this brand appeal, unlike any other terrorist group we've seen so far, ISIS has created a sophisticated propaganda campaign that is dominating in the social media space.

The ISIS Defector Interview Project will continue to expose the corrupt inner workings of ISIS and most important for the purposes of this project, why defectors grow so tired and so disillusioned with its vision that they risk their lives to defect from ISIS and risk them again to tell us their stories.

ISIS is an evil organization unlikely to disappear anytime soon. Many strong factors fuel its continued survival: the deep Shia/Sunni divide further unleashed by the U.S. Coalition invasion of Iraq; the proxy wars being fought through ISIS; the many regional powers that gain from ISIS continuing to exist. Likewise, despite the U.S. Coalition's persistent airstrikes and resultant narrowing of territory held by ISIS, the loss of oil revenues and its taxation base, defectors told us that even if their territory is lost—ISIS cadres plan to shave their beards and blend into civil society where they will continue to mount terrorist attacks upon innocent civilians as they keep up their fight for a "Caliphate" reborn.

While defeating the group militarily and bringing political peace and good governance solutions to the Middle East are gargantuan tasks, the ISIS "brand" can be broken. And we now possess tools to do so.

At *ICSVE*, we believe in action-based research and are taking the fight against ISIS to the ideological battlefield, using our research in strategic and creative ways to counter recruitment and discredit ISIS. Real stories of real people who felt the same urges and desires to join ISIS are the most persuasive voices to prevent vulnerable others from moving further along the terrorist trajectory. As of the publishing of this book, we have conducted an unprecedented thirty-eight interviews with ISIS insiders, but many more are underway.

As you read this, we are inside ISIS chat rooms and are loading slick, short defector videos and memes onto the Internet using ISIS hashtags, to fight ISIS recruitment where it lives. On the surface, these clips will blend in with ISIS' propaganda. By naming them with enticing titles such as *A Sex Slave as a Gift for You from al-Baghdadi, Come to the Caliphate, The Glorious Cubs of the Caliphate,* we are luring those who are already consuming ISIS products to mistakenly consume ours as well—and hear the truth, from insiders.

Our Internet campaign must be followed with the creation of helplines and rapid intervention teams that provide safe support to concerned friends, colleagues and family members of those being ensnared by ISIS and its virulent ideology. At present those concerned about potential radicalization of a loved one have only the police or FBI to call. The FBI states that in most cases family members are aware of serious changes and radicalization of their loved one, but few call for help, fearing arrests, sting operations, or worse. We stand ready to support and assist efforts to create these kinds of counter actions to compete with the "swarming" that ISIS executes on vulnerable individuals drawn in by its Internet campaigns. We also stand ready to support and improve educational materials to "inoculate" youth against ISIS and groups like it.

We have been doing counter-terrorist work for decades and will continue our face-to-face meetings with those who have been inside the deadliest and most brutal terrorist group in recent history. Visit our website at www.ICSVE.org to keep an eye out for our next book and our many reports—video and written—based on this project.

You can help us stay in the fight against ISIS. Please consider donating to support our work at www.ICSVE.org.

Anne Speckhard, Ph.D.
Ahmet S. Yayla, Ph.D.
International Center for the Study of Violent Extremism (ICSVE)

Please Like this Book on Amazon!

If you found ISIS Defectors a good read, please give it some good words and loads of stars on Amazon, Barnes & Noble, or wherever you purchase your books. Thanks for your time in doing so!

Other Books by, or coauthored by, Anne Speckhard, Ph.D.

<u>Talking to Terrorists: Understanding the Psycho-Social Motivations of Militant Jihadi Terrorists, Mass Hostage Takers, Suicide Bombers and "Martyrs"</u>,

<u>Undercover Jihadi: Inside the Toronto 18—Al Qaeda Inspired, Homegrown Terrorism in the West</u>

<u>Bride of ISIS: One Young Woman's Path into Homegrown Terrorism</u>

<u>Warrior Princess: A U.S. Navy SEAL's Journey to Coming out Transgender</u>

<u>Fetal Abduction: The True Story of Multiple Personalities and Murder</u>,

<u>Timothy Tottle's Terrific Dream</u>

<u>Timothy Tottle's Terrific Crocodiles</u>

Other Books by, or coauthored by, Ahmet S. Yayla, Ph.D.

<u>First Responders' Guide to Professionally Interacting with Muslim Communities: Law Enforcement, Emergency and Fire Fighters</u>

<u>Understanding and Responding to Terrorism:A Complete Model to Deal with Terrorism</u>

<u>Understanding and Responding to Terrorism</u>

Acknowledgements

A special thanks to our esteemed colleagues and friends for reviewing and commenting on the book: Richard Barrett; Peter Bergen; Stephen van den Bosch; Michael A. Brown; Joe Charlaff; Rita Cosby; Dr. Alistair D. Edgar; U.S. Ambassador Alberto Fernandez (Ret.); Carol Rollie Flynn; Professor James Forest; Professor Rohan Gunaratna; Stephan Van Hauwe; Shashi Jayakumar; Arie W. Kruglanski; Maqsoud Kruse; Arno Arr Michaelis IV; Abigail Rodriguez; Howard J. Shatz; Sheikh Ali; Professor Emeritus Alex P. Schmid; Yoram Schweitzer; Mubin Shaikh; Howard J. Shatz; Allison McDowell-Smith; Jeff Swicord; Farhana Qazi and Sara Zeiger. We've been encouraged and influenced by many of you over the years and are grateful for you. A special thanks to Sheik Ali for insights on Islamic scriptures often twisted and used by terrorist groups and Allison Mc-Dowell-Smith for carefully reading the entire manuscript and supporting our work.

Thank you so very much to Susan Barnett for working and reworking the text, helping us to craft this book, and tell the stories herein. Thank you Susan for all your thoughtful insights, great job editing, hours of support and valuable advice throughout the process of writing this book. Thanks also for helping with the publicity campaign to bring it to readers and news outlets.

Thanks to Sourabh Aryabhatta, for the layout and book design of all of the various digital versions of this book. And kudos to my artist daughter, Jessica Speckhard, for her creative vision for the cover artwork.

Thank you to both of our families for supporting our work. Ahmet's family literally ran for their lives as a result of his work and mine hung in there for research trips that turned fraught with danger, late night writing binges, and always had support and advice to offer along with needed laughs. Ahmet thanks his wife and three children and his brother.... Thank you Daniel, who always tells me don't worry about the money—follow your heart. Daniel, Jessica, Danny and Leah, you have all put up with me when I've traveled into dangerous territories, prison cells and ghettos to talk to nefarious folks and always supported me as I prepared, departed and returned from such trips, even when it took time and care away from our family to do so. And Katarina you keep me remembering what a pure and clean heart looks like and you make me laugh even when the world is in a sorry and sad state.

Thanks also to the people we cannot mention by name here as they wish, or need, to remain anonymous—our film director who filmed our European interviews and single-handedly wrote, directed, and produced the mini-doc video clips released with this book—doing so even when there was no budget to pay her, working with a fully dedicated heart to fighting ISIS. Thanks also to our English to Arabic sub-titler, video editor and producer of small film clips who also went above and beyond the call to duty.

Thanks to our fixers and videographers and especially thanks from the bottom of our hearts to Abu Said and Murat (not their real names) who risked everything to help us invite defectors in Turkey to be interviewed and capture them on videos—even staying engaged when Ahmet had to run for his life from ISIS. To all of you—your passion, care, diligence and the risks you took to help us fight ISIS will never be forgotten.

Lastly, thanks to the courage of the ISIS defectors who, despite having recently returned from evil and the confusion, trauma, emotional pain and the dangers of opening up about their experiences under ISIS, risked talking to us and telling the world the truth about ISIS.

About the Authors

Anne **Speckhard, Ph.D.** is Adjunct Associate Professor of Psychiatry in the School of Medicine, Georgetown University, and Director of the *International Center for the Study of Violent Extremism (ICSVE)*. Dr. Speckhard has been working in the field of posttraumatic stress disorder (PTSD) since the 1980's and has extensive experience working in Europe, the Middle East and the former Soviet Union. She was the chair of the NATO Human Factors & Medicine Research and Technology Experts Group (HFM-140/RTG) on the Psychosocial, Cultural and Organizational Aspects of Terrorism, served as the co-chair of the NATO-Russia Human Factors & Medicine Research Task Group on Social Sciences Support to Military Personnel Engaged in Counter-Insurgency and Counter-Terrorism Operations and served on the NATO Human Factors & Medicine Research Task Group Moral Dilemmas and Military Mental Health Outcomes. She is a member of the United Nations Roster of Experts for the Terrorism Prevention Branch Office on Drugs and Crime and was previously awarded a Public Health Service Fellowship in the United States Department of Health & Human Services where she served as a Research Fellow.

She has provided expert consultation to European and Middle Eastern governments as well as the U.S. Department of Defense regarding programs for prevention and rehabilitation of individuals committed to political violence and militant jihad. In 2006-2007 she worked with the U.S. Department of Defense to design and pilot test the Detainee Rehabilitation Program in Iraq. In 2002, she interviewed hostages taken in the Moscow Dubrovka Theater about their psychological responses and observations of the suicidal terrorists and did the same in 2005 with surviving hostages from the Beslan school take-over. Since 2002, she has collected nearly five hundred research interviews of family members, friends, close associates and hostages of terrorists and militant jihadi extremists in Palestine, Israel, Iraq, Lebanon, Jordan, Morocco,

Russia, Chechnya, Belarus, Canada, the United States, Netherlands, United Kingdom, Belgium, Turkey, Kosovo, Denmark, and France.

Dr. Speckhard is the director of the *Holocaust Survivors Oral Histories Project – Belarus*, a project constructing the history of the Minsk Ghetto and Holocaust in Belarus through oral histories and archival research.

She also researched traumatic stress issues in survivors of the Chernobyl disaster and has written about stress responses to toxic disasters. Dr. Speckhard worked with American expatriates after 9-11 (at SHAPE, NATO, the U.S. Embassy to Belgium and Mission to the EU) and conducted research on acute stress responses to terrorism in this population.   She also studies psychological resilience to terrorism in various populations including American civilians, military and diplomats serving in Iraq under high threat security conditions. Dr. Speckhard co-directed the NATO Advanced Research Workshops - Ideologies of Terrorism: Understanding and Predicting the Social, Psychological and Political Underpinnings of Terrorism and Understanding and Addressing the Root Causes of Radicalization among Groups with an Immigrant Heritage in Europe and served on the NATO/Russia Counter-Terrorism Advisory Group.

Dr. Speckhard has consulted to NATO, OSCE, foreign governments and the U.S. Departments of State, Defense, Justice, Homeland Security, Health & Human Services, CIA and FBI. In the past year she has also briefed ,along with Dr. Yayla, on their joint research on ISIS with the terrorism-related committees of the U.S. Senate and House; the Defense Intelligence Agency; Swiss Federal and local police; Austrian, Dutch and Belgian counter-radicalization authorities; and local police from various American cities, among others. She is a sought after expert on the subject of terrorism appearing on CNN, BBC, NPR, Fox News, MSNBC, CTV, and in *Time*, *The New York Times*, *The Washington Post*, *London Times* and many other publications. She frequently lectures on subjects related to her books and research studies. She is the author of seven books including: *Talking to Terrorists: Understanding the Psycho-Social Motivations of Militant Jihadi Terrorists, Mass Hostage Takers, Suicide Bombers and "Martyrs", Fetal Abduction: The True Story of Multiple Personalities and Murder, Bride of ISIS, Timothy Tottle's Terrific Crocodiles and Timothy Tottle's Terrific Dream* and co-author of *Undercover Jihadi: Inside the Toronto 18—Al Qaeda Inspired, Homegrown Terrorism in the West* and *Warrior Princess: A U.S. Navy SEAL's Journey to Coming out Transgender*.   Website: www.AnneSpeckhard.com

Ahmet S. Yayla, Ph.D. is the Deputy Director of the *International Center for the Study of Violent Extremism (ICSVE)*. He is also Adjunct Professor at the Department of Criminology, Law and Society at George Mason University and formerly served as Professor and the Chair of the Sociology Department at Harran University in Şanlıurfa, Turkey. Dr. Yayla earned both his Master's and Ph.D. degrees in Criminal Justice and Information Science from the University of North Texas in the United States. Dr. Yayla served as Chief of Counter-terrorism and Operations Division for the Turkish National Police in charge of administrative oversight of counter-terrorism actions along the Turkey-Syria border from 2010 to 2015. His work was primarily concerned with terrorist and related activities of ISIS, al-Qaeda, al-Nusra, Hezbollah, the PKK, and other global terrorist organizations and he was responsible for several successful operations against the above-listed terrorist organizations. Dr. Yayla designed and administered counter-terrorism activities and operations for precautionary measures in city of Şanlıurfa, located at the Turkish-Syrian border and at the borders of the current ongoing war-zone in Syria.

Dr. Yayla's research mainly focuses on terrorism, radicalization and countering violence extremism (CVE). He has authored and co-authored several articles and books on the subject of terrorism and violence including: *First Responders' Guide to Professionally Interacting with Muslim Communities: Law Enforcement, Emergency and Fire Fighters; Understanding and Responding to Terrorism:A Complete Model to Deal with Terrorism;* and *Understanding and Responding to Terrorism.* Among the most recent articles are "Deadly Interactions: ISIS" World Policy Journal, December, 2015 and "Inside ISIS: First Person Accounts from ISIS Defectors", Journal of Perspectives in Terrorism, December 2015.

Dr. Yayla over the years has interviewed cadres representing over twenty terrorist organizations. The ISIS defectors interviews of late, are unique in the world as he was one of the first researchers (with Dr. Anne Speckhard) who managed to reach ISIS defectors hiding in Turkey and persuade them to tell their stories. Most agreed to be video recorded for future documentaries. One of the results of this research is the book you are reading, *ISIS Defectors: Inside Stories of the Terrorist Caliphate.*

Due to his accomplishments in the field of counter-terrorism, Dr. Yayla was invited on October 21, 2006 to the U.S. Senate, Homeland Security Committee and Subcommittee on Prevention of Nuclear and Biological Attacks as an expert witness upon request of the U.S. Department of Homeland Security to testify on local law enforcement preparedness for countering terrorism threats in the USA and Turkey, including dealing with urban terrorism as a criminal activity. Moreover, Dr. Yayla was appointed as an Official Advisor by the U.S. Department of Homeland Security between November 2006 – March 2007 to advise on understanding and building connections with terrorism-targeted international communities living in the United States. Over the years, Dr. Yayla has taught terrorism and counterterrorism related courses to different agencies in various countries around the world. He also advised, consulted and was involved in projects related with CVE in numerous countries and with diverse international organizations. In the past year he has briefed, along with Dr. Speckhard, on their joint research on ISIS with the terrorism-related committees of the U.S. Senate and House; the Defense Intelligence Agency; Swiss Federal and local police; Austrian, Dutch and Belgian counter-radicalization authorities; and local police from various American cities, among others.

Glossary

Abaya - A woman's robe worn loose over clothing, especially thick and black under ISIS rule.

Abu – Father of (eg. Abu Omar, Father of Omar).

Adhan – Islamic call to daily prayers, five times a day.

AK-47 – Semi-automatic and automatic 7.62 mm machine gun. Also called Kalashnikov or in slang, Kalash.

Alawite – A Syrian version of Shia Islam, sometimes known as the third branch of Islam.

Allah – Standard Arabic word used for God.

Allahu Akbar – "Allah/God is Greater." Can be used in exclamation of anything positive.

Ansar/Ansari – Literally means the helpers, was used to refer to the inhabitants of the city of Medina to refer to the Muslims who accepted and helped to the Muslims coming from Mecca during the time of the Prophet Mohammad. ISIS uses Ansar to address the locals. For example, the Syrian ISIS members are referred to as ansar by the group.

Baba – Father.

Bayat – (also Bay'ah) Literally means a pact of providing allegiance and commitment. In ISIS's case, it refers the oath and pledge of allegiance to the Islamic State and to the so-called Caliph El-Bagdadi.

Bint – Daughter of. Fatimah bint Qays, meaning daughter of Qays, Fatima.

BKC – Iraqi clone of the Soviet PKM machine gun.

Burqa – An outer garment that envelopes the head, face and whole body, used by some Islamic women to cover themselves in public.

Caliph – A spiritual leader of Islam, claiming succession from the Prophet Muhammad.

Caliphate – The rank, jurisdiction, or government of a caliph.

Dabiq – A town in Northern Syria. Considered as the place of the final epic battle between the Muslims and Christians marking the end of the world. Hence, ISIS uses and refers to Dabiq frequently, claiming itself being the Muslim force countering the West close to the resurrection day. ISIS also had named its online magazine *Dabiq*.

Dawah – Inviting to submit to Islam, proselytizing or preaching.

ad-Dawlah – Literally means "the State". ISIS uses *ad-Dawlah* to refer to itself as the Islamic State and bans the use of other terms, including IS,

ISIS, DAESH.

Daesh - An adapted acronym of the Arabic name for ISIS (Dawlat al-Islamiyah f'al-Iraq w Belaad al-Sham) which is used by Gulf states to refer to the group. This name is so hated by ISIS leaders that they have threatened to cut out the tongues of anyone who uses it.

Dua – Personal prayers that follow formal prayer.

Eid – Festival in Arabic.

Eid al-Adha – Sacrificing festival during when Muslims sacrifice animals following the tradition of the Prophet Abraham.

Eid al-Fitr – End of the month of Ramadan festival. Muslims fast during the month of Ramadan and Eid al-Fitr refers to the three-day festival at the end of one month fasting.

Fajr – Dawn prayers

Fard – Religious duty in Islamic Law. For example, daily prayers, fasting in Ramadan etc.

Fard al-ayn – Obligatory Islamic duty imposed on every individual in Islamic Law, means that duty must be committed by every Muslim, for example daily prayers. Also referred to as individual duty.

Fard al-kifayah – Obligatory Islamic duty imposed on Muslim communities in Islamic Law, means that duty must be committed by some members of the Muslim community, for example funeral prayers.

Fusha Arabic – Classical form of Arabic referring to the Qur'anic form of Arabic.

Hadith – A traditional account, including recorded and protected sayings, habits and actions, said or done by the Prophet Muhammad.

Halal – Permissible according to the Islamic Law.

Haram – Forbidden according to the Islamic Law.

Hijab – Also veil. A traditional scarf worn by Muslim women to cover the hair, head and sometimes the neck.

Hisbah – Religious or morality police of ISIS.

Hookah – Arabic water pipe for smoking.

Houri – Beautiful and young virgin companions of Muslims in the paradise.

Ibn – Son of. Ibni-I Ali. Son of Ali.

Iddah – Four months and ten days waiting period for Muslim women after divorce, or loss of husband based upon Verse number 2 Ayah 234 of the Qur'an. "If any of you die and leave widows behind, they shall wait concerning themselves four months and ten days – when they have fulfilled their term, there is no blame on you if they dispose of themselves in a just and reasonable manner. And Allah is well acquainted with what ye do."

Insha'Allah – "If Allah wills it." Usually said in response to a request or desire. Sometimes cynically described as a polite way of saying, "No."

Imam – The title for a Muslim religious leader or anyone who leads prayer. Iman – Faith of an Islamic believer. There are six requirements of Iman in Islam: Belief in Allah, the Angels, Divine Books, the Prophets, the Day of Judgement, and Allah's predestination (destiny and fate).

ISIS – "Islamic State in Iraq and Syria." A modern day terrorist group that originated in Iraq and crossed into Syria in defiance of al-Qaeda's orders to make war upon the mujahideen fighting in Syria and returned back to Iraq to continue their insurgency. In June 2014, their leader Abu Bakr al-Baghdadi unilaterally declared himself to be the Caliph of the entire Muslim world.

Islam – The religious faith of Muslims, based on the Qur'an (the speech of Allah) and the Sunnah (the life example of the Prophet Muhammad, the basic principle of which is absolute submission to a unique and personal God (Allah).

Istishadi – Becoming a self-'martyr.' ISIS refers to suicide attacks as istishadi.

Jamaat – Refers to an assembly. Usually used in the Islamic sense to address the congregation of a mosque or a group of people who follow a certain imam.

Jawshan al-Kabir – Literally means steel plate. A lengthy prayer that recites the 1000 names of Allah which are thought to have been revealed directly by the Archangel Gabriel to the Prophet Muhammed as an armor to protect against evil.

Jihad – There are two forms of jihad—the inner struggle every Muslim makes to attempt a life of morality and a second form that involves fighting as a militant for the defense of Muslim lands, people and honor.

Kafir – Unbeliever/rejecter of Islam. Technically: one who knows the truth but conceals it. Falsely made synonymous with "infidel," a Judeo-Christian concept describing a person unfaithful to God.

Kufr – Action of unbelieving.

Kassas – Executioner.

Keffiyeh – Checkered scarf-like (usually black and white) head wrap, generally used by Arab men to cover their heads.

al-Khansaa Brigade – The all-female morality police of ISIS operating since 2014 in Mosul and Raqqa and in the other parts of the ISIS.

Khawarij – Islamic insurrectionists, referring to the renegade tribe in the time of the Prophet Muhammed who practiced *takfir* [excommunication] and believed they could kill other Muslims who did not adhere to their interpretation of Islam.

Iman – Faith of an Islamic believer. There are six requirements of Iman in Islam: Belief in Allah, the Angels, Divine Books, the Prophets, the Day of Judgement, and Allah's predestination (destiny and fate).

Kitabiyat – Refers to Ahl al-Kitâb, the People of the Book, i.e. Jews and Christians.

al-Lakhdar Brahimi – The kind of whip ISIS uses. Its name is a word play referring to the UN peace envoy and negotiator for Syria from 2012 to 2014 who is deeply hated by ISIS. The whip is made of a green rubber tubing and akhdhar means green in Arabic so it's a play on words.

Maghrib – West.

Mahram – A woman's chaperone, meaning her father, husband or a man she cannot marry (i.e. son, or uncle).

Malayinat – Unnecessary things which take people away from Allah's way.

Martyr – A person who died for the cause of a religion. In Islam, someone who has died carrying out jihad, in the military expansion of Islam, or carrying out a religious commandment.

Martyrdom – Dying for the cause of a religion.

Masjid – Mosque.

Militiant Jihadi – An Islamic fundamentalist who participates in or supports jihad, especially armed and violent confrontation.

Mubayaeen – Followers.

Mubayah – Giving out bayat and pledge.

Muezzin – Person who calls Muslims to daily prayers five times a day.

Muhajirun – The first Muslims who immigrated to the city of Medina with the Prophet Muhammed at the very early years of Islam. ISIS uses the term to refer to its foreign fighters.

Mujahid – One who participates in Jihad. Plural: Mujahideen.

Mujahideen – Plural of mujahid- one who is engaged in jihad.

Multazama – Conforming to Islam and wearing the niqaab and hijab.

Murtad – an apostate, someone who gives up Islam willingly.

Murtadeen – Plural form of Murtad. Those who abandoned the true Islam as defined by ISIS in the case of ISIS.

Nikah – Engagement between man and woman.

Niqab – A traditional head, face and shoulder covering worn by Islamic women that shows only the eyes, if that. It is debated by some, but generally believed to be nonobligatory to cover the face in Islam.

Nizam – Literally means order. In this book, defectors use nizam to refer to the Assad regime and army.

PKM machine gun – Also known or referred to as Bixi. Uses 7.62×54mm cartridges making it significantly more powerful than an AK-47.

al-Qaeda – Normally understood to be the group headed by the late Osama Bin Laden that declared war on the West. Better illustrated in the statement of al Qaeda ideologue al-Suri: It is a system and methodology, not a group per se. Al Qaeda has many affiliates under various names.

Qur'an – The holy book and central religious text of Islam.

Radicalization – Very simply, the process by which an individual comes to support non-traditional political views. "Violent Radicalization" refers to a process whereby an individual comes to support violent political views. "Violent Extremism" refers to a state of being where an individual acts out their violent thoughts in support of particular political extremist groups. Terrorism is thus a type of violent extremism. These terms apply equally to Muslim and non-Muslim extremists and can include ultranationalists, white supremacists and even street gangs.

Ribat – ISIS uses this term to refer to guarding its battle fronts, usually at the borders of its territory.

Ribbaya – Follower who has pledged allegiance

RPG – Anti-tank rocket propelled grenades, launched from shoulder.

Saafer – Uncovered/ barefaced.

Sabaya – Female slave.

Sahih al-Bukhari – One of the major Hadith collection books compiled by Muhammad Al-Bukhari. Considered as the most authentic book after the Quran.

Salaam Alekium – Islamic greeting, Peace be Upon You.

Salaf – First generations of Muslims.

Salafist movement (Salafism) – Fundamentalist and ultra-conservative approach of Islam within Sunni tradition, also followed by militant jihadi terrorists.

Salat – Obligatory Muslim ritual prayers performed five times daily.

Sawm – Islamic fasting.

Shahid/Shahida – Originates from the Arabic root that means "witness". Denotes a martyr, someone who has died in jihad or in the military expansion of Islam or carrying out a religious commandment.

Sheikh – (shaikh) Usually refers to an Islamic teacher or a prominent leader in a community.

Shariah – Literally means path in Arabic. Refers to Islamic law, the religious legal system of Islam.

Sheb – Youth.

Shia – Followers of Shia Islam. Shi Islam is the second largest denomination (branch) of Islam. The division between Sunni and Shia Islam goes back to the disputes over the proper succession after the Prophet Mohammad, Shias argue that the son-in-law and cousin of the Prophet Mohammad Ali had the right to become the first of the Caliphs whereas he was the fourth.

Sin – Wrongdoings which are against Allah's will and shariah Law.

Subhan'Allah – Glory be to Allah. Can be used in exclamation as well as when receiving negative news.

Sunni – Followers of the major denomination in Islam, over eighty-five percent of all Muslims. The major contrast with Shia Islam is about the successor of the Prophet Mohammad. The closest companion and father-in-law of the Prophet Muhammed, Abu Bakr was chosen as the first caliph of Islam.

Takfir - Declaring other Muslims who don't adhere to their version of Islam as apostates, worthy of death.

Tassatur – Covering of body based on the Islamic rules both for men and women.

Tawbah – Repentance.

Tesbih – Prayer beads.

Thobe – Male Islamic robe.

Tuk-tuk - A small three-wheeled auto rickshaw.

Umm – Mother of. Umm Fatimah, mother of Fatimah.

Wali – Governor or administrator.

al Wala wal bara – Islamic and Arabic term referring to "Loving and Hating for the Sake of Allah" only.

Wudu – Ablution before Muslim prayers.

Yazidi – An ancient religious community living generally in Northern Mesopotamia regions. ISIS claims the Yazidis to be devil worshippers and especially targeted them to cleanse its territories from nonbelievers.

al-Zarqawiya – A big knife ISIS terrorists use to behead people, named after Abu Musab al-Zarqawi, the killed leader of al-Qaeda in Iraq, the precursor organization of ISIS.

Endnotes

1 The Soufan Group. (December 2015). Foreign fighters: An updated assessment of the flow of foreign fighters into Syria and Iraq. Retrieved from http://soufangroup.com/wp-content/uploads/2015/12/TSG_ForeignFightersUpdate_FINAL3.pdf

2 See: Kosinski, M. (November 17, 2015). CIA director anticipates more ISIS attacks 'in the pipeline'. CNN. Retrieved from http://www.cnn.com/2015/11/15/politics/isis-us-threat-paris-attacks/index.html and LoBianco, T. (December 2, 2015). Former intel chief says WH worried over re-elect 'narrative'. CNN. Retrieved from http://www.cnn.com/2015/12/01/politics/michael-flynn-obama-isis/

3 Hayward, J. (October 23, 2015). FBI Director estimates 900 active investigations of ISIS operativesi n U.S. Breitbart. Retrieved from http://www.breitbart.com/national-security/2015/10/23/fbi-director-estimates-900-active-investigations-isis-operatives-u-s/

4 Engel, P. (December 17, 2015). Here's the ISIS message the female San Bernardino shooter posted on Facebook during the attack. Business Insider. Retrieved from http://www.businessinsider.com/isis-message-tashfeen-malik-posted-on-facebook-during-attack-2015-12

5 See: Speckhard, A. (2012). Talking to terrorists: Understanding the psycho-social motivations of militant jihadi terrorists, mass hostage takers, suicide bombers and "martyrs". McLean, VA: Advances Press.

6 See: Speckhard, A. (2012). Talking to terrorists: Understanding the psycho-social motivations of militant jihadi terrorists, mass hostage takers, suicide bombers and "martyrs". McLean, VA: Advances Press; Speckhard, A., Tarabrina, N., Krasnov, V., & Mufel, N. (2005). Posttraumatic and acute stress responses in hostages held by suicidal terrorists in the takeover of a Moscow theater Traumatology, 11(1), 3-21.

7 The private donor has asked to remain anonymous for security concerns.

8 See: Kirk, A. (March 24, 2016). Iraq and Syria: How many foreign fighters are fighting for Isil? The Telegraph. http://www.telegraph.co.uk/news/2016/03/29/iraq-and-syria-how-many-foreign-fighters-are-fighting-for-isil/ Retrieved from http://www.telegraph.co.uk/news/2016/03/29/iraq-and-syria-how-many-foreign-fighters-are-fighting-for-isil/; The Soufan Group. (December 2015). Foreign fighters: An updated assessment of the flow of foreign fighters into Syria and Iraq. http://soufangroup.com/wp-content/uploads/2015/12/TSG_ForeignFightersUpdate_FINAL3.pdf Retrieved from http://soufangroup.com/wp-content/uploads/2015/12/TSG_ForeignFightersUpdate_FINAL3.pdf; Neumann, P. (January 26, 2015). Foreign fighter total in Syria/Iraq now exceeds 20,000; surpasses Afghanistan conflict in the 1980s. ISCR. http://icsr.info/2015/01/foreign-fighter-total-syriairaq-now-exceeds-20000-surpasses-afghanistan-conflict-1980s/ Retrieved

from http://icsr.info/2015/01/foreign-fighter-total-syriairaq-now-exceeds-20000-surpasses-afghanistan-conflict-1980s/ and Ginkel, B. v., Entenmann, E., Boutin, B., Chauzal, G., Dorsey, J., Jegerings, M., . . . Zavagli, S. (April 1, 2016). The foreign fighters phenomenon in the European Union. http://icct.nl/wp-content/uploads/2016/03/ICCT-Report_Foreign-Fighters-Phenomenon-in-the-EU_1-April-2016_including-AnnexesLinks.pdf Retrieved from http://icct.nl/wp-content/uploads/2016/03/ICCT-Report_Foreign-Fighters-Phenomenon-in-the-EU_1-April-2016_including-AnnexesLinks.pdf

9 Storm, M., Lister, T., & Cruickshank, P. (June 15, 2015). Agent Storm: My Life Inside al Qaeda and the CIA: Grove Press.

10 Speckhard, A., & Shaikh, M. (October 17, 201). Undercover Jihadi: Inside the Toronto 18 - Al Qaeda inspired, homegrown terrorism in the West: Advances Press, LLC.

11 Speckhard, A. (2015). Bride of ISIS: One young woman's journey into homegrown terrorism. McLean, VA: Advances Press, LLC.

12 Russia: Turkish president benefits from ISIL oil deals. (December 3, 2015). Al Jazeera. http://www.aljazeera.com/news/2015/12/russia-turkish-president-benefits-isil-oil-deals-151202144412848.html Retrieved from http://www.aljazeera.com/news/2015/12/russia-turkish-president-benefits-isil-oil-deals-151202144412848.html

13 Janine di Giovanni, Leah McGrath Goodman, & Sharkov, D. (November 16, 2014). How does ISIS fund its reign of terror? Newsweek. https://http://www.newsweek.com/2014/11/14/how-does-isis-fund-its-reign-terror-282607.html Retrieved from https://http://www.newsweek.com/2014/11/14/how-does-isis-fund-its-reign-terror-282607.html

14 US Army's Leavenworth Foreign Military Military Studies Office. (Winter, 2015). Ribat: Defending the Islamic State. Retrieved from http://fmso.leavenworth.army.mil/OEWatch/201503/MiddleEast_08.html

15 Reuters. (March 24, 2015). 'Cubs of the Caliphate' - ISIS recruits 400 children since January. Jersusalem Post. http://www.jpost.com/Middle-East/Cubs-of-the-Caliphate-ISIS-recruits-400-children-since-January-394908 Retrieved from http://www.jpost.com/Middle-East/Cubs-of-the-Caliphate-ISIS-recruits-400-children-since-January-394908

16 Chastain, M. (September 10, 2015). Report: ISIS Abducts 127 Children to Turn into 'Caliphate Cubs'. Breitbart. http://www.breitbart.com/national-security/2015/09/10/report-isis-abducts-127-children-to-turn-into-caliphate-cubs/ Retrieved from http://www.breitbart.com/national-security/2015/09/10/report-isis-abducts-127-children-to-turn-into-caliphate-cubs/

17 Reuters. (March 24, 2015). 'Cubs of the Caliphate' - ISIS recruits 400 children since January. Jersusalem Post. http://www.jpost.com/Middle-East/Cubs-of-the-Caliphate-ISIS-recruits-400-children-since-January-394908 Retrieved from http://www.jpost.com/Middle-East/Cubs-of-the-Caliphate-ISIS-recruits-400-children-since-January-394908

18 Dearden, L. (July 17, 2015). Isis video shows young boy beheading Syrian

soldier near ancient city of Palmyra. The Independent. http://www.independent.co.uk/news/world/middle-east/isis-video-shows-young-boy-beheading-syrian-soldier-near-ancient-city-of-palmyra-10397354.html Retrieved from http://www.independent.co.uk/news/world/middle-east/isis-video-shows-young-boy-beheading-syrian-soldier-near-ancient-city-of-palmyra-10397354.html, and Hall, J. (July 17, 2015). ISIS film a CHILD carrying out a beheading for the first time: 'Cub of the Caliphate' is the first seen executing a prisoner by decapitation as the terror group increasingly use boys to kill. Daily Mail. Retrieved from http://www.dailymail.co.uk/news/article-3164999/ISIS-film-CHILD-carrying-beheading-time-Cub-Caliphate-seen-executing-prisoner-decapitation-terror-group-increasingly-use-boys-kill.html#ixzz3vN3nhKKn

19 Dearden, L. (July 17, 2015). Isis video shows young boy beheading Syrian soldier near ancient city of Palmyra. The Independent. http://www.independent.co.uk/news/world/middle-east/isis-video-shows-young-boy-beheading-syrian-soldier-near-ancient-city-of-palmyra-10397354.html Retrieved from http://www.independent.co.uk/news/world/middle-east/isis-video-shows-young-boy-beheading-syrian-soldier-near-ancient-city-of-palmyra-10397354.htmlHall, J. (July 17, 2015). ISIS film a CHILD carrying out a beheading for the first time: 'Cub of the Caliphate' is the first seen executing a prisoner by decapitation as the terror group increasingly use boys to kill. Daily Mail. Retrieved from http://www.dailymail.co.uk/news/article-3164999/ISIS-film-CHILD-carrying-beheading-time-Cub-Caliphate-seen-executing-prisoner-decapitation-terror-group-increasingly-use-boys-kill.html#ixzz3vN3nhKKn

20 ISIS defectors usually referred to the YPG/PYD fighters as PKK whereas Ahmet chose to refer to the fighters as the PYD, even though that is really the government that supports their fighting force (i.e. the YPG).

21 Reuter, C. (April 18, 2015). The terror strategist: Secret files reveal the structure of Islamic State. Der Spiegel.URL: http://www.spiegel.de/international/world/islamic-state-files-show-structure-of-islamist-terror-group-a-1029274.html

22 Oseni, Z. I. The poetic life of Tumadir al-Khansa' bint 'Amr Retrieved from unilorin.edu.ng/publications/zioseni/NATAIS.doc

23 MacAskill, E. (March 9, 2016). Isis document leak reportedly reveals identities of 22,000 recruits. The Guardian. http://www.theguardian.com/world/2016/mar/09/isis-document-leak-reportedly-reveals-identities-syria-22000-fighters Retrieved from http://www.theguardian.com/world/2016/mar/09/isis-document-leak-reportedly-reveals-identities-syria-22000-fighters

24 Speckhard, A. (2015). Bride of ISIS. McLean, VA: Advances Press, LLC.

25 Leonard, I. (July 11, 2015). ISIS 'female Gestapo' leading campaign of terror against own sex - and 60 are British. Mirror. http://www.mirror.co.uk/news/world-news/isis-female-gestapo-leading-campaign-6046944 Retrieved from http://www.mirror.co.uk/news/world-news/isis-female-gestapo-leading-campaign-6046944

26 Leonard, I. (July 11, 2015). ISIS 'female Gestapo' leading campaign of terror against own sex - and 60 are British. Mirror. http://www.mirror.co.uk/news/world-news/isis-female-gestapo-leading-campaign-6046944 Retrieved from http://www.mirror.co.uk/news/world-news/isis-female-gestapo-leading-campaign-6046944

27 Leonard, I. (July 11, 2015). ISIS 'female Gestapo' leading campaign of terror against own sex - and 60 are British. Mirror. http://www.mirror.co.uk/news/world-news/isis-female-gestapo-leading-campaign-6046944 Retrieved from http://www.mirror.co.uk/news/world-news/isis-female-gestapo-leading-campaign-6046944

28 In 2014 the al Sheitaat tribe staged an uprising against ISIS and up to 900 members were slaughtered as a result. http://www.ibtimes.co.uk/syria-isis-kills-shaitat-tribe-teen-bazooka-deir-al-zour-1502356

29 Speckhard, A. (September 29, 2015). How dragging out feet on refugees creates more terrorists. New York Times.

30 Reuter, C. (April 18, 2015). The terror strategist: Secret files reveal the structure of Islamic State. Der Spiegel.URL: http://www.spiegel.de/international/world/islamic-state-files-show-structure-of-islamist-terror-group-a-1029274.html

31 Hawramy, F., Mohammed, S., & Harding, L. (November 19, 2014). Inside Islamic State's oil empire: how captured oilfields fuel ISIS insurgency. The Guardian. http://www.theguardian.com/world/2014/nov/19/-sp-islamic-state-oil-empire-iraq-isis Retrieved from http://www.theguardian.com/world/2014/nov/19/-sp-islamic-state-oil-empire-iraq-isis

32 Speckhard, A. (2012). Talking to terrorists: Understanding the psycho-social motivations of militant jihadi terrorists, mass hostage takers, suicide bombers and "martyrs". McLean, VA: Advances Press.

33 Ferris, E., & Kirişci, K. (July 8, 2015). What Turkey's open-door policy means for Syrian refugees. Brookings. http://www.brookings.edu/blogs/order-from-chaos/posts/2015/07/08-turkey-syrian-refugees-kirisci-ferris Retrieved from http://www.brookings.edu/blogs/order-from-chaos/posts/2015/07/08-turkey-syrian-refugees-kirisci-ferris

34 Speckhard, A. (2012). Talking to terrorists: Understanding the psycho-social motivations of militant jihadi terrorists, mass hostage takers, suicide bombers and "martyrs". McLean, VA: Advances Press.

35 The Quran, chapter 22 (Al-Hajj), verse 58, translated by Abdullah Yusuf Ali.

36 Speckhard, A. (September 24, 2013). "Sex jihad"—A new role for extremist women in militant jihadi groups? Huffington Post. http://www.huffingtonpost.co.uk/anne-speckhard/extremism-jihadi-women_b_3973825.html

37 The Guardian. (October 15, 2015). Ankara bombings: 10 more people arrested 'suspected of Isis and PKK links'. http://www.theguardian.com/world/2015/oct/15/ankara-bombings-10-more-people-arrested-suspected-isis-pkk-links

38 Hurriyet Daily News. (October 19, 2015). ISIL child training camp discovered in Istanbul: Report. http://www.hurriyetdailynews.com/

isil-child-training-camp-discovered-in-istanbul-report-.aspx?Page-ID=238&NID=90052&NewsCatID=341

39 Sunday Express. (October 25, 2015). Turkey terror alert: Four ISIS jihadists enter country 'in bid to attack Westerners'. http://www.express.co.uk/news/world/614465/Turkey-terror-alert-Four-ISIS-jihadists-entered-country-and-are-preparing-attacks

40 Associated Press. (October 27, 2015). Istanbul has more Syrian refugees than all of Europe says David Miliband. The Guardian. http://www.theguardian.com/world/2015/oct/27/istanbul-has-more-syrian-refugees-than-all-of-europe-says-david-miliband

41 Speckhard, A. (September 29, 2015). How dragging our feet on Syrian refugees creates more terrorists. New York Times. http://www.nytimes.com/2015/09/29/opinion/how-dragging-our-feet-on-refugees-creates-more-terrorists.html

42 Speckhard, A. (2015). Bride of ISIS. McLean, VA: Advances Press, LLC.

43 Janine di Giovanni, Leah McGrath Goodman, & Sharkov, D. (November 16, 2014). How does ISIS fund its reign of terror? Newsweek. https://http://www.newsweek.com/2014/11/14/how-does-isis-fund-its-reign-terror-282607.html

44 Spencer, R. (June 22, 2015). Chechen group of 15,000 jihadis pledges allegiance to Islamic State. Jihad Watch.

45 Virtual Jerusalem. (November 2, 2015). ISIS claims first beheadings inside Turkey. http://virtualjerusalem.com/news.php?option=com_content&view=article&id=18411:isis-claims-first-beheadings-inside-turkey&catid=148:headlines&Itemid=18411 Retrieved from http://virtualjerusalem.com/news.php?option=com_content&view=article&id=18411:isis-claims-first-beheadings-inside-turkey&catid=148:headlines&Itemid=18411

46 Loveluck, L. (October 30, 2015). Islamic state critic found beheaded in Turkey. The Telegraph. http://www.telegraph.co.uk/news/worldnews/islamic-state/11965804/Beheaded-bodies-of-Syria-anti-Islamic-State-activist-and-friend-found-in-Turkey.html Retrieved from http://www.telegraph.co.uk/news/worldnews/islamic-state/11965804/Beheaded-bodies-of-Syria-anti-Islamic-State-activist-and-friend-found-in-Turkey.html

47 We've changed his exact title to protect his identity, however he was a high-level commander in Raqqa.

48 Speckhard, A. (April 27, 2016). ISIS revenues include sales of oil to the al-Assad regime. ICSVE Brief Reports. Retrieved from http://www.icsve.org/brief-reports/isiss-revenues-include-sales-of-oil-to-the-al-assad-regime/

49 Speckhard, A. (April 27, 2016). ISIS revenues include sales of oil to the al-Assad regime. ICSVE Brief Reports. Retrieved from http://www.icsve.org/brief-reports/isiss-revenues-include-sales-of-oil-to-the-al-assad-regime/

50 Hugh N and Justin W. M. (January 8, 2016). Islamic State fighter publicly executes own mother, Syrian activists say. The Washington Post. Retrived from: https://www.washingtonpost.com/news/morning-mix/

wp/2016/01/08/islamic-state-fighter-publicly-executes-his-mother-report-says/

51 Gallagher, I and Beckford, M. (November 14, 2015). The Daily Mail UK. Revealed: Two of the Jihadis sneaked into Europe via Greece by posing as refugees and being rescued from a sinking migrant boat - and survivors say one of the attackers was a WOMAN. Retrieved from: http://www.dailymail.co.uk/news/article-3318379/Hunt-Isis-killers-Syrian-passport-body-suicide-bomber-Stade-France.html#ixzz40rDDgh5B

52 Topcu, H. (January 14, 2016). Almanya İstanbul saldırganının kimliğine şüpheyle bakıyor (Germany is skeptical about the Istanbul attackers). BBC Turkey. Retrieved from http://www.bbc.com/turkce/haberler/2016/01/160114_almanya_turkiye_saldiri

53 Arsu, S. (February 21, 2015). Turkish military enters Syria to evacuate eoldiers and move tomb's remains, reports say. New York Times. Retrieved from http://www.nytimes.com/2015/02/22/world/europe/turkish-military-enters-syria-to-evacuate-soldiers-guarding-tomb-reports-say.html?_r=1

54 For a full discussion of these events see: Dettmer, J. (February 24, 2015). Did Turkey cut a deal with ISIS to save soldiers? The Daily Beast. Retrieved from http://www.thedailybeast.com/articles/2015/02/23/did-turkey-cut-a-deal-with-isis-to-save-soldiers.html; Abdulrahim, R. (September 20, 2014). Questions arise as to how Turkey got ISIS to release hostages. LA Times. Retrieved from Dettmer, J. (February 24, 2015). Did Turkey cut a deal with ISIS to save soldiers? The Daily Beast. Retrieved from http://www.thedailybeast.com/articles/2015/02/23/did-turkey-cut-a-deal-with-isis-to-save-soldiers.html; and Varghese, J. (October 6, 2014). Turkey swapped 180 ISIS fighters, including two British jihadists for its Mosul embassy staff. International Business Times. Retrieved from http://www.ibtimes.co.in/turkey-swapped-180-isis-fighters-including-2-british-jihadists-its-mosul-embassy-staff-610616

55 Speckhard, A. (April 27, 2016). ISIS revenues include sales of oil to the al-Assad regime. ICSVE Brief Reports. Retrieved from http://www.icsve.org/brief-reports/isiss-revenues-include-sales-of-oil-to-the-al-assad-regime/

56 For more on this see: Bokhari, F. (July 4, 2008). Al Qaeda expanding recruitment of children. CBS News. Retrieved from http://www.cbsnews.com/news/al-qaeda-expanding-recruitment-of-children/; Butt, Y. (January 20, 2015). How Saudi Wahhabism Is the fountainhead of Islamist ferrorism. Huffington Post. Retrieved from http://www.huffingtonpost.com/dr-yousaf-butt-/saudi-wahhabism-islam-terrorism_b_6501916.html and Georges, A. (April 14, 2015). Lethal recruitment: Child recruitment in terrorist organizations. Trends Research. Retrieved from http://trendsinstitution.org/?p=1093

57 Lopez, G. (November 21, 2015). Captagon, ISIS's favorite amphetamine, explained. Vox. http://www.vox.com/world/2015/11/20/9769264/captagon-isis-drug Retrieved from http://www.vox.com/

world/2015/11/20/9769264/captagon-isis-drug
58 BBC News. (February 3, 2015). Jordan pilot hostage Moaz al-Kasasbeh 'burned alive'. http://www.bbc.com/news/world-middle-east-31121160 Retrieved from http://www.bbc.com/news/world-middle-east-31121160
59 See: Speckhard, A., & Ahkmedova, K. (2005). Talking to Terrorists. Journal of Psychohistory, Fall 33(2), 125-156; Speckhard, A., & Akhmedova, K. (2006). The New Chechen Jihad: Militant Wahhabism as a Radical Movement and a Source of Suicide Terrorism in Post-War Chechen Society. Democracy and Security, 2(1), 103-155 and Speckhard, A. (2012). Talking to terrorists: Understanding the psycho-social motivations of militant jihadi terrorists, mass hostage takers, suicide bombers and "martyrs". McLean, VA: Advances Press.
60 Speckhard, A. (2012). Talking to terrorists: Understanding the psycho-social motivations of militant jihadi terrorists, mass hostage takers, suicide bombers and "martyrs". McLean, VA: Advances Press.
61 AFP. (August 8, 2014). ISIS captures key Syria army base. al Arabiya. http://english.alarabiya.net/en/News/middle-east/2014/08/08/ISIS-captures-key-base-from-Syrian-army-.html Retrieved from http://english.alarabiya.net/en/News/middle-east/2014/08/08/ISIS-captures-key-base-from-Syrian-army-.html
62 Sly, L. (October 20, 2014). Syria tribal revolt against Islamic State ignored, fueling resentment. The Washington Post. https://www.washingtonpost.com/world/syria-tribal-revolt-against-islamic-state-ignored-fueling-resentment/2014/10/20/25401beb-8de8-49f2-8e64-c1cfbee45232_story.html Retrieved from https://www.washingtonpost.com/world/syria-tribal-revolt-against-islamic-state-ignored-fueling-resentment/2014/10/20/25401beb-8de8-49f2-8e64-c1cfbee45232_story.html
63 Holmes, O., & al-Khalidi, S. (August 16, 2014). Islamic State executed 700 people from Syrian tribe: monitoring group. Reuters News. http://www.reuters.com/article/us-syria-crisis-execution-idUSKBN0GG0H120140817 Retrieved from http://www.reuters.com/article/us-syria-crisis-execution-idUSKBN0GG0H120140817 and
64 In 2014 the al Sheitaat tribe staged an uprising against ISIS and from 700 to 900 members were slaughtered as a result. See: Mezzofiore, G., & Limam, A. (May 21, 2015). Syria: Isis executes al-Sheitaat tribe teenager with bazooka in Deir al-Zour. International Business Times. http://www.ibtimes.co.uk/syria-isis-kills-shaitat-tribe-teen-bazooka-deir-al-zour-1502356 Retrieved from http://www.ibtimes.co.uk/syria-isis-kills-shaitat-tribe-teen-bazooka-deir-al-zour-1502356
65 InformOverload. (June 24, 2015). Shocking Video Of ISIS Drowning People In Cages. YouTube. https://www.youtube.com/watch?v=GlIplhkeQrw Retrieved from https://www.youtube.com/watch?v=GlIplhkeQrw
66 See Mezzofiore, G., & Limam, A. (May 21, 2015). Syria: Isis executes al-Sheitaat tribe teenager with bazooka in Deir al-Zour. International Business Times. http://www.ibtimes.co.uk/syria-isis-kills-shaitat-tribe-teen-bazooka-deir-al-zour-1502356 Retrieved from http://www.ibtimes.

co.uk/syria-isis-kills-shaitat-tribe-teen-bazooka-deir-al-zour-1502356

67 See: Degreef, C. (January 13, 2016). NewEurope. Declining press freedom in Turkey. http://neurope.eu/article/declining-press-freedom-in-turkey/ Retrieved from http://neurope.eu/article/declining-press-freedom-in-tur-key/ and Akkoc, R. (October 30, 2015). 'Of course I feel restricted': How press freedom in Turkey is declining - and getting worse. The Telegraph. http://www.telegraph.co.uk/news/worldnews/europe/turkey/11958185/ Of-course-I-feel-restricted-How-press-freedom-in-Turkey-is-declining-and-getting-worse.html Retrieved from http://www.telegraph.co.uk/news/worldnews/europe/turkey/11958185/Of-course-I-feel-restricted-How-press-freedom-in-Turkey-is-declining-and-getting-worse.html

68 Speckhard, A., & Akhmedova, K. (2006). Black Widows: The Chechen Female Suicide Terrorists. In Y. Schweitzer (Ed.), Female Suicide Terrorists. Tel Aviv: Jaffe Center Publication. Speckhard, A., & Akhmedova, K. (2008). Black Widows and Beyond: Understanding the Motivations and Life Trajectories of Chechen Female Terrorists. In C. Ness (Ed.), Female Terrorism and Militancy: Agency, Utility and Organization: Agency, Utility and Organization Routledge.

69 For more on female suicide bombers see: Speckhard, A. (Dec/January 2016). Brides of ISIS: The Internet seduction of Western females into ISIS. Homeland Security Today, 13(1).; Speckhard, A. (2008). The Emergence of Female Suicide Terrorists. Studies in Conflict and Terrorism, 31, 1-29; Speckhard, A. (2009). Female suicide bombers in Iraq. Democracy and Security, 5(1), 19-50.; Speckhard, A. (May 4, 2015). Female terrorists in ISIS, al Qaeda and 21rst century terrorism. Trends Research. https://www.academia.edu/12606010/Female_Terrorists_in_ISIS_al_Qae-da_and_21st_Century_Terrorism Retrieved from https://www.academia.edu/12606010/Female_Terrorists_in_ISIS_al_Qaeda_and_21st_Centu-ry_Terrorism; Speckhard, A., & Akhmedova, K. (2006). Black Widows: The Chechen Female Suicide Terrorists. In Y. Schweitzer (Ed.), Female Suicide Terrorists. Tel Aviv: Jaffe Center Publication.; Speckhard, A., & Akhmedova, K. (2008). Black Widows and Beyond: Understanding the Motivations and Life Trajectories of Chechen Female Terrorists. In C. Ness (Ed.), Female Terrorism and Militancy: Agency, Utility and Organi-zation: Agency, Utility and Organization Routledge.; Schweitzer, Y. (Ed.) (2006). Female Suicide Bombers:Dying for Equality? : The Jaffee Center for Strategic Studies

70 Verkaik, R., & Akbar, J. (May 13, 2015). Is ISIS about to send women to die on suicide missions? Daily Mail. http://www.dailymail.co.uk/news/article-3079857/Is-ISIS-send-women-die-suicide-missions-Chilling-fa-natic-wedding-certificate-states-jihadi-brides-carry-bombings-without-husband-s-permission.html#ixzz3aS3BKtfx Retrieved from http://www.dailymail.co.uk/news/article-3079857/Is-ISIS-send-women-die-suicide-missions-Chilling-fanatic-wedding-certificate-states-jihadi-brides-carry-bombings-without-husband-s-permission.html#ixzz3aS3BKtfx

71 Wyke, T. (October 27, 2015). Desperate ISIS forms new female suicide squad

to carry out bombings because the terror group is running out of children for use in the attacks. Daily Mail. http://www.dailymail.co.uk/news/article-3290323/Desperate-ISIS-forms-new-female-suicide-squad-carry-bombings-terror-group-running-children-use-attacks.html#ixzz3pkz7vtke Retrieved from http://www.dailymail.co.uk/news/article-3290323/Desperate-ISIS-forms-new-female-suicide-squad-carry-bombings-terror-group-running-children-use-attacks.html#ixzz3pkz7vtke

72 Wyke, T. (October 27, 2015). Desperate ISIS forms new female suicide squad to carry out bombings because the terror group is running out of children for use in the attacks. Daily Mail. http://www.dailymail.co.uk/news/article-3290323/Desperate-ISIS-forms-new-female-suicide-squad-carry-bombings-terror-group-running-children-use-attacks.html#ixzz3pkz7vtke Retrieved from http://www.dailymail.co.uk/news/article-3290323/Desperate-ISIS-forms-new-female-suicide-squad-carry-bombings-terror-group-running-children-use-attacks.html#ixzz3pkz7vtke

73 Speckhard, A. (2009). Female suicide bombers in Iraq. Democracy and Security, 5(1), 19-50.

74 Letsch, C. (January 16, 2015). Pregnant Istanbul suicide bomber was Russian citizen. The Guardian. http://www.theguardian.com/world/2015/jan/16/pregnant-istanbul-suicide-bomber-russian-citizen Retrieved from http://www.theguardian.com/world/2015/jan/16/pregnant-istanbul-suicide-bomber-russian-citizen

75 Speckhard, A., & Yayla, A. S. (March 20, 2016). American ISIS sefector - Mohamad Jamal Khweis & the threat posed by "clean skin" terrorists: Unanswered questions and confirmations. ICSVE Brief Reports. Retrieved from http://www.icsve.org/american-isis-defector---mohamad-jamal-khweis-and-the-threat-of-clean-skin-terrorists-.html

76 See these two articles for different views on this issue: Spencer, R. (May 22, 2015). Jihadi bride: "I rejoiced when we had our first sex slave". Jihad Watch. http://www.jihadwatch.org/2015/05/jihadi-bride-i-rejoiced-when-we-had-our-first-sex-slave Retrieved from http://www.jihadwatch.org/2015/05/jihadi-bride-i-rejoiced-when-we-had-our-first-sex-slave and Ibrahim, R. (February 10, 2016). Relax: Islam only sometimes allows Muslims to enslave, rape and rob infidels, says female Muslim professor. Raymond Ibrahim. http://www.raymondibrahim.com/2016/02/10/relax-islam-only-sometimes-allows-muslims-to-enslave-rape-and-rob-infidels-says-female-muslim-professor/ Retrieved from http://www.raymondibrahim.com/2016/02/10/relax-islam-only-sometimes-allows-muslims-to-enslave-rape-and-rob-infidels-says-female-muslim-professor/

77 MEMRI. (December 4, 2014). Islamic State (ISIS) releases pamphlet on female slaves. MEMRI Jihad and Terrorism Threat Monitor. http://www.memrijttm.org/islamic-state-isis-releases-pamphlet-on-female-slaves.html Retrieved from http://www.memrijttm.org/islamic-state-isis-releases-pamphlet-on-female-slaves.html

78 Speckhard, A. (April 27, 2016). ISIS revenues include sales of oil to the al-Assad regime. ICSVE Brief Reports. Retrieved from http://www.icsve.

org/brief-reports/isiss-revenues-include-sales-of-oil-to-the-al-assad-regime/

79 Hassan, S. (March, 2015). Combating Cult Mind Control: Freedom of Mind Press.

80 Speckhard, A. (April 27, 2016). ISIS revenues include sales of oil to the al-Assad regime. ICSVE Brief Reports.

81 Speckhard, A. (2012). Talking to terrorists: Understanding the psycho-social motivations of militant jihadi terrorists, mass hostage takers, suicide bombers and "martyrs". McLean, VA: Advances Press.

82 Speckhard, A., Reidy, K., & Jacuch, B. (2007). Taking on the Persona of a Suicide Bomber: A Thought Experiment. Traumatology.

83 BBC News. (December 9, 2015). Paris attacks: What happened on the night. http://www.bbc.com/news/world-europe-34818994 Retrieved from http://www.bbc.com/news/world-europe-34818994

84 Speckhard, A. (2012). Talking to terrorists: Understanding the psycho-social motivations of militant jihadi terrorists, mass hostage takers, suicide bombers and "martyrs". McLean, VA: Advances Press.

85 Yayla, A., & Speckhard, A. (March 21, 2016). ISIS operative Salah Abdelslam a not so true believer. ICSVE Brief Reports. Retrieved from http://www.icsve.org/brief-reports/isis-operative-salah-abdeslam/

86 German ISIS 'storm trooper' gets jail time. (March 4, 2016). Arutz Sheva. Retrieved from http://www.israelnationalnews.com/News/News.aspx/208909#.VusuMFLZqf5

87 See: Speckhard, A. (2012). Talking to terrorists: Understanding the psycho-social motivations of militant jihadi terrorists, mass hostage takers, suicide bombers and "martyrs". McLean, VA: Advances Press.

88 Personal communication from the Belgian national police, January 2016.

89 See: Akbar, J. (November 22, 2015). Mastermind of Paris terror attacks was linked to at least six UK hate preachers including 'Tottenham Ayatollah' Omar Bakri Muhammad. Mail Online. Retrieved from http://www.dailymail.co.uk/news/article-3329327/Mastermind-Paris-terror-attacks-linked-six-UK-hate-preachers-including-Tottenham-Ayatollah-Omar-Bakri-Muhammad.html#ixzz3sKlTss7V; BBC News. (December 9, 2015). Paris attacks: What happened on the night. Retrieved from http://www.bbc.com/news/world-europe-34818994; Jayalakshmi, K. (November 20, 2015). Paris attacks: Salah Abdeslam tells friend he regrets terror act and could be on the run from Isis. International Business Times. Retrieved from http://www.ibtimes.co.uk/paris-attacks-saleh-abdeslam-who-regrets-act-could-be-run-isis-1529618; Lichfield, J. (November 20, 2015). On the run from Isis: Jihadists 'targeting Paris attacker Salah Abdeslam for chickening out of killings'. Independent. Retrieved from http://www.independent.co.uk/news/world/europe/paris-attack-eighth-attacker-salah-abdeslam-could-also-be-on-the-run-from-isis-amid-fears-the-group-a6740781.html; and Perring, R. (November 21, 2015). Europe's most wanted man was ready to BLOW HIMSELF UP after Paris terror attacks. Sunday Express. Retrieved from http://www.

express.co.uk/news/world/621149/Paris-terror-attack-Salah-Abdeslam-suicide-bomber-Islamic-State

90 See Speckhard, A. (2012). Talking to terrorists: Understanding the psycho-social motivations of militant jihadi terrorists, mass hostage takers, suicide bombers and "martyrs". McLean, VA: Advances Press.

91 Johnson, Z. (January 25, 2005). Chronology: The Plots. Frontline. Retrieved from http://www.pbs.org/wgbh/pages/frontline/shows/front/special/cron.html

92 See: Naylor, S. (June 9, 2015). Airstrikes killing rhousands of Islamic State dighters, but it just recruits more. Foreign Policy. Retrieved from http://foreignpolicy.com/2015/06/09/airstrikes-killing-thousands-of-islamic-state-fighters-but-it-just-recruits-more/; Kirk, A. (March 24, 2016). Iraq and Syria: How many foreign fighters are fighting for Isil? The Telegraph. Retrieved from http://www.telegraph.co.uk/news/2016/03/29/iraq-and-syria-how-many-foreign-fighters-are-fighting-for-isil/; Ginkel, B. v., Entenmann, E., Boutin, B., Chauzal, G., -.5

94 See: Leherte, O. (October 15, 2015). Etat Islamique : le djihadiste belge qui ne regrette rien (The Islamic State: The Belgian Jihadist who regrets nothing. RTBR. Retrieved from https://www.rtbf.be/info/societe/detail_etat-islamique-le-djihadiste-belge-qui-ne-regrette-rien?id=9108437; Sminate, N., & Metsu, K. (October 15, 2015). Hoort een manipulator als Younnes Delefortrie niet veeleer thuis in de gevangenis? DeMorgen.

95 See: Esman, A. (December 17, 2011). Never mind "occupy." The new solution Is sharia. Forbes. Retrieved from http://www.forbes.com/sites/abigailesman/2011/12/17/never-mind-occupy-the-new-solution-is-shari-a/#28ec32292697 and Your Daily Muslim. (November 28, 2013). Your daily Muslim: Fouad Belkacem. Retrieved from https://yourdailymuslim.com/2013/11/28/your-daily-muslim-fouad-belkacem/

96 See Speckhard, A. (2012). Talking to terrorists: Understanding the psycho-social motivations of militant jihadi terrorists, mass hostage takers, suicide bombers and "martyrs". McLean, VA: Advances Press.

97 De Bode, L. (March 5, 2015). From Belgium to Syria and back: How an altar boy became an ISIL admirer. Al Jazeera. http://america.aljazeera.com/articles/2015/3/5/how-one-belgian-went-from-altar-boy-to-isil-fan.html Retrieved from http://america.aljazeera.com/articles/2015/3/5/how-one-belgian-went-from-altar-boy-to-isil-fan.html

98 De Bode, L. (March 5, 2015). From Belgium to Syria and back: How an altar boy became an ISIL admirer. Al Jazeera. http://america.aljazeera.com/articles/2015/3/5/how-one-belgian-went-from-altar-boy-to-isil-fan.html Retrieved from http://america.aljazeera.com/articles/2015/3/5/how-one-belgian-went-from-altar-boy-to-isil-fan.html

99 Leherte, O. (October 15, 2015). Etat Islamique : le djihadiste belge qui ne regrette rien (The Islamic State: The Belgian Jihadist who regrets nothing. RTBR. Retrieved from https://www.rtbf.be/info/societe/detail_etat-islamique-le-djihadiste-belge-qui-ne-regrette-rien?id=9108437

100 See Speckhard, A. (2012). Talking to terrorists: Understanding the

psycho-social motivations of militant jihadi terrorists, mass hostage tak-ers, suicide bombers and "martyrs". McLean, VA: Advances Press.

101 Speckhard, A., & Akhmedova, K. (2006). The New Chechen Jihad: Militant Wahhabism as a Radical Movement and a Source of Suicide Terrorism in Post-War Chechen Society. Democracy and Security, 2(1), 103-155.

102 Their names and their town are all changed to protect their identities.

103 Speckhard, A. (February 25, 2016). The lethal cocktail of terrorism: the four necessary ingredients that go into making a terrorist & fifty individu-al vulnerabilities/motivations that may also play a role. *International Center for the Study of Violent Extremism*: Brief Report. Retrieved from http://www.icsve.org/brief-

104 De Bode, L. (March 5, 2015). From Belgium to Syria and back: How an altar boy became an ISIL admirer. Al Jazeera. http://america.aljazeera.com/articles/2015/3/5/how-one-belgian-went-from-altar-boy-to-isil-fan.html Retrieved from http://america.aljazeera.com/articles/2015/3/5/how-one-belgian-went-from-altar-boy-to-isil-fan.html

105 See: Symons, E.-K. (January 10, 2016). The "Madame Deradicalization" of France is rehabilitating ISIS's youngest recruits. The New York Times. Retrieved from http://nytlive.nytimes.com/womenintheworld/2016/01/10/the-madame-deradicalization-of-france-is-rehabilitating-isiss-youngest-recruits/ and Reuters. (November 3, 2015). To tackle jihadis, French activist says, ditch reason and religion. Retrieved from http://blogs.reuters.com/faithworld/2015/11/03/to-tackle-jihadis-french-activist-says-ditch-reason-and-religion/

106 Gude, H., & Wiedmann-Schmidt, W. (December 16, 2015). Back from the 'Caliphate': Returnee says IS recruiting for terror attacks in Germany. Der Spiegel. Retrieved from http://www.spiegel.de/international/world/german-jihadist-returns-from-syria-and-gives-testimony-a-1067764.html

107 Rawlinson, K. (September 6, 2014). Jewish museum shooting suspect 'is Islamic State torturer'. The Guardian. http://www.theguardian.com/world/2014/sep/06/jewish-museum-shooting-suspect-islamic-state-tor-turer-brussels-syria Retrieved from http://www.theguardian.com/world/2014/sep/06/jewish-museum-shooting-suspect-islamic-state-tortur-er-brussels-syria

108 Samuel, H. (March 16, 2016). One gunman killed after shootout during Brussels raid linked to Paris attacks. The Telegraph. Retrieved from http://www.telegraph.co.uk/news/worldnews/europe/belgium/12194789/Brussels-police-shot-at-during-raid-linked-to-Paris-attacks.html

109 See also: Rubin, A. J. (March 21, 2016). The arrest of Salah Abdeslam, a Paris suspect, ends manhunt, not questions. The New York Times. http://www.nytimes.com/2016/03/22/world/europe/arrest-salah-ab-deslam-paris-suspect.html?_r=0 Retrieved from http://www.nytimes.com/2016/03/22/world/europe/arrest-salah-abdeslam-paris-suspect.

html?_r=0

110 See Speckhard, A. (2012). Talking to terrorists: Understanding the psycho-social motivations of militant jihadi terrorists, mass hostage takers, suicide bombers and "martyrs". McLean, VA: Advances Press.

111 Speckhard, A. (April 27, 2016). ISIS revenues include sales of oil to the al-Assad regime. ICSVE Brief Reports. Retrieved from http://www.icsve.org/brief-reports/isiss-revenues-include-sales-of-oil-to-the-al-assad-regime/

112 Speckhard, A., & Yayla, A. (December 22, 2015). Discrediting ISIS from the inside. ICSVE Brief Reports. http://www.icsve.org/brief-reports/discrediting-isis-from-the-inside-using-stories-from-recent-isis-defectors-why-they-joined-what-they-saw-why-they-quit/ Retrieved from http://www.icsve.org/brief-reports/discrediting-isis-from-the-inside-using-stories-from-recent-isis-defectors-why-they-joined-what-they-saw-why-they-quit/

Index

9 781935 866718